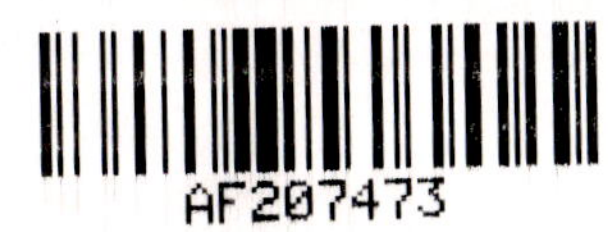

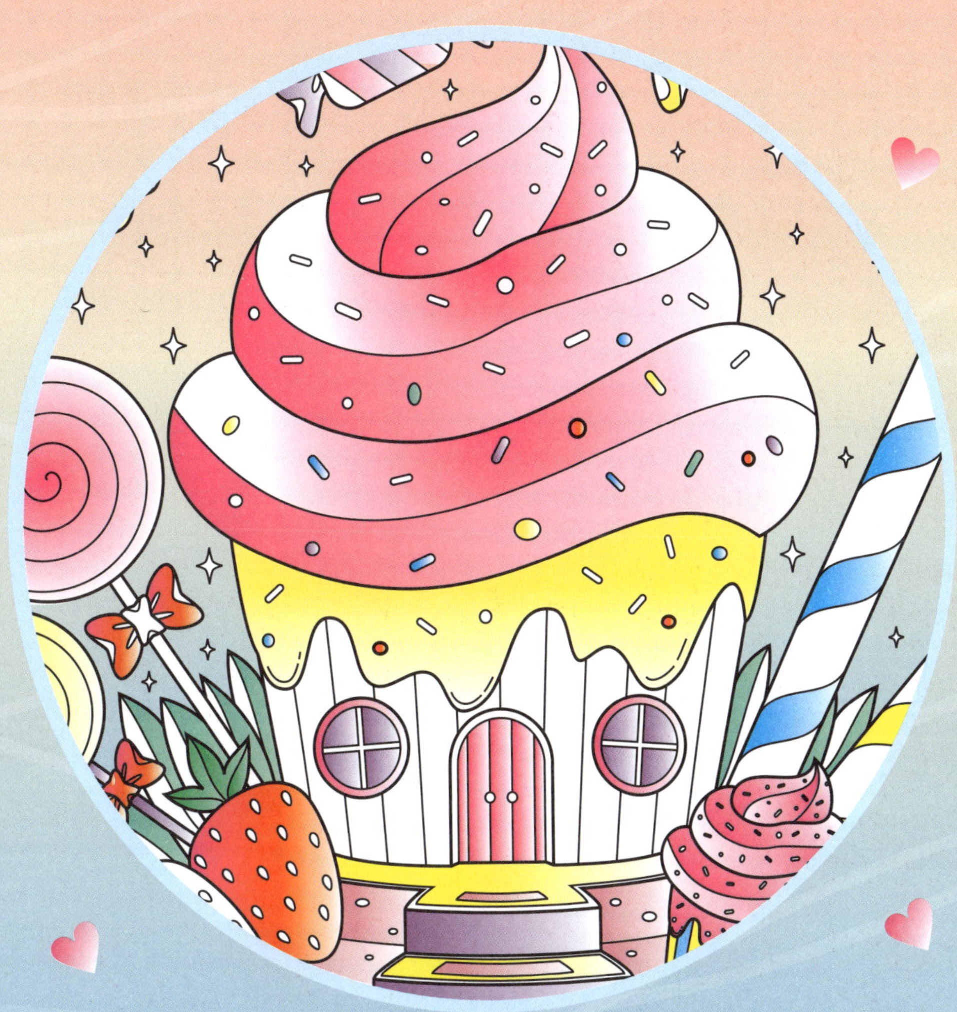

Sweets & Treats

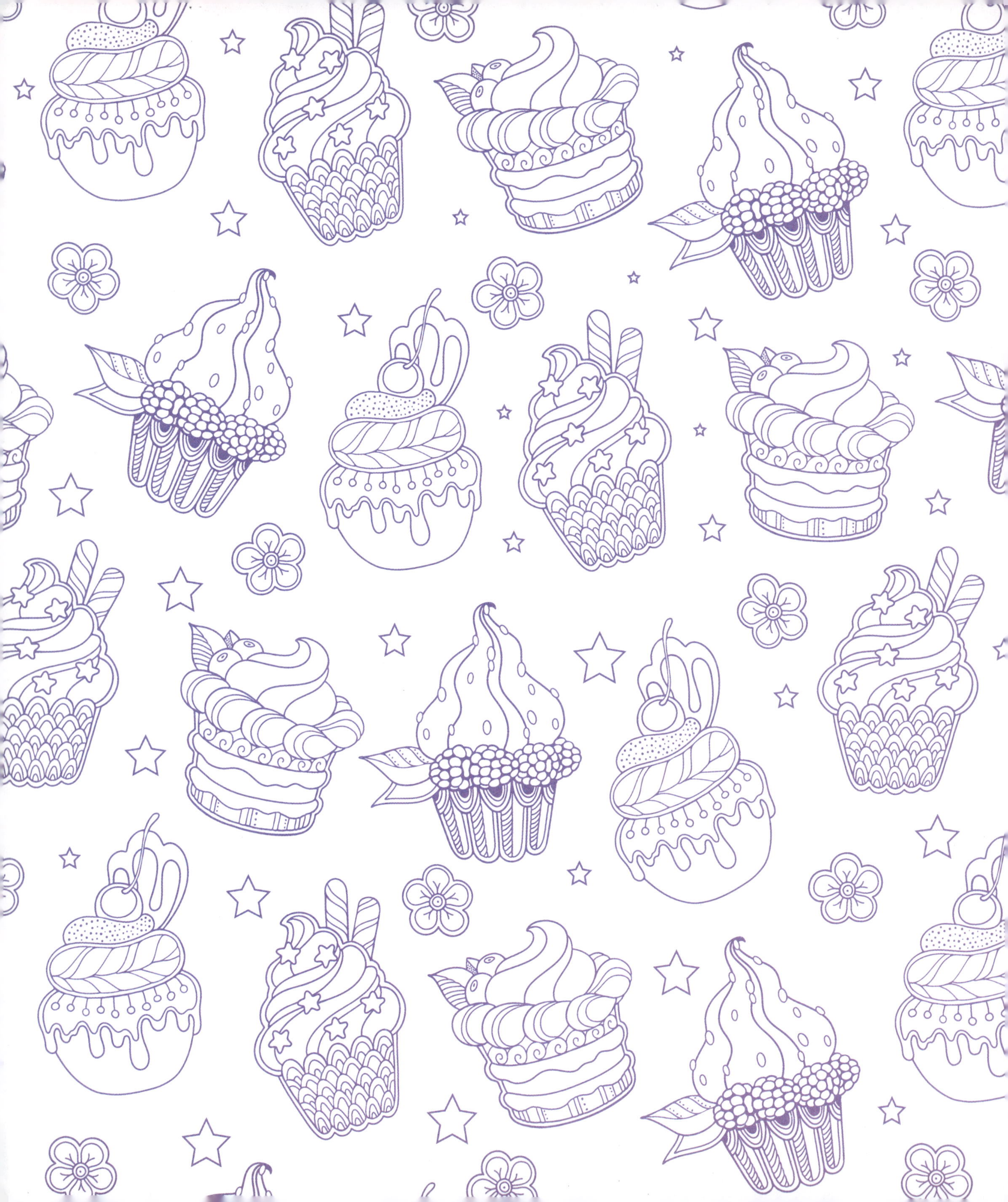

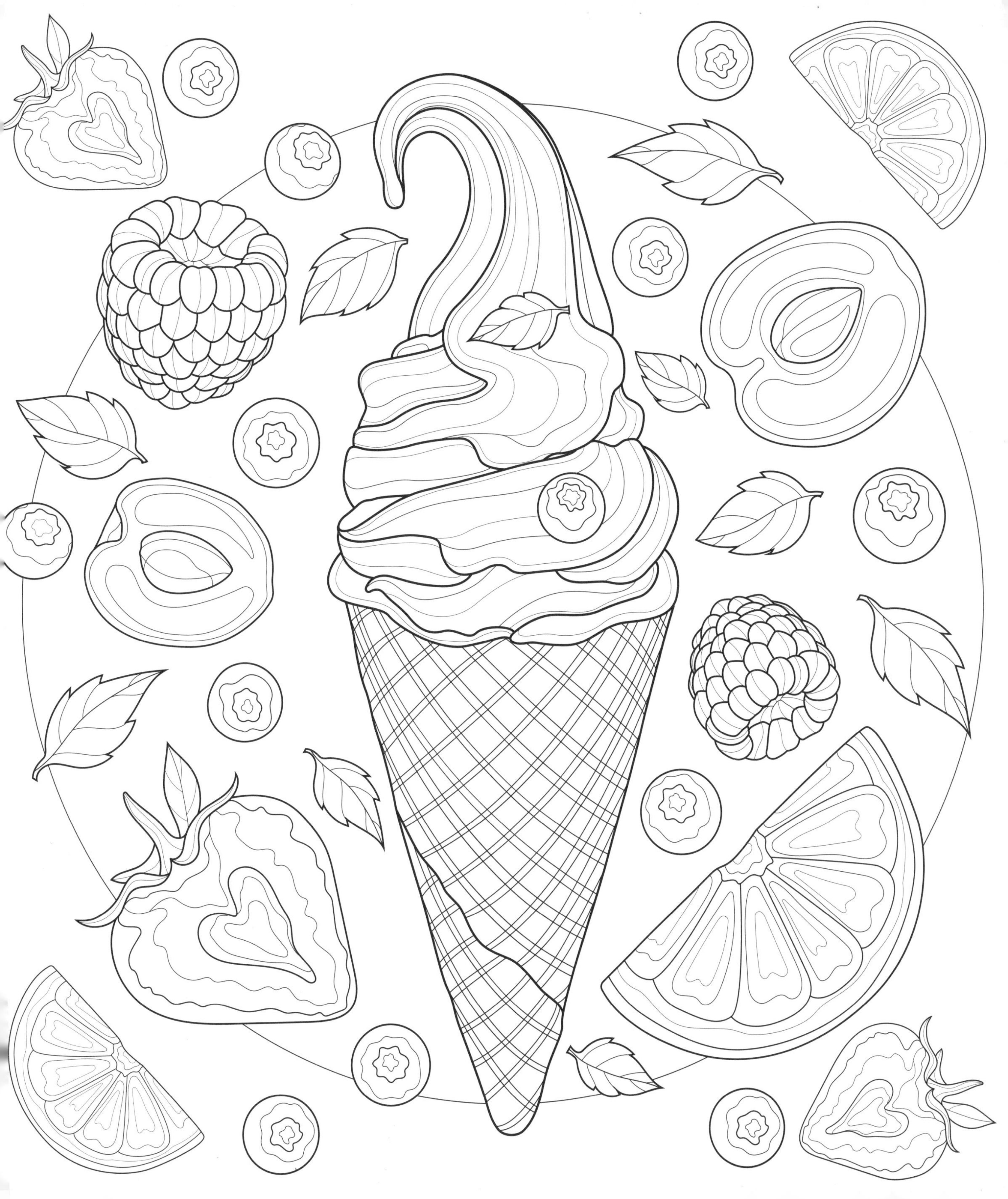

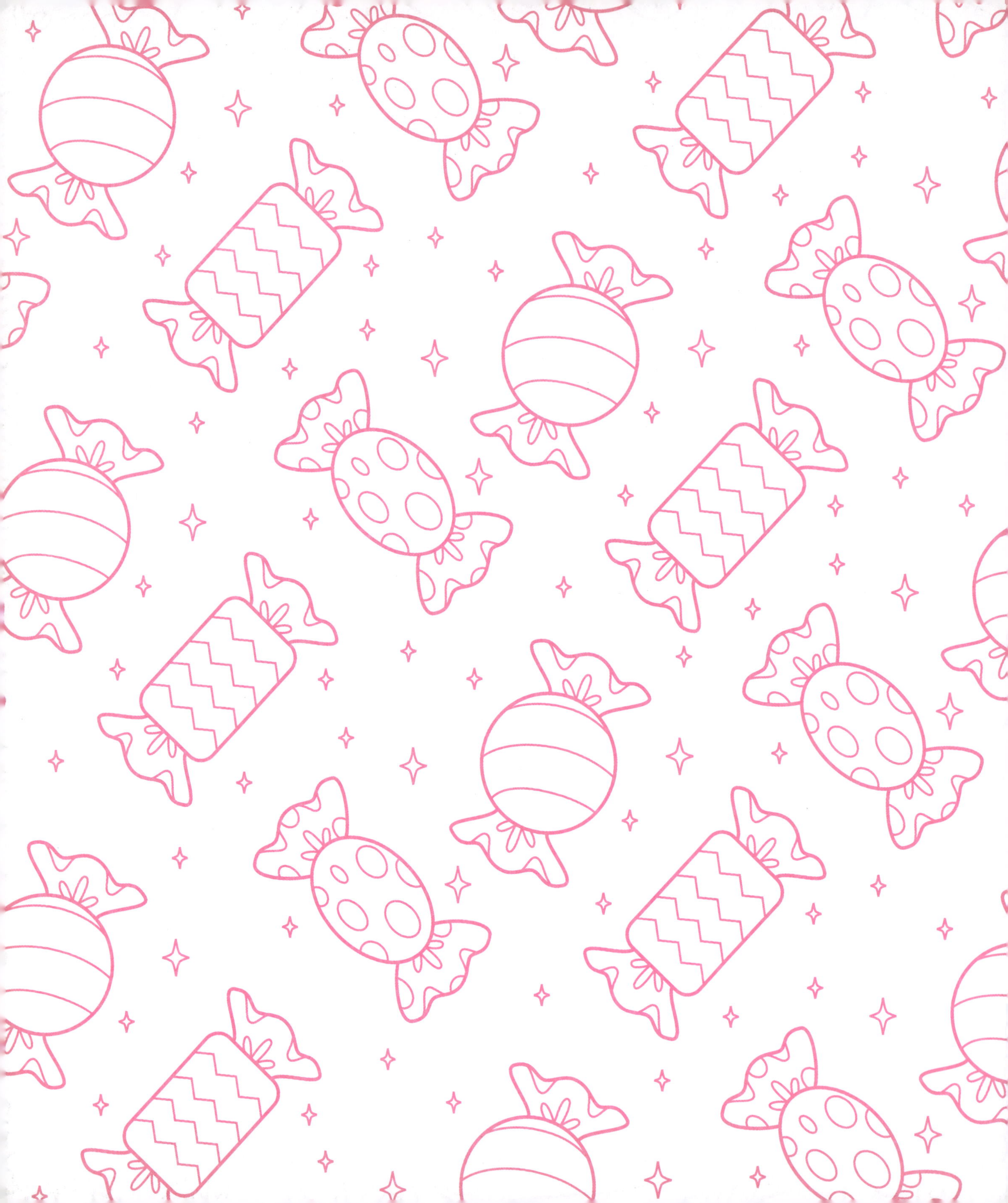

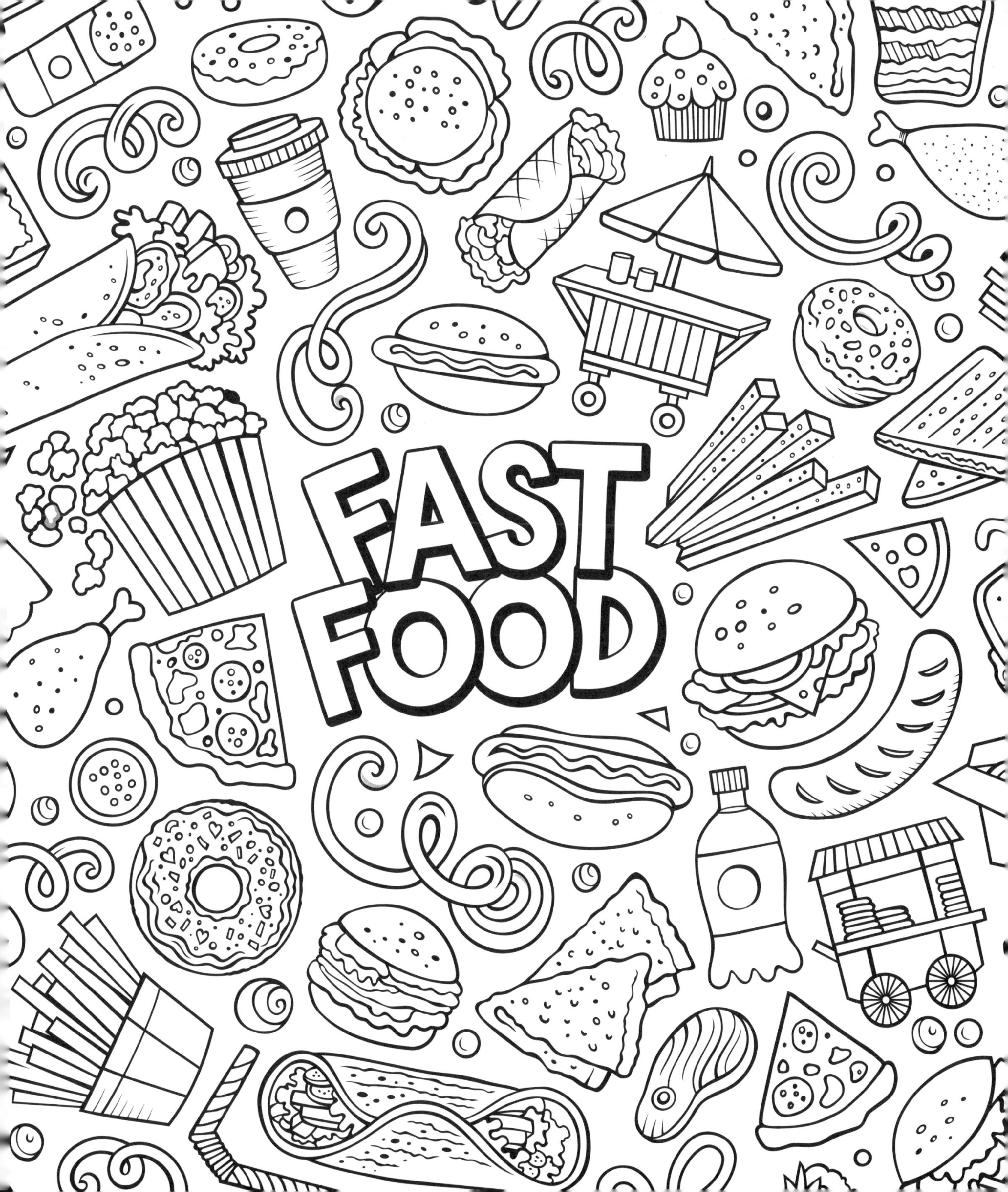

FAST FOOD

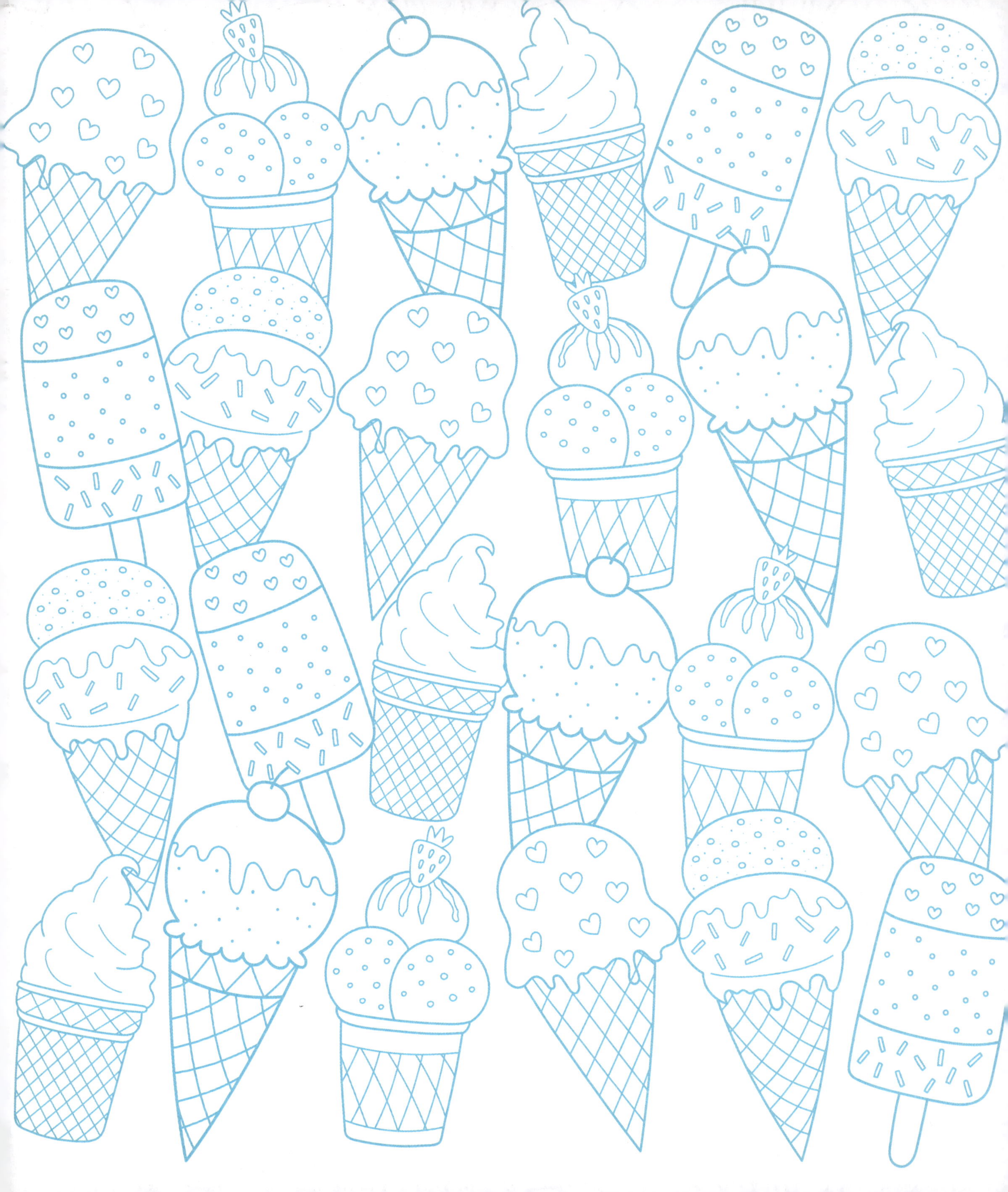

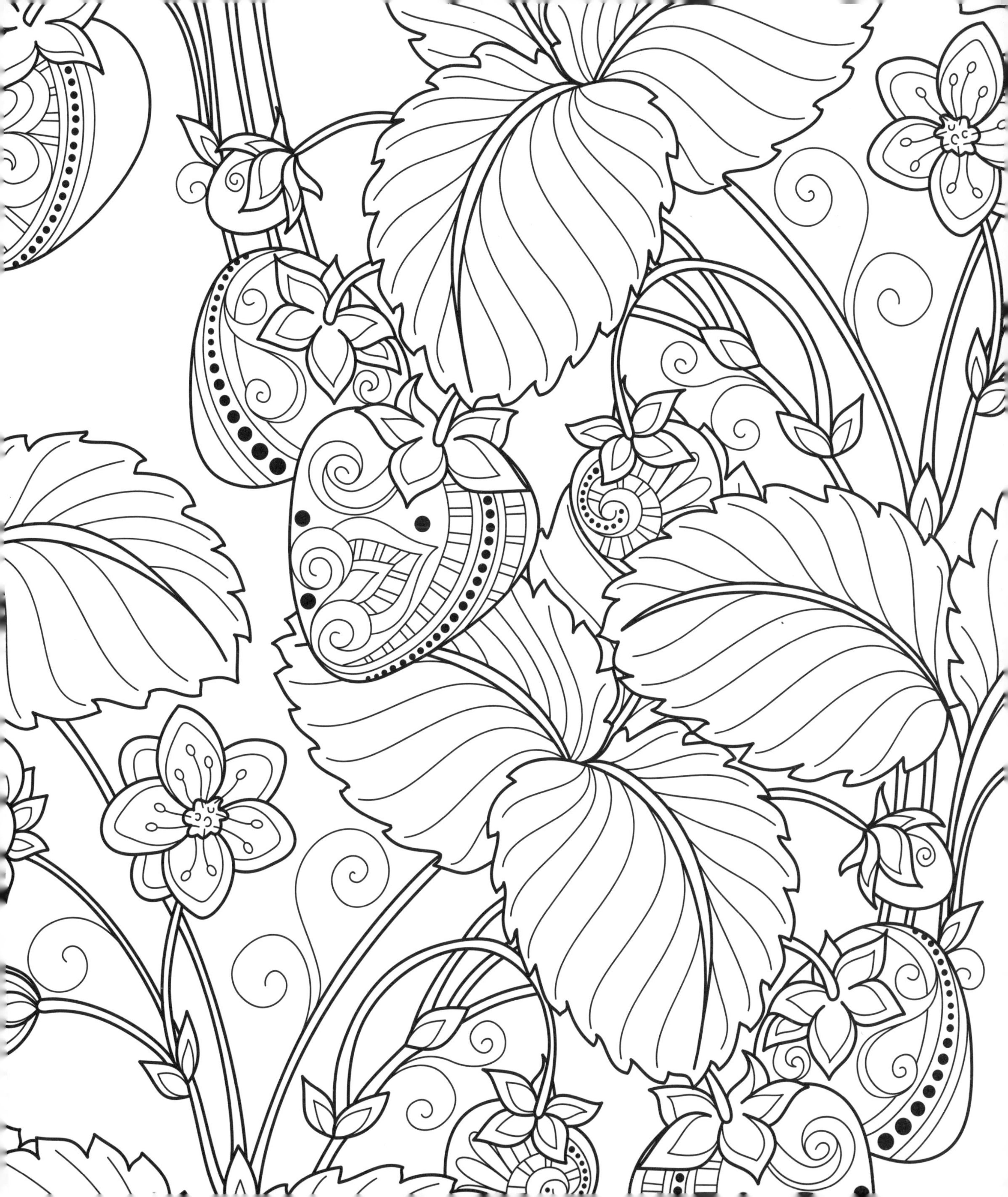

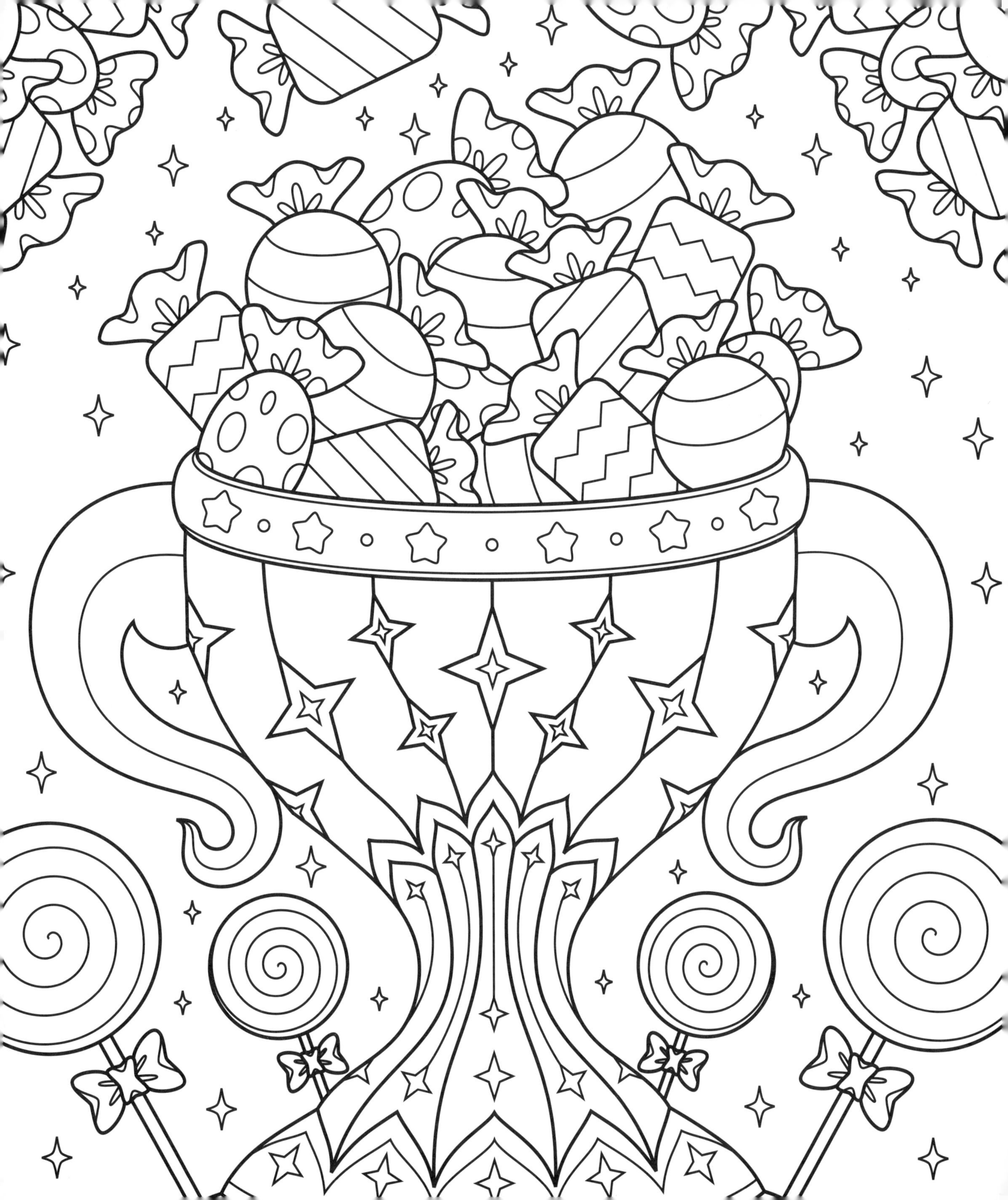

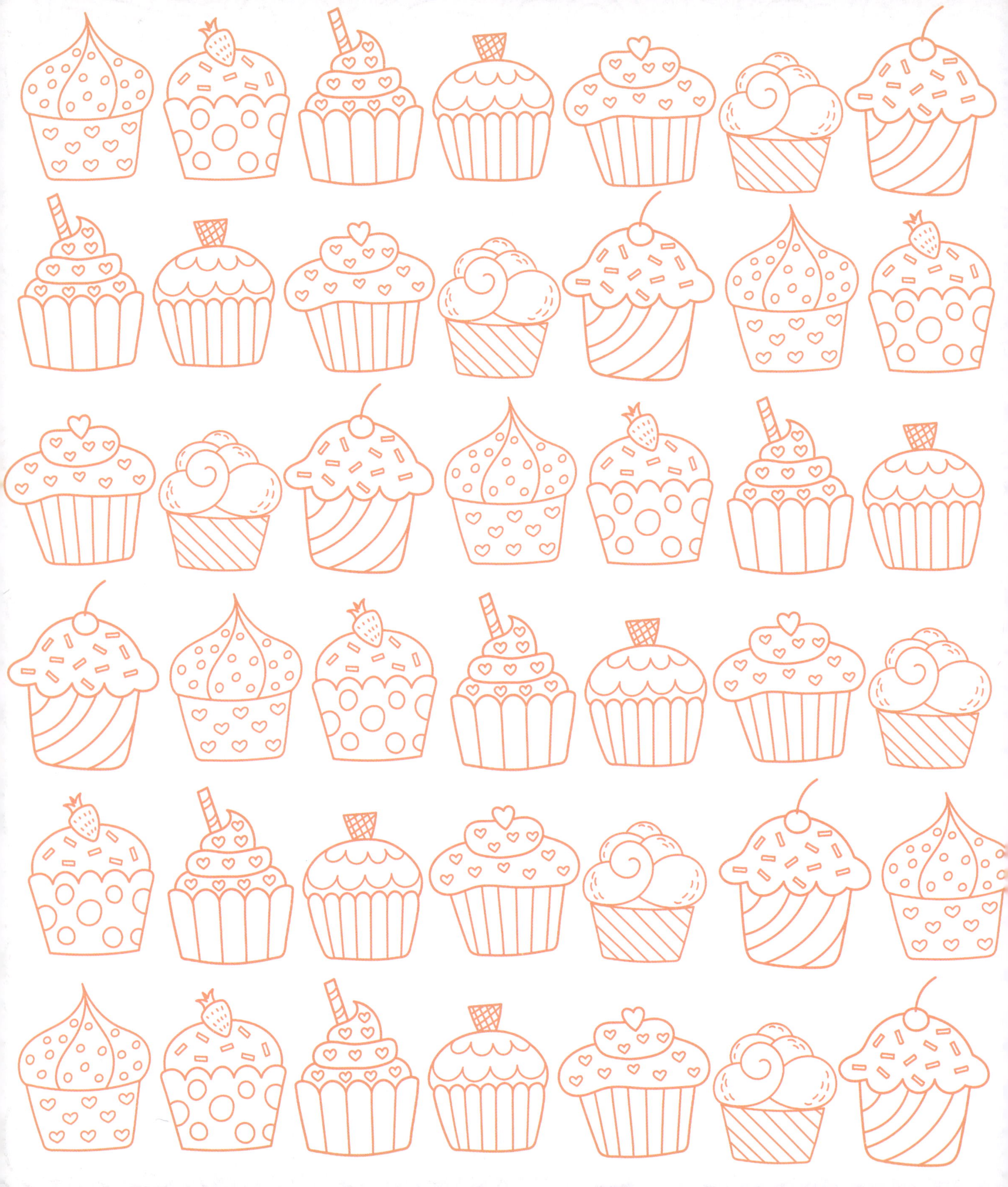

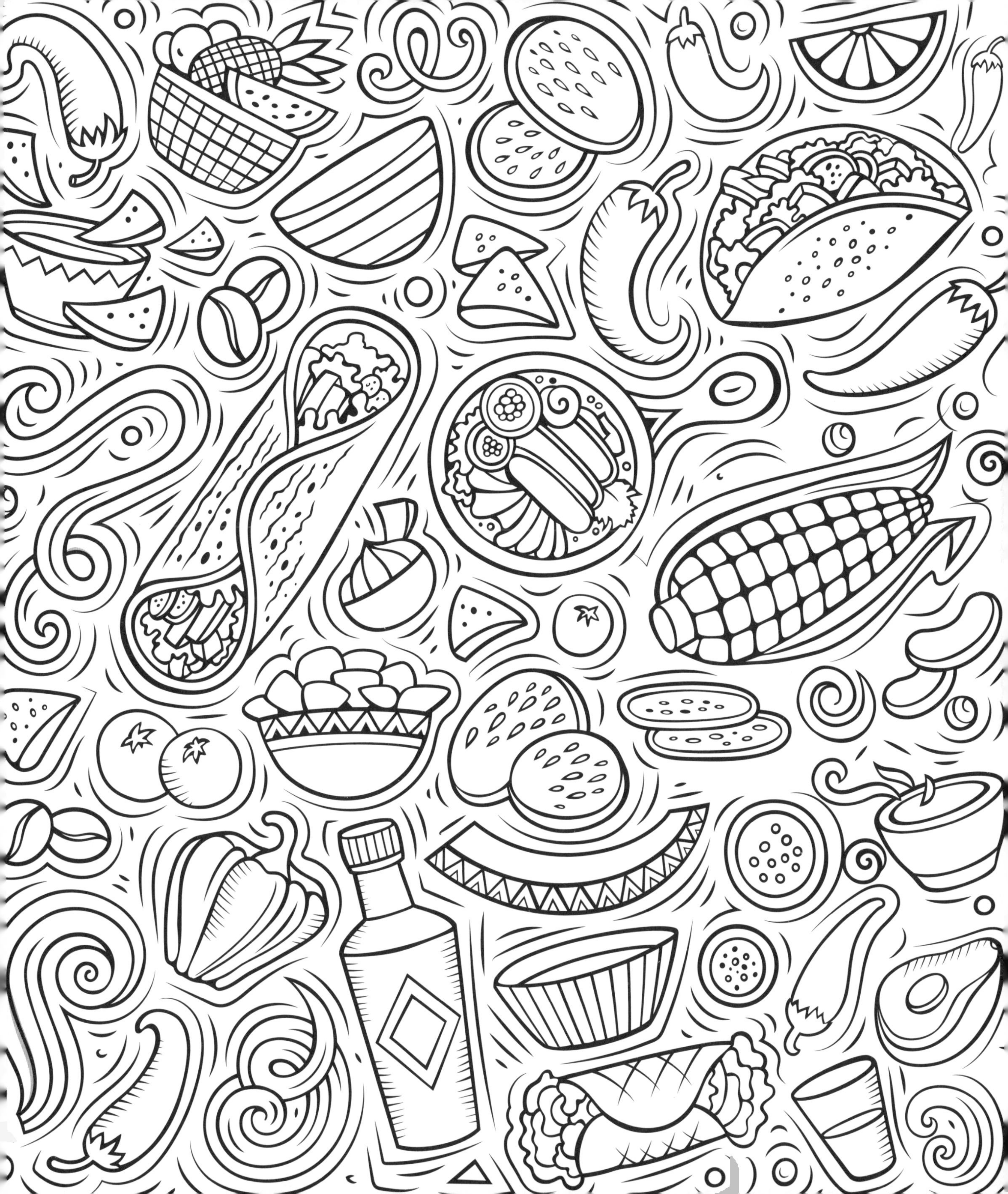

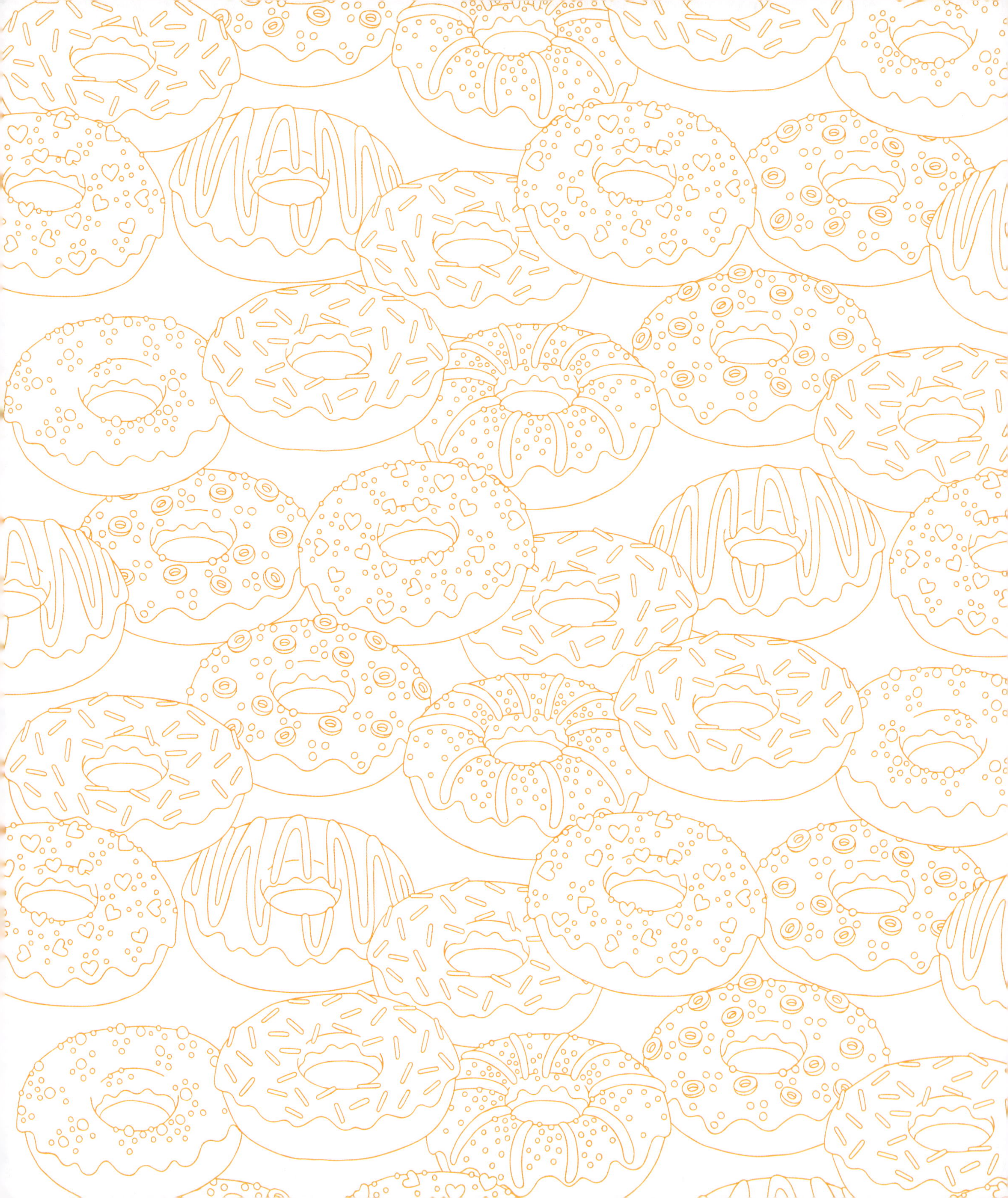

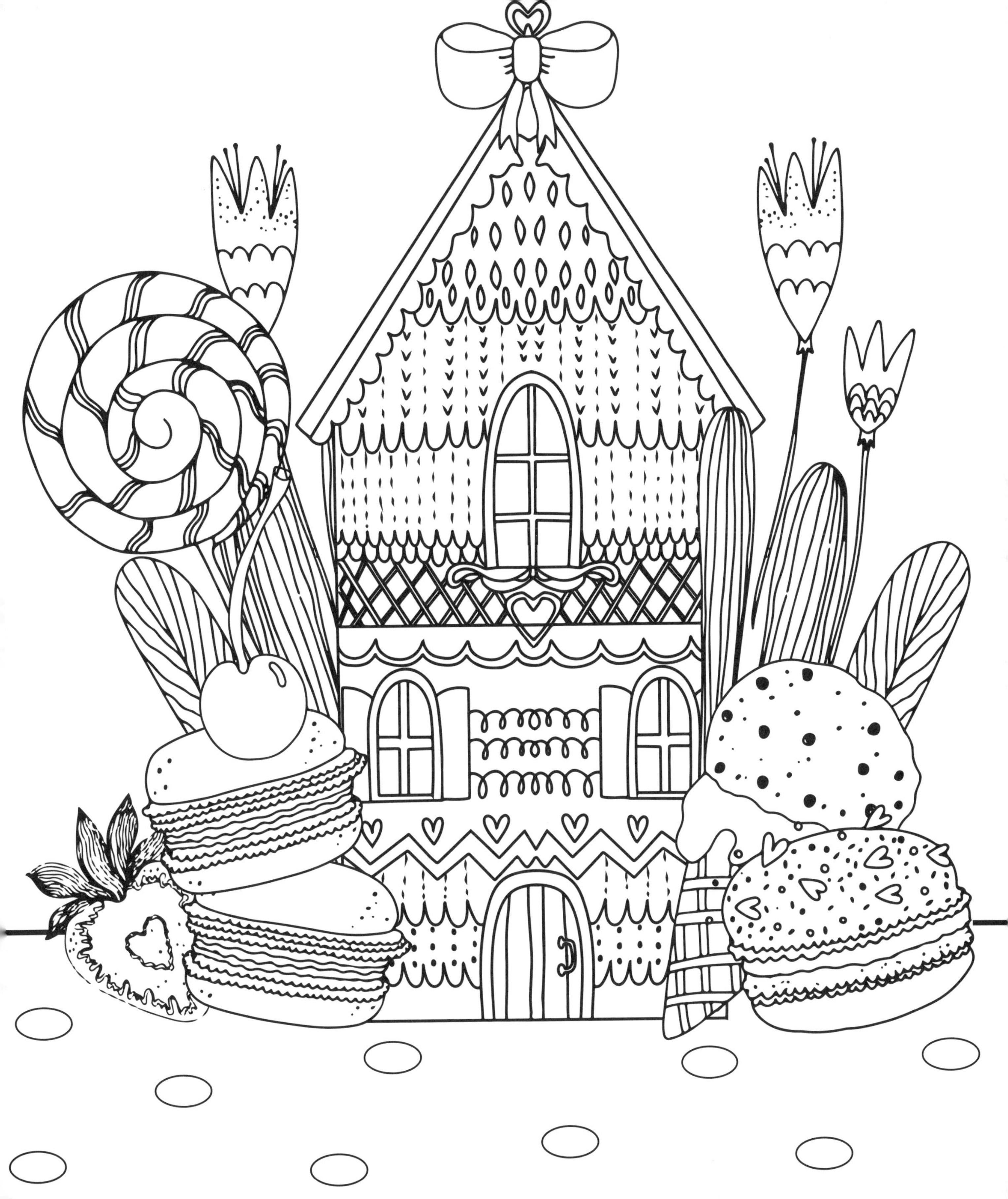

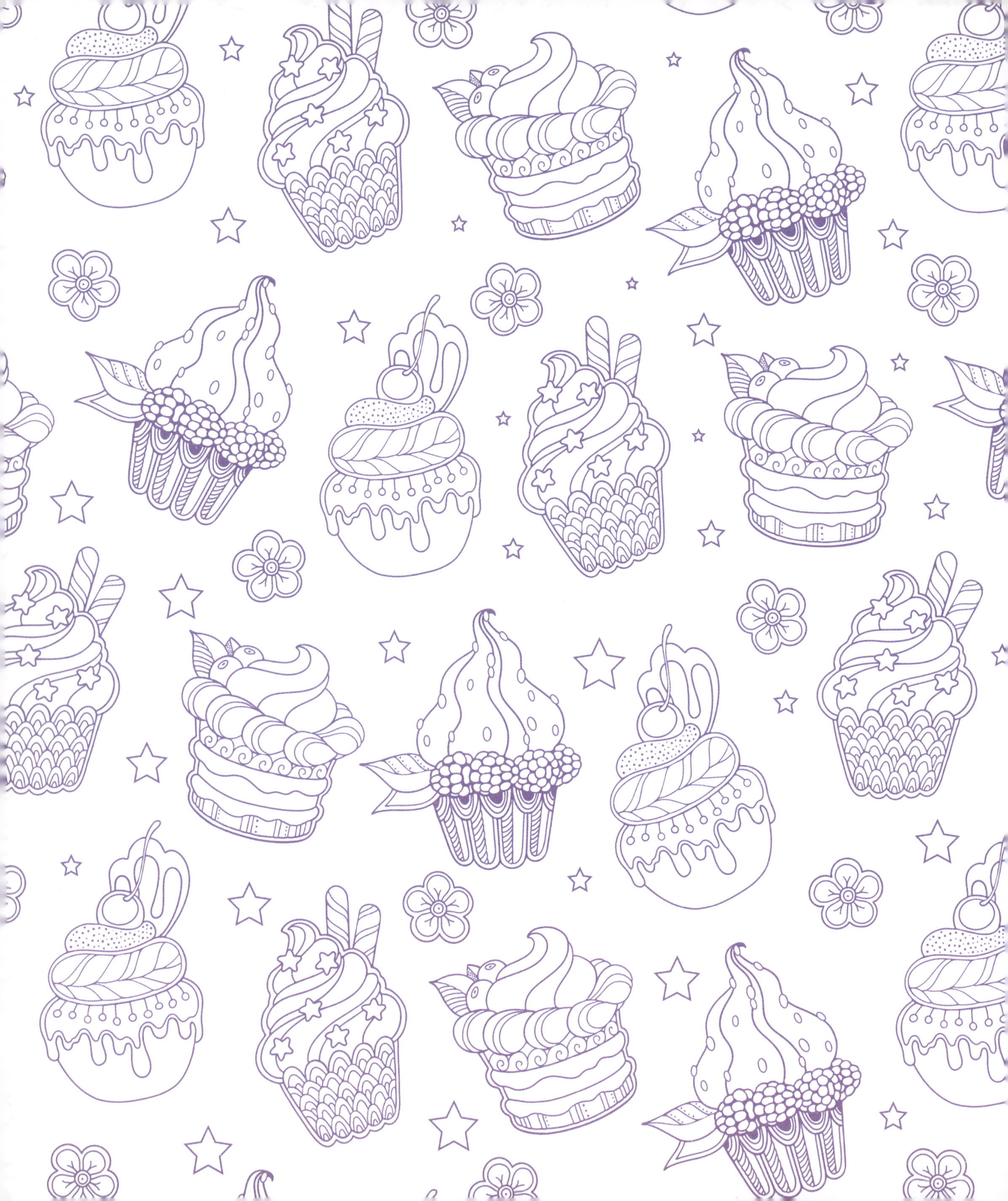

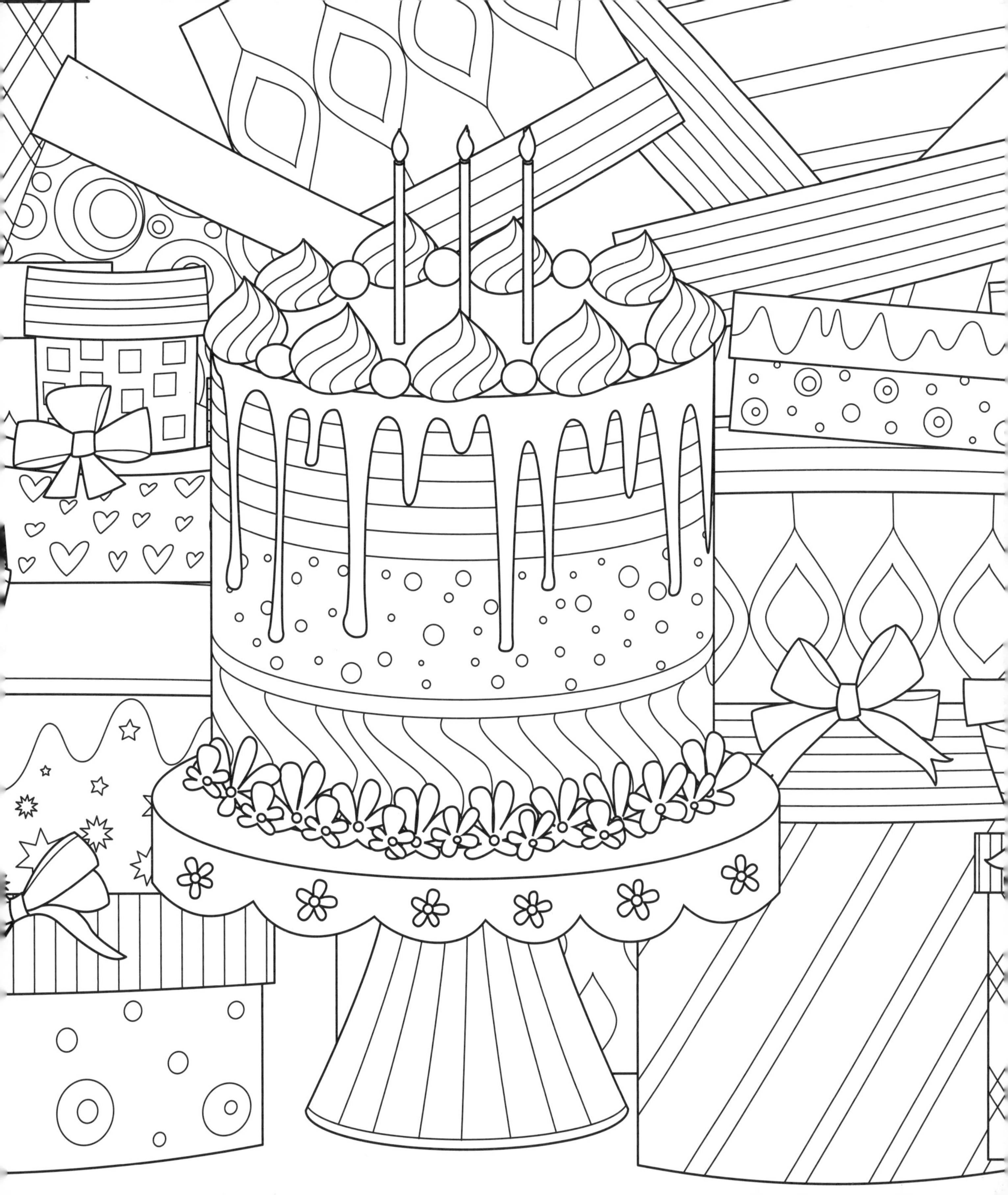

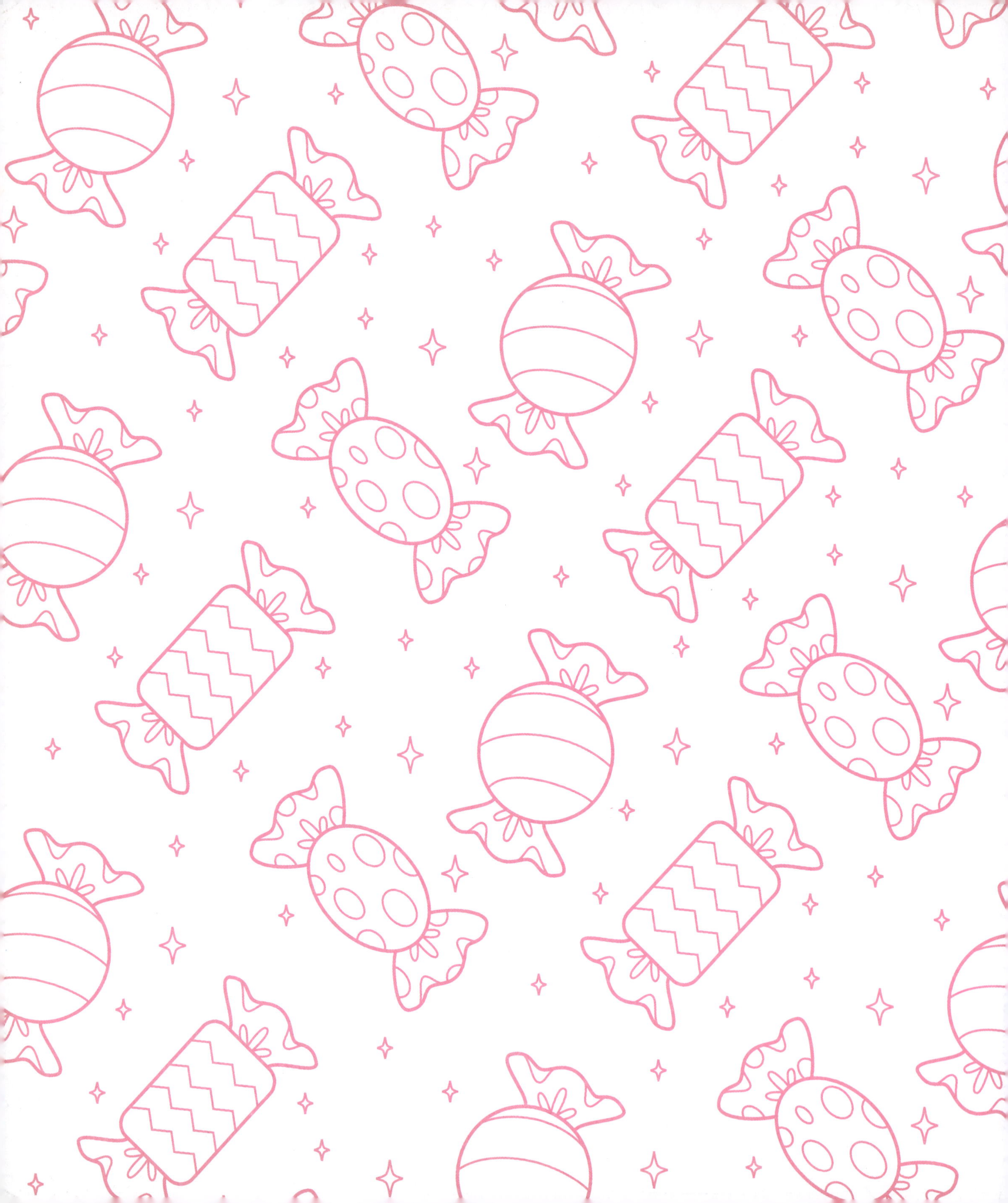

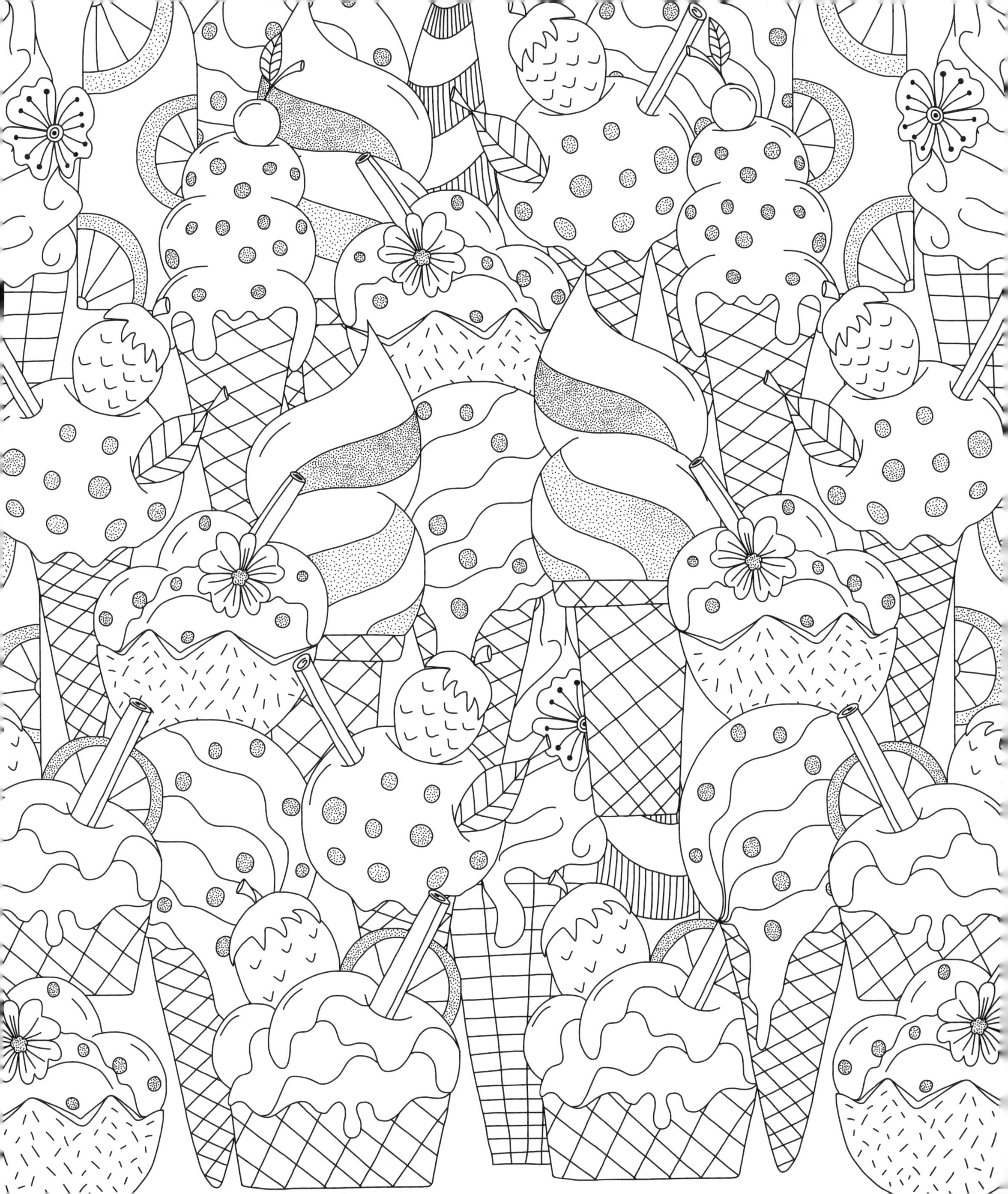

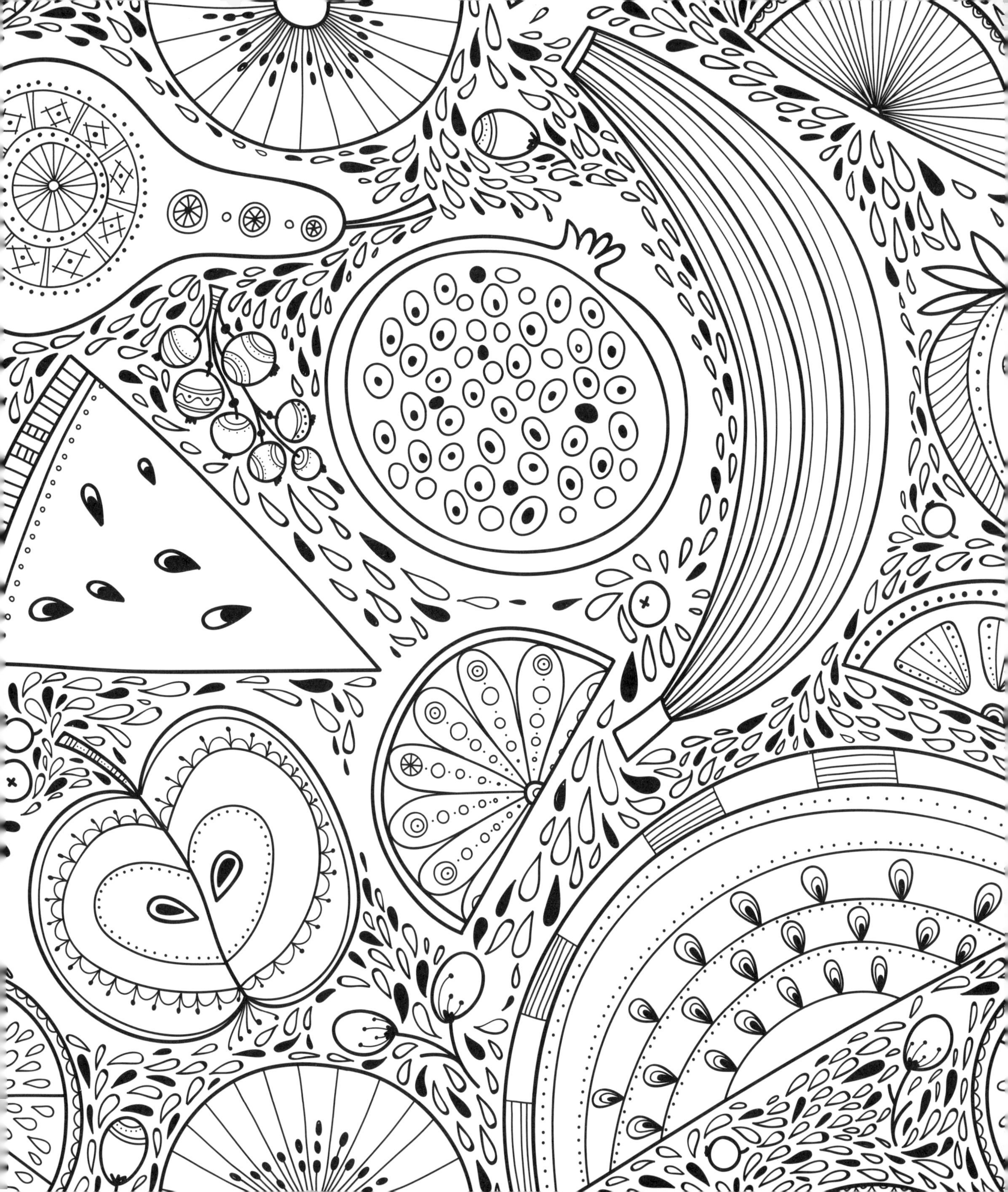

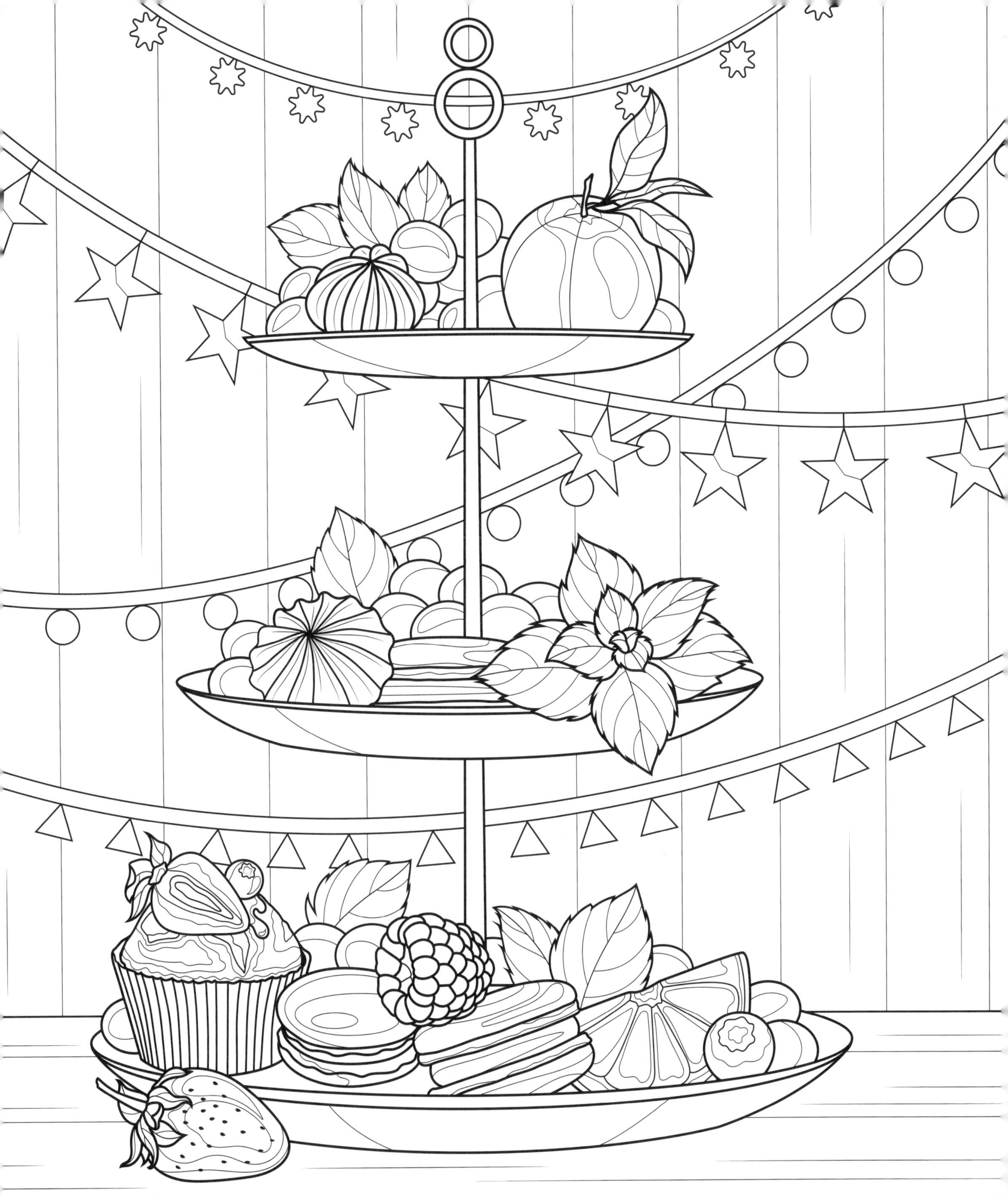

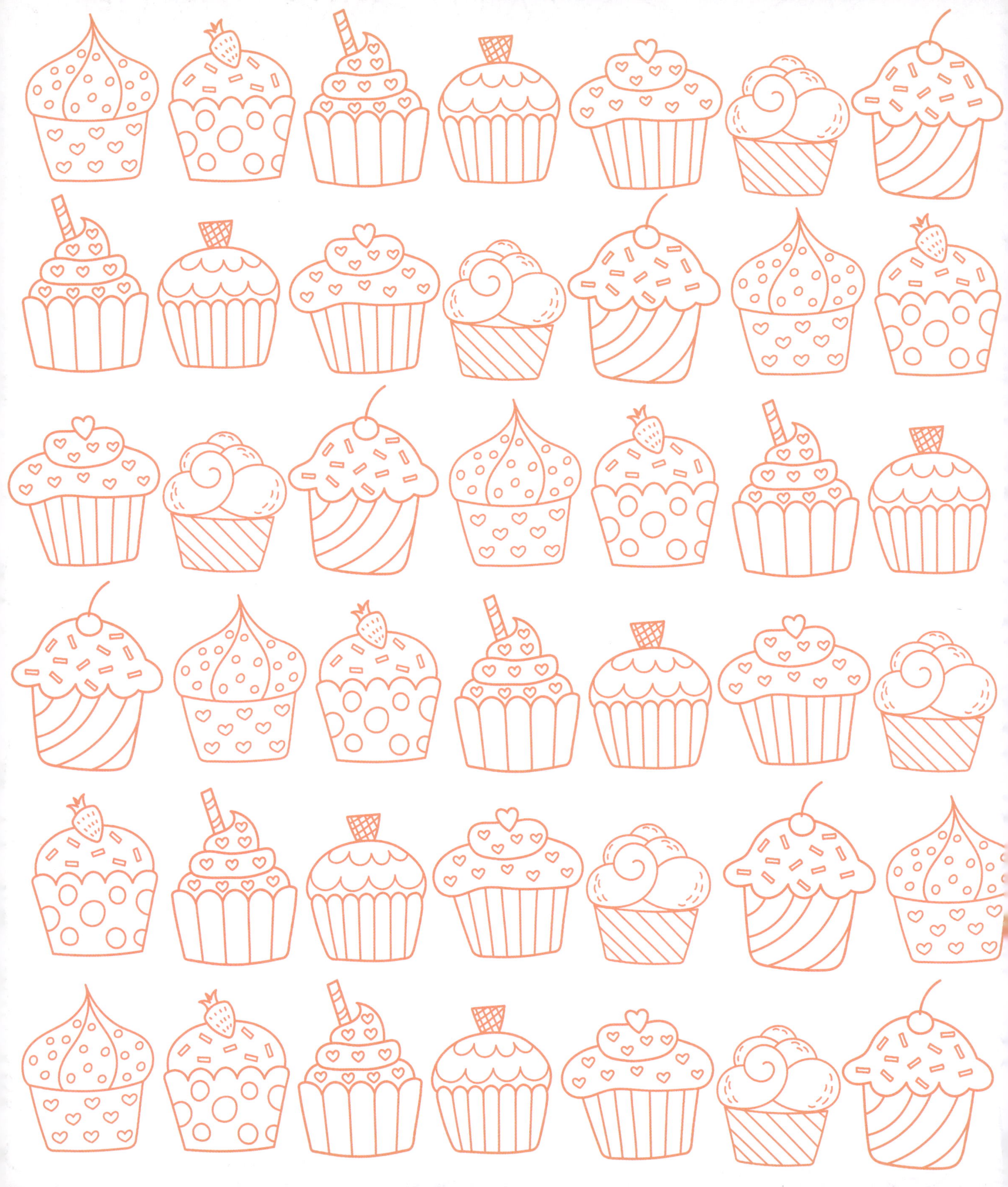

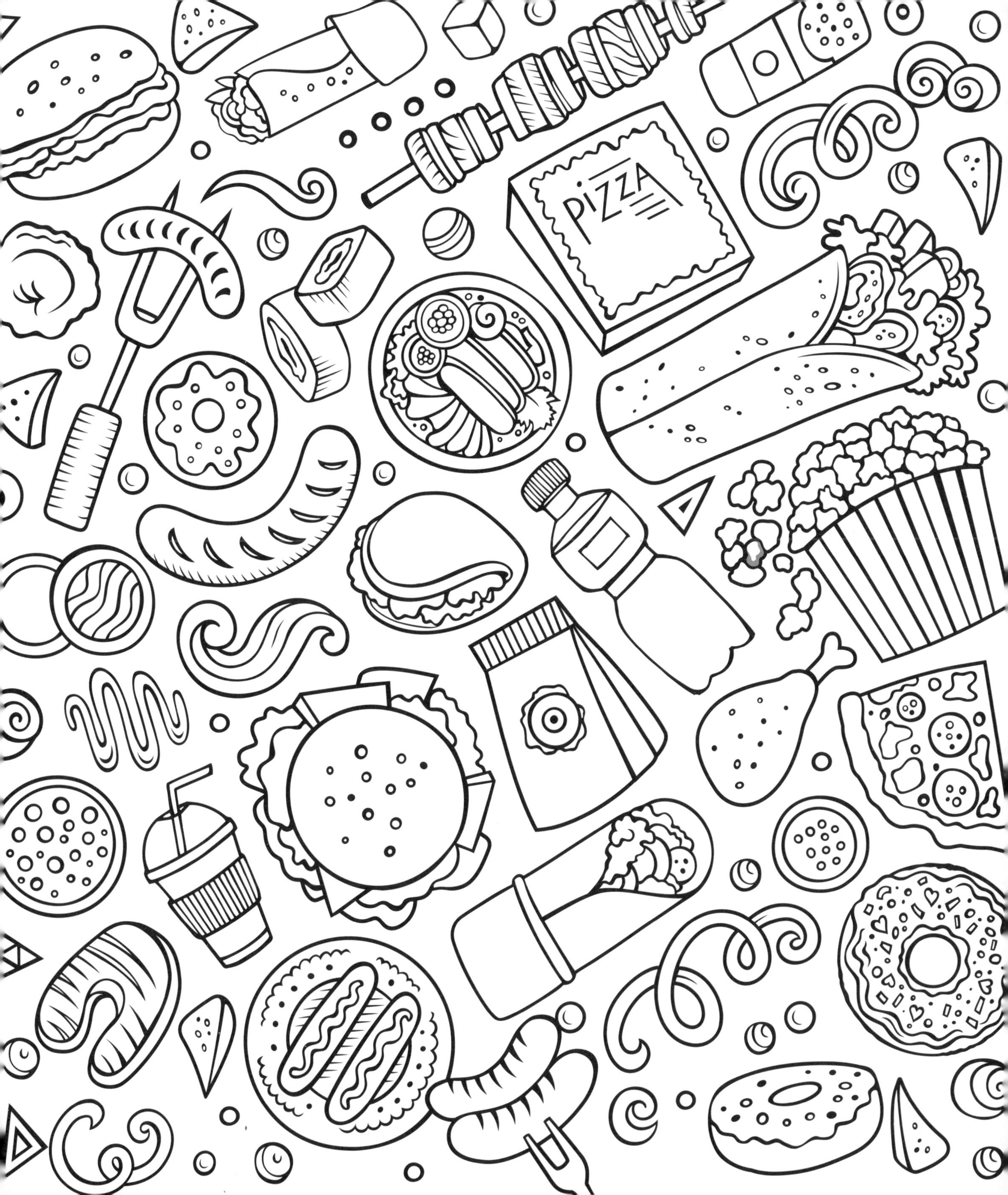

pizza

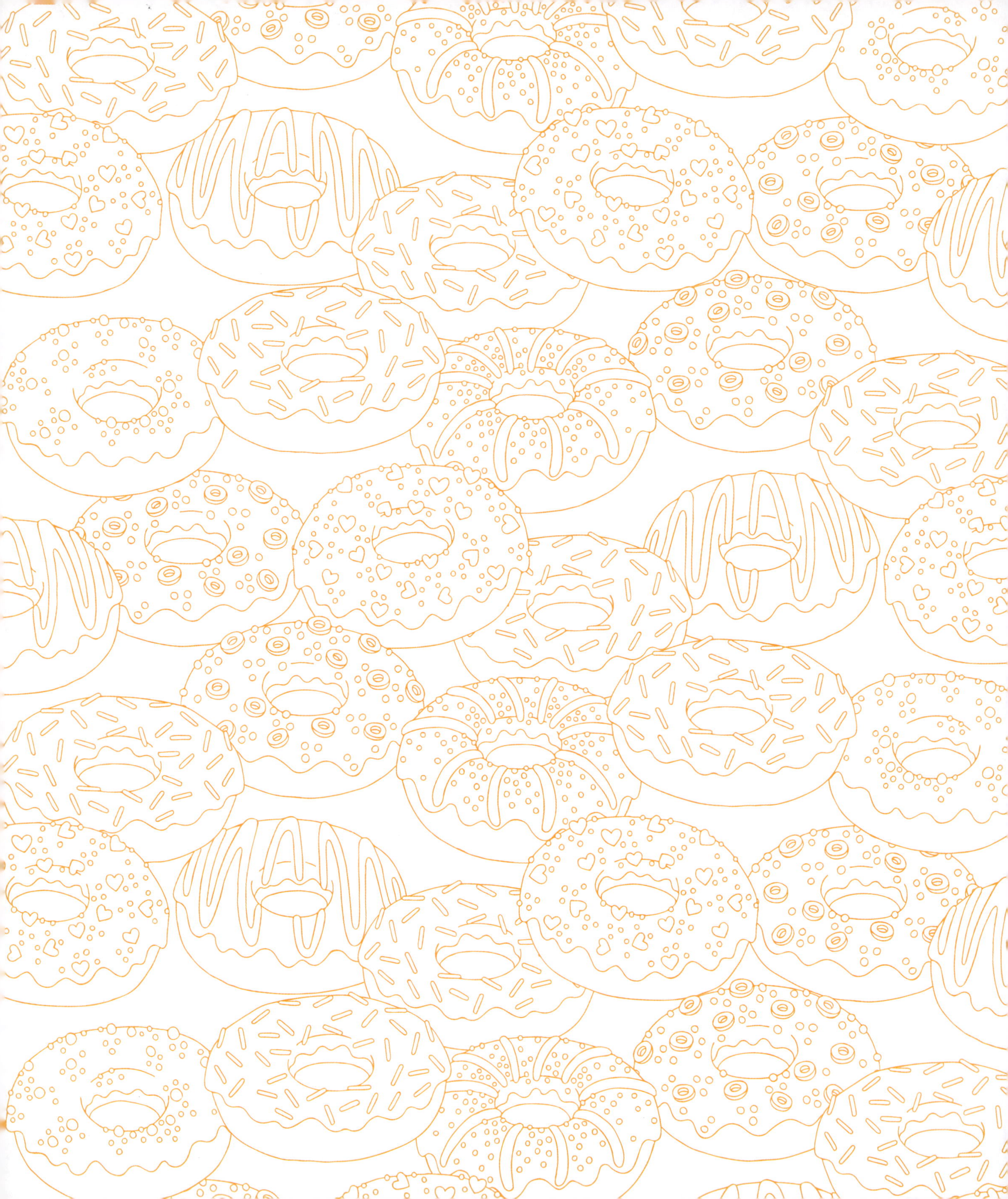

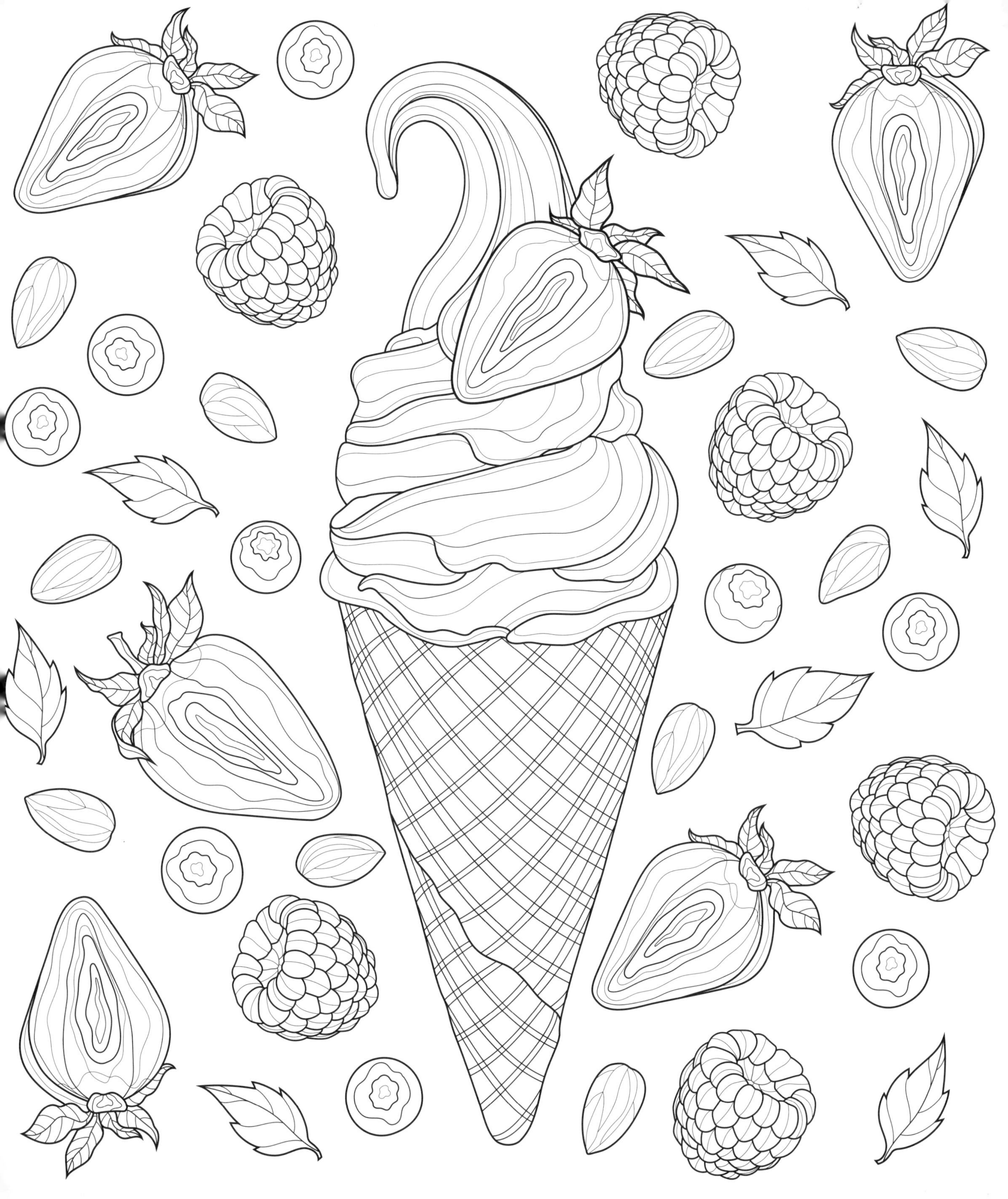

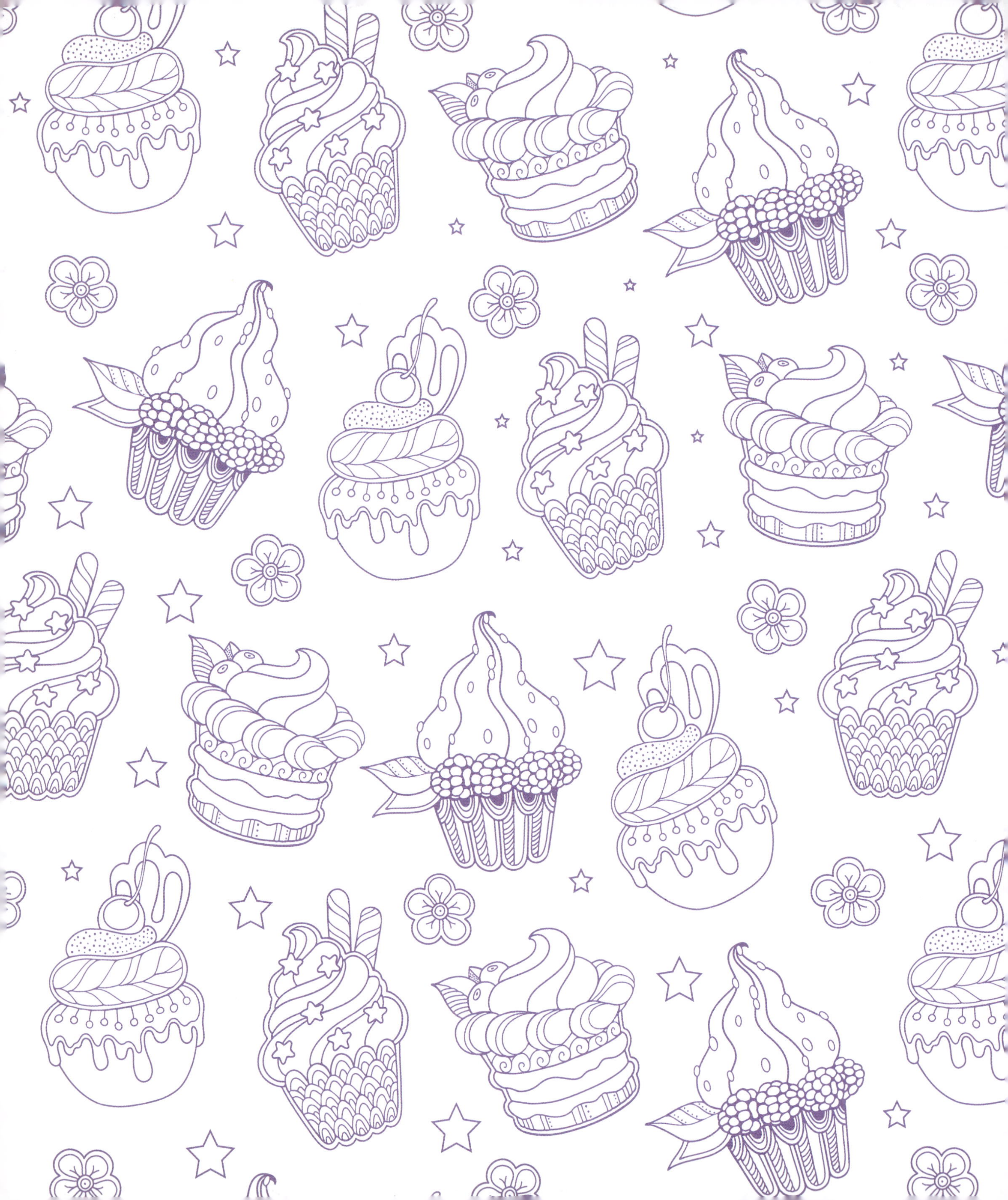

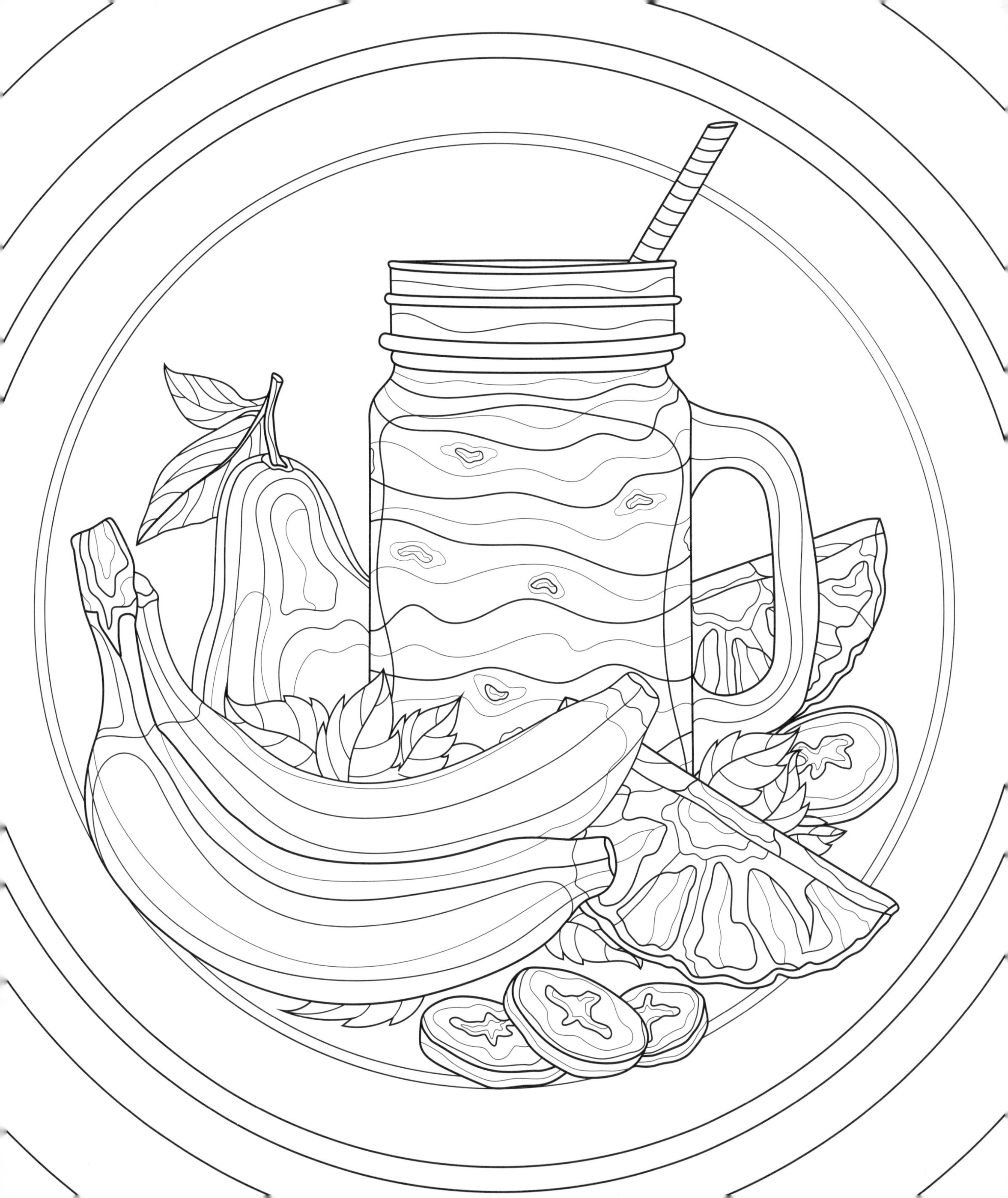

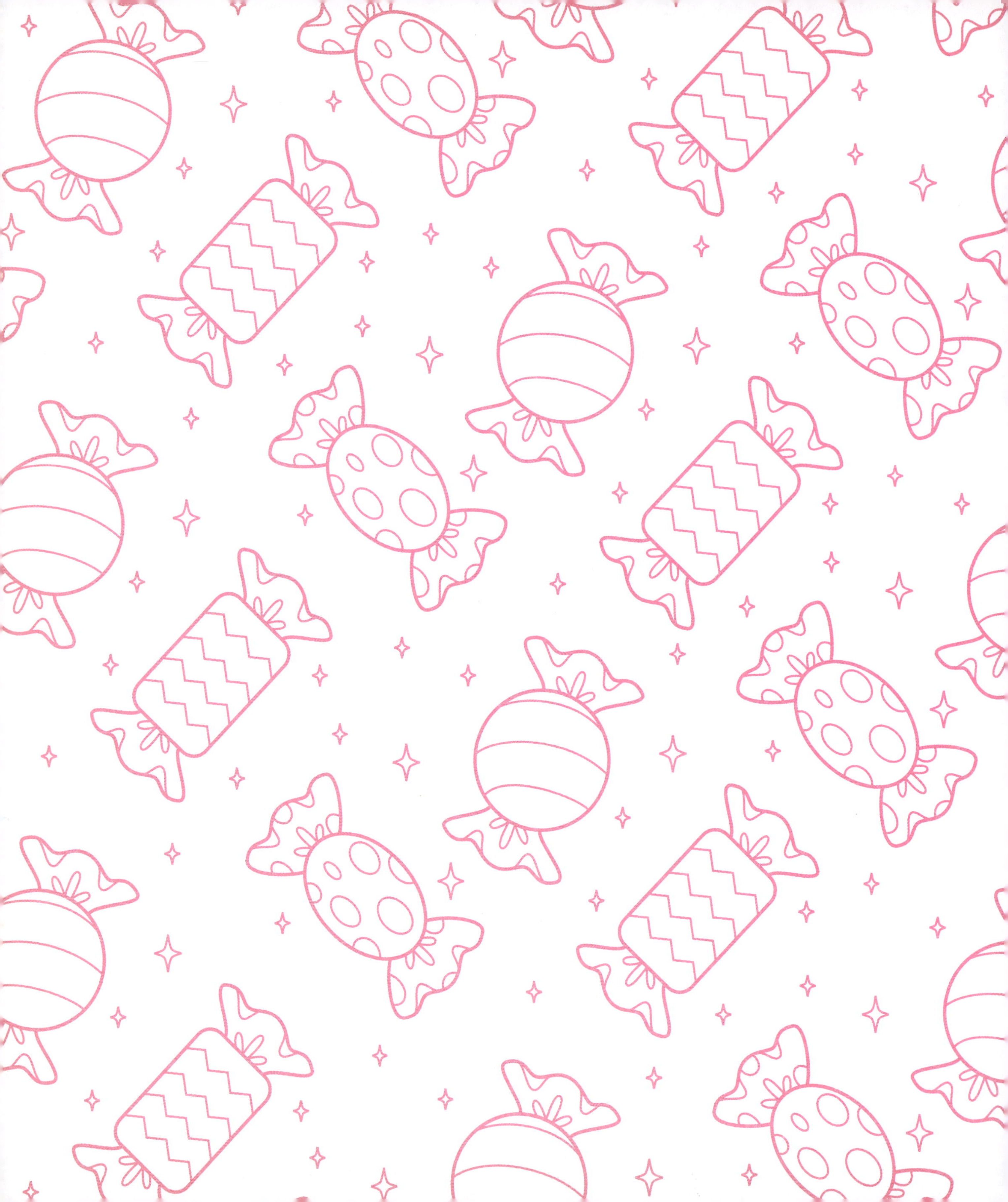

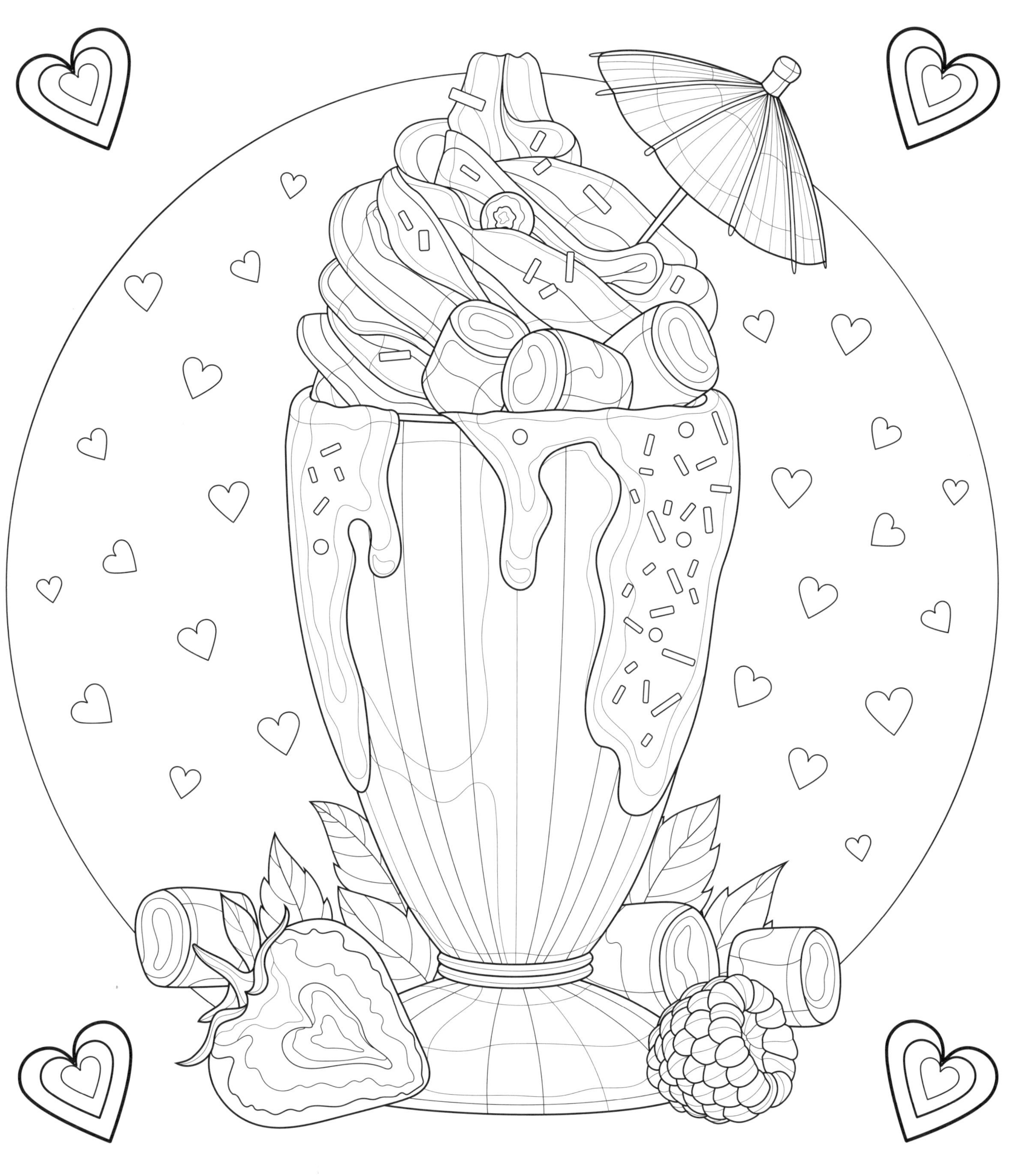

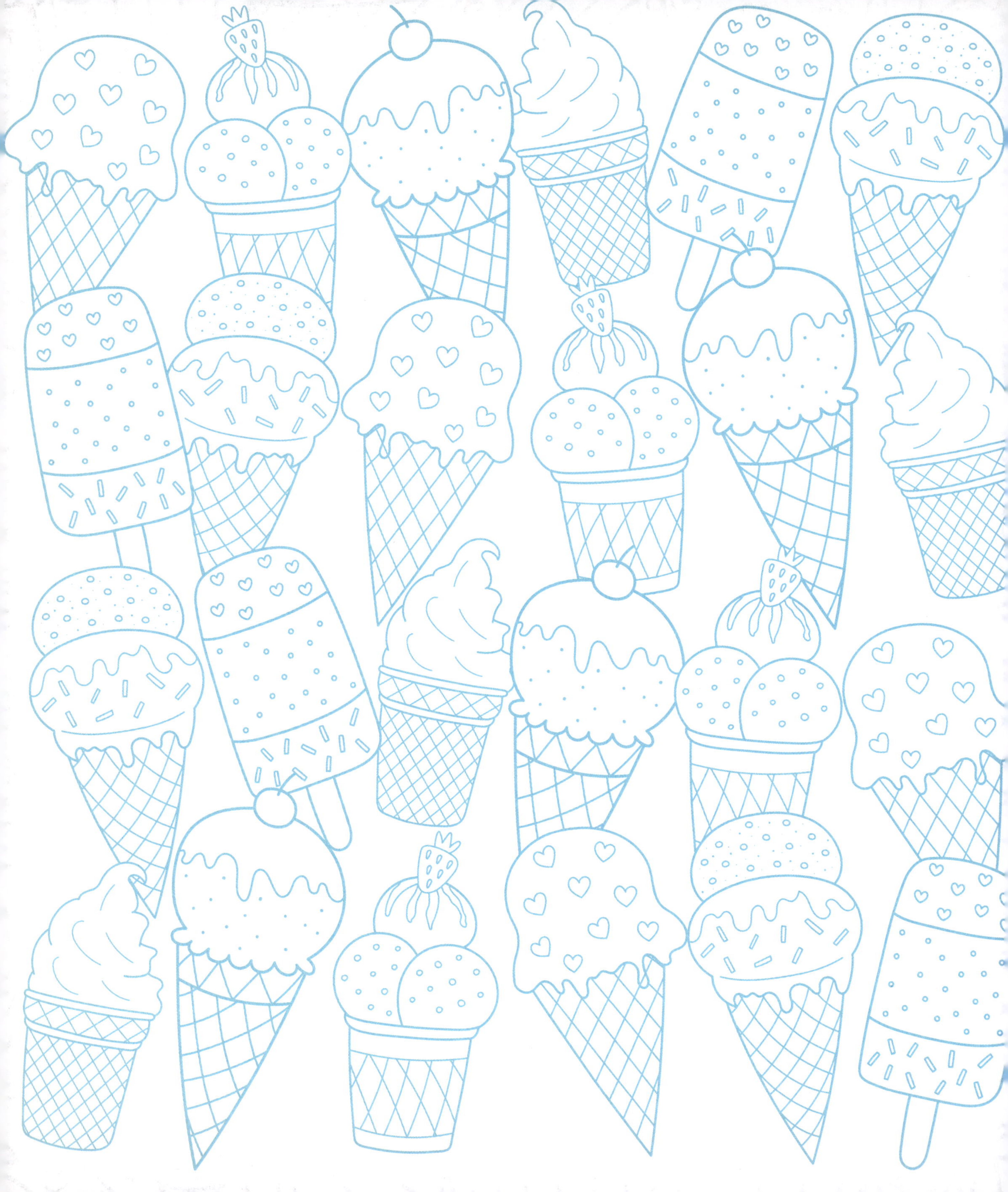

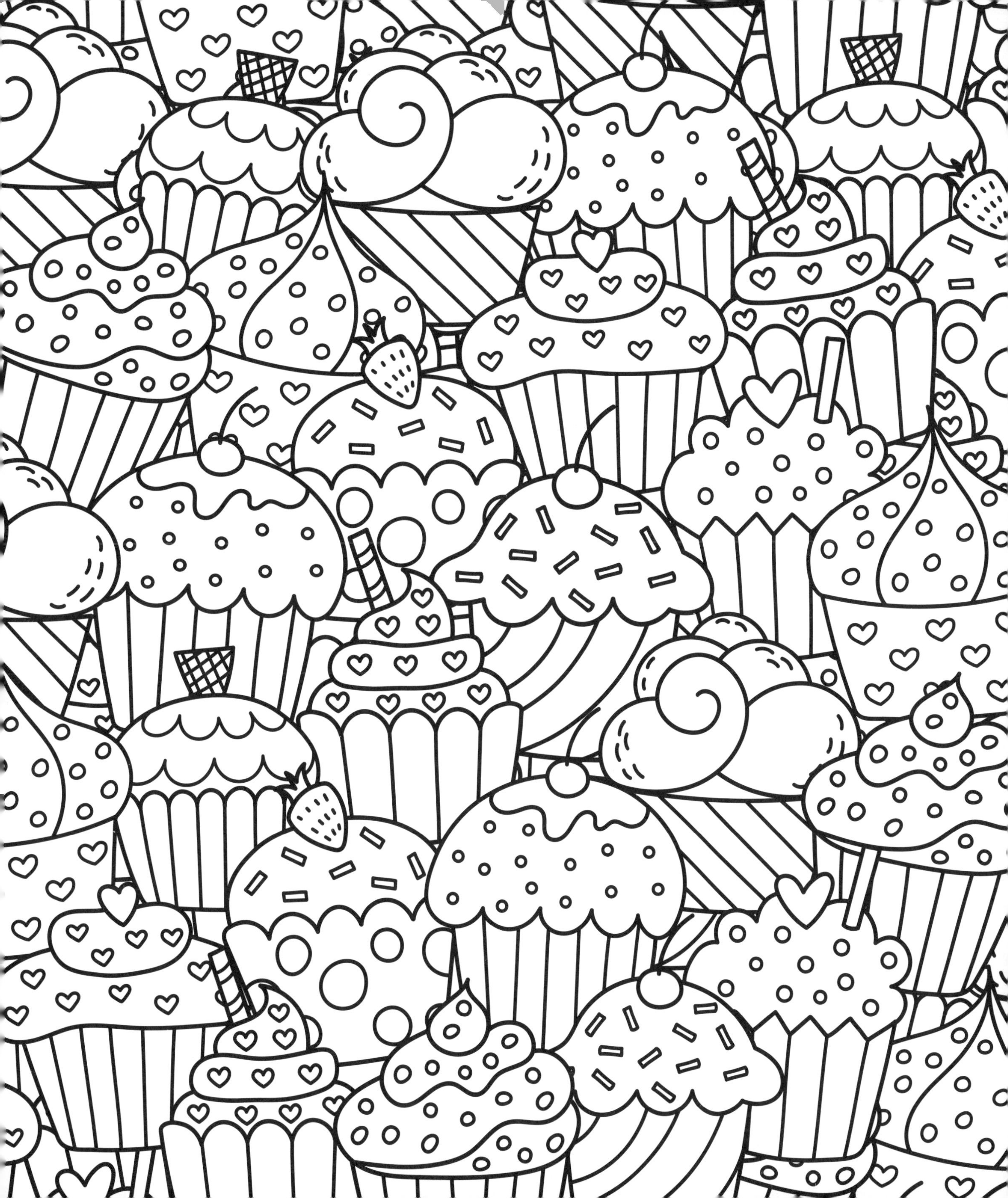

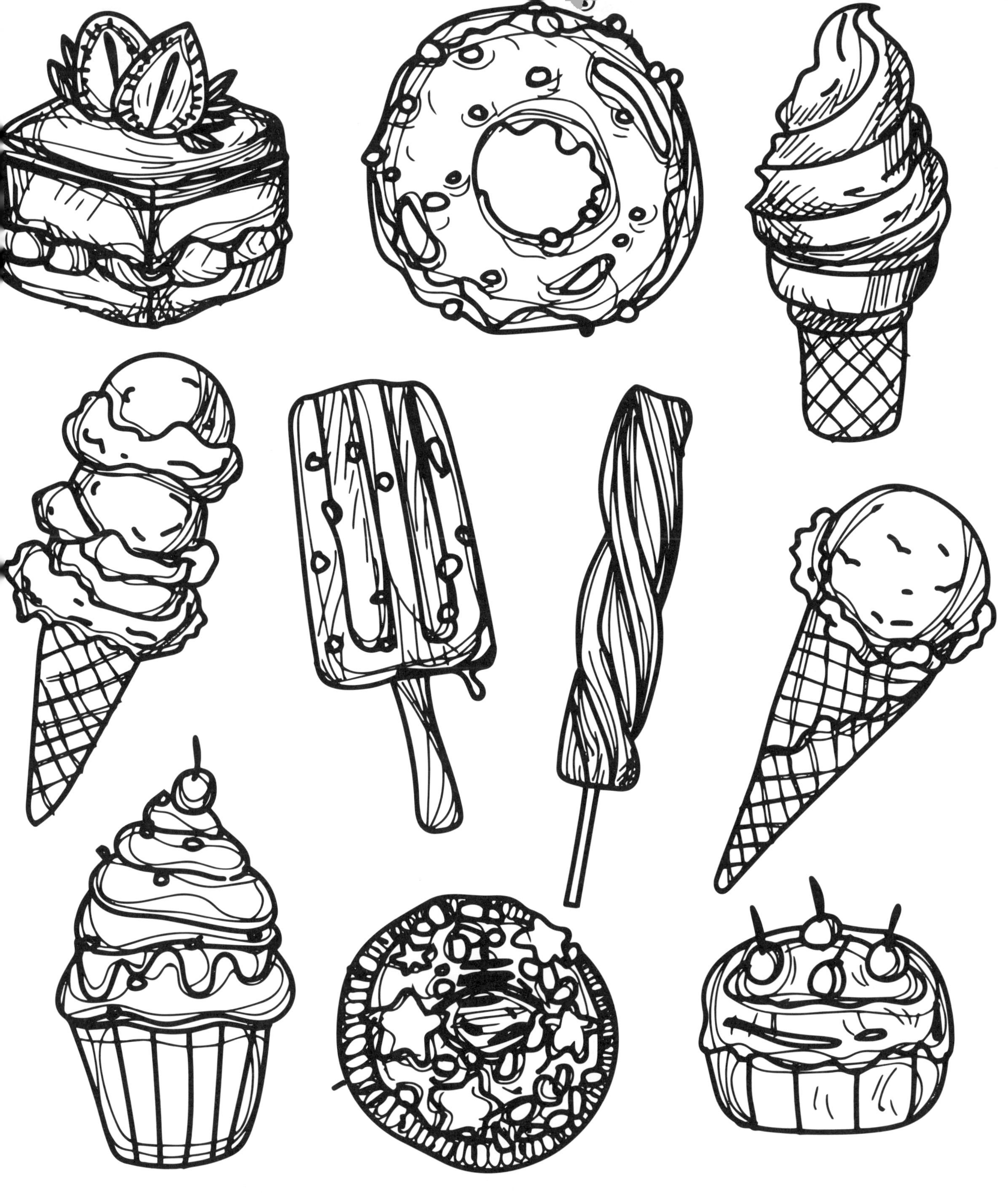

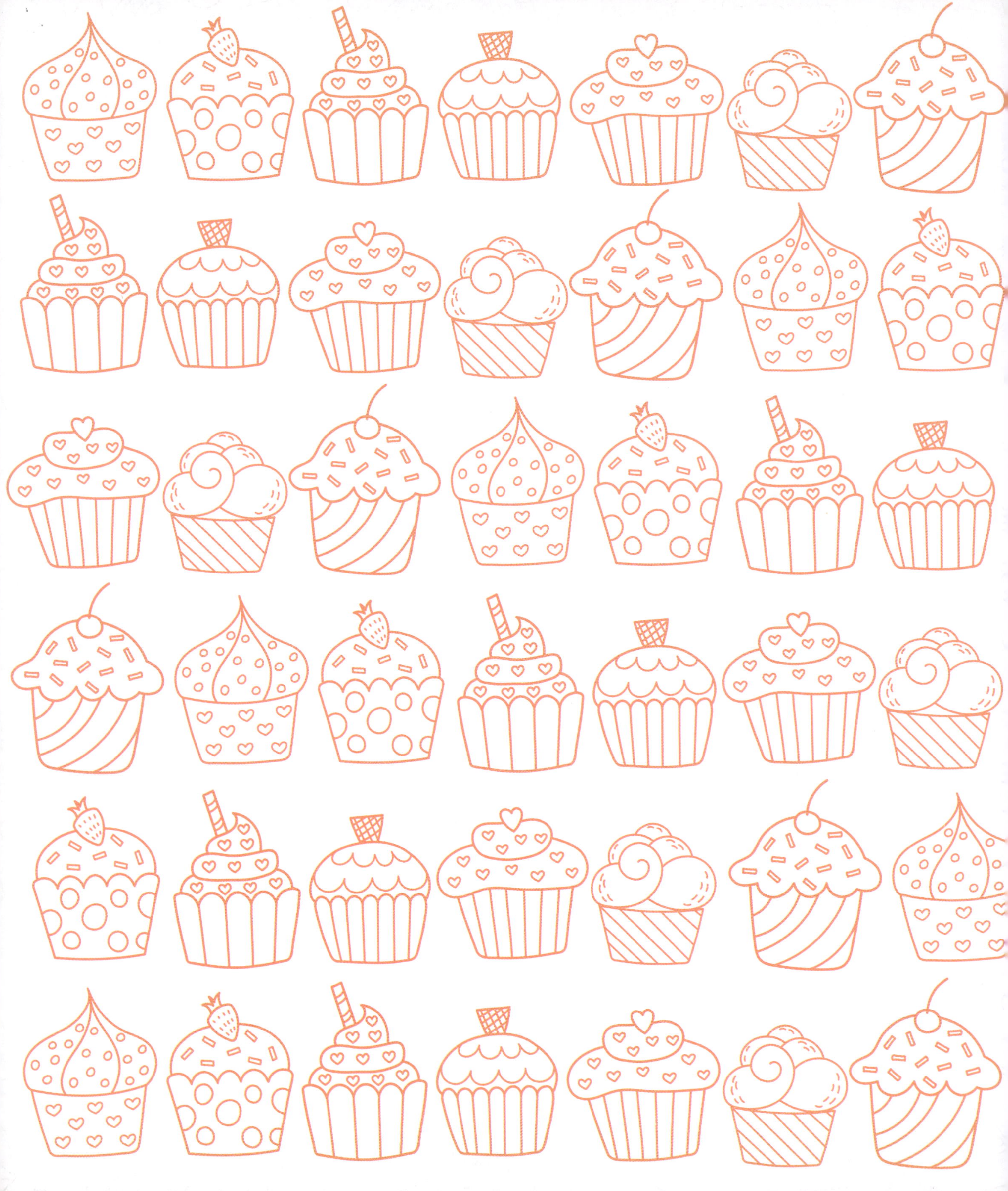

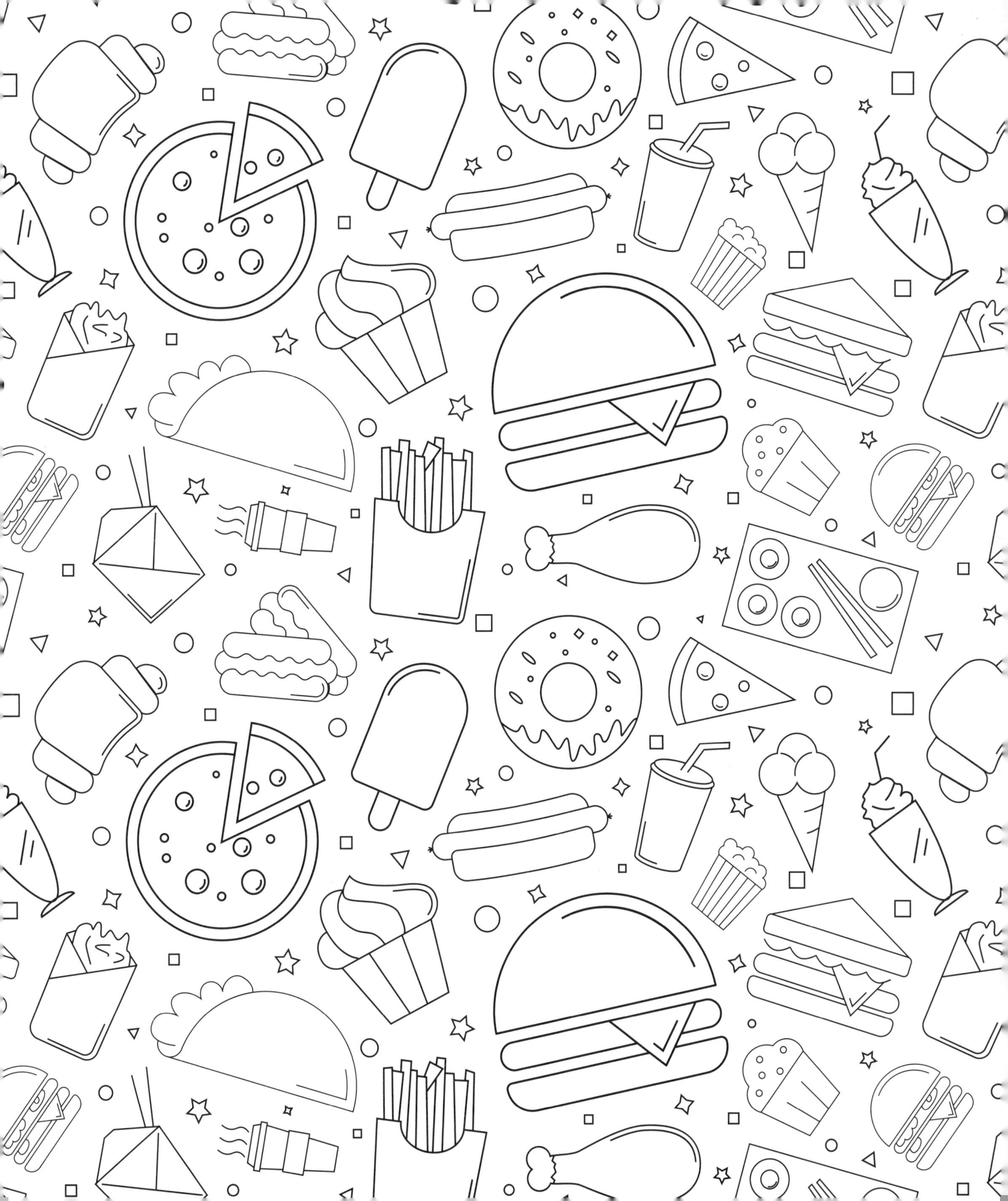

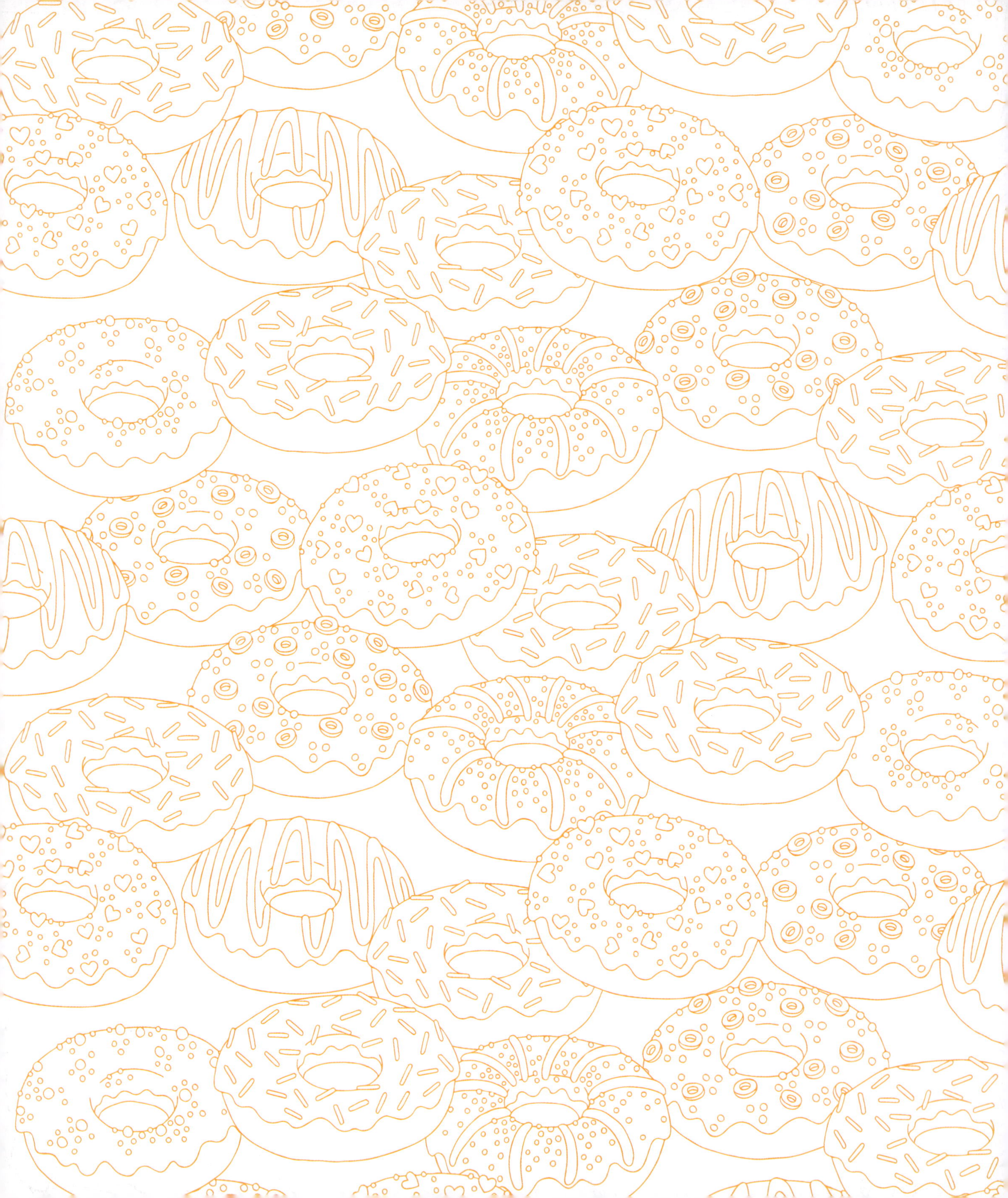

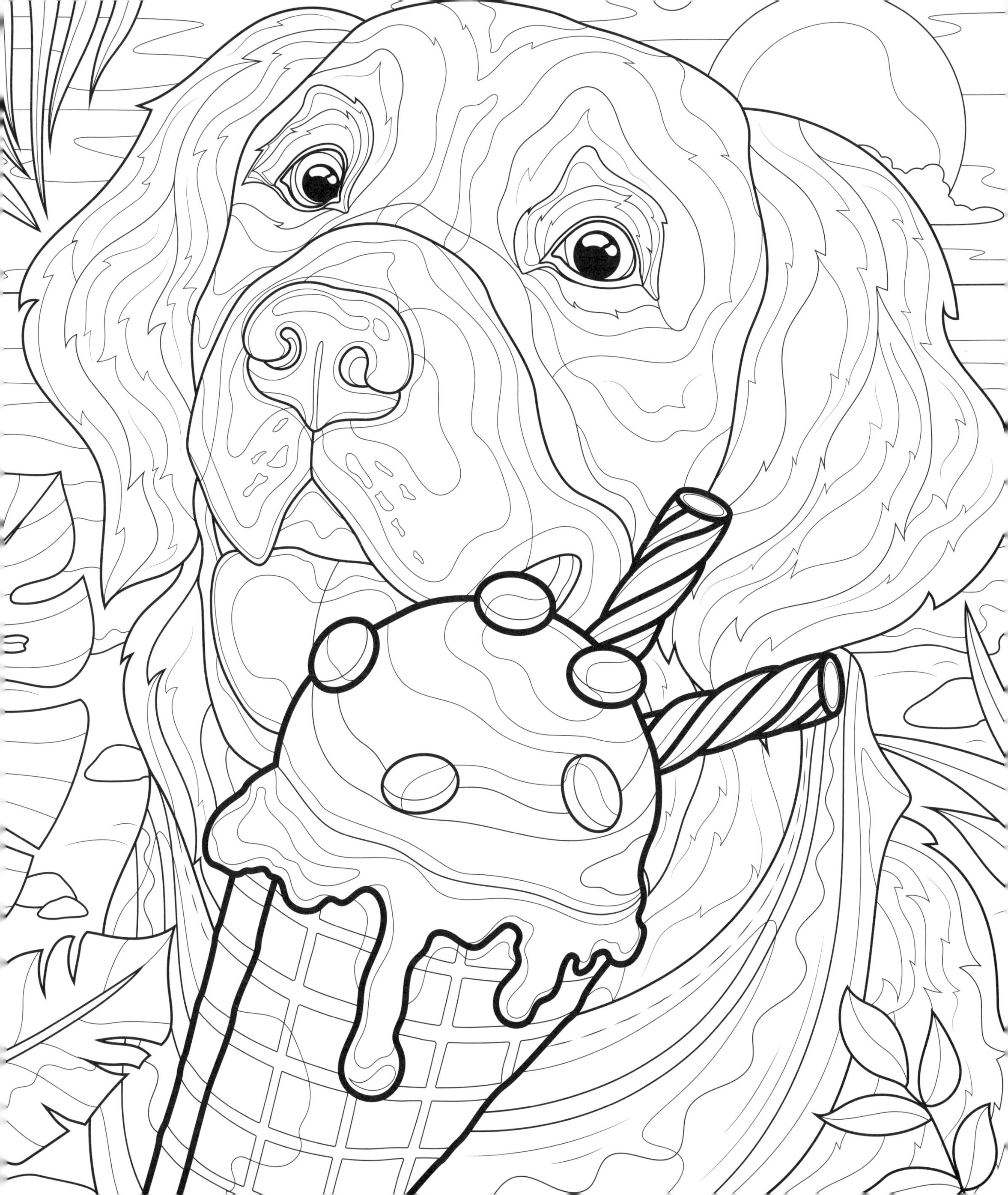

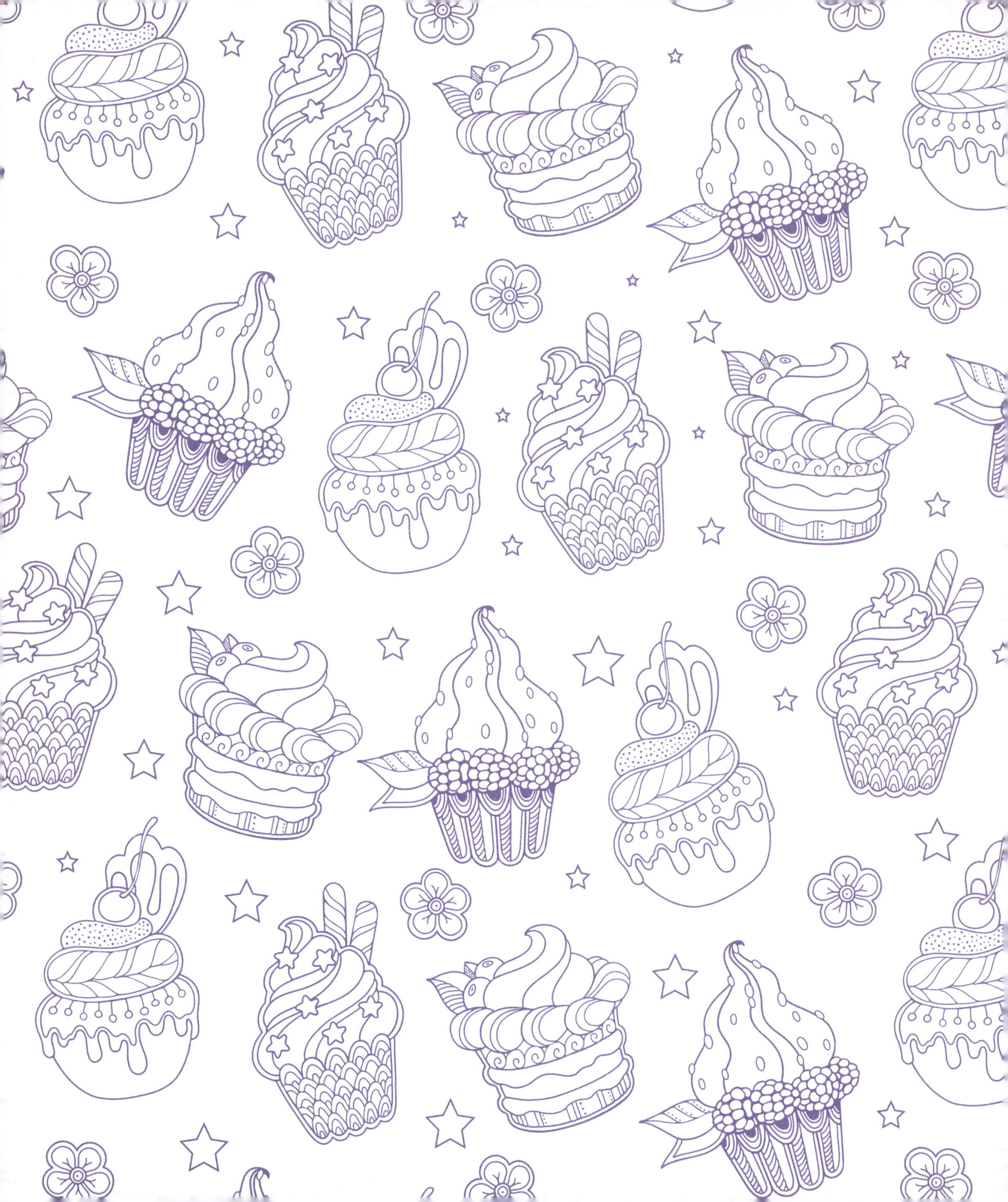

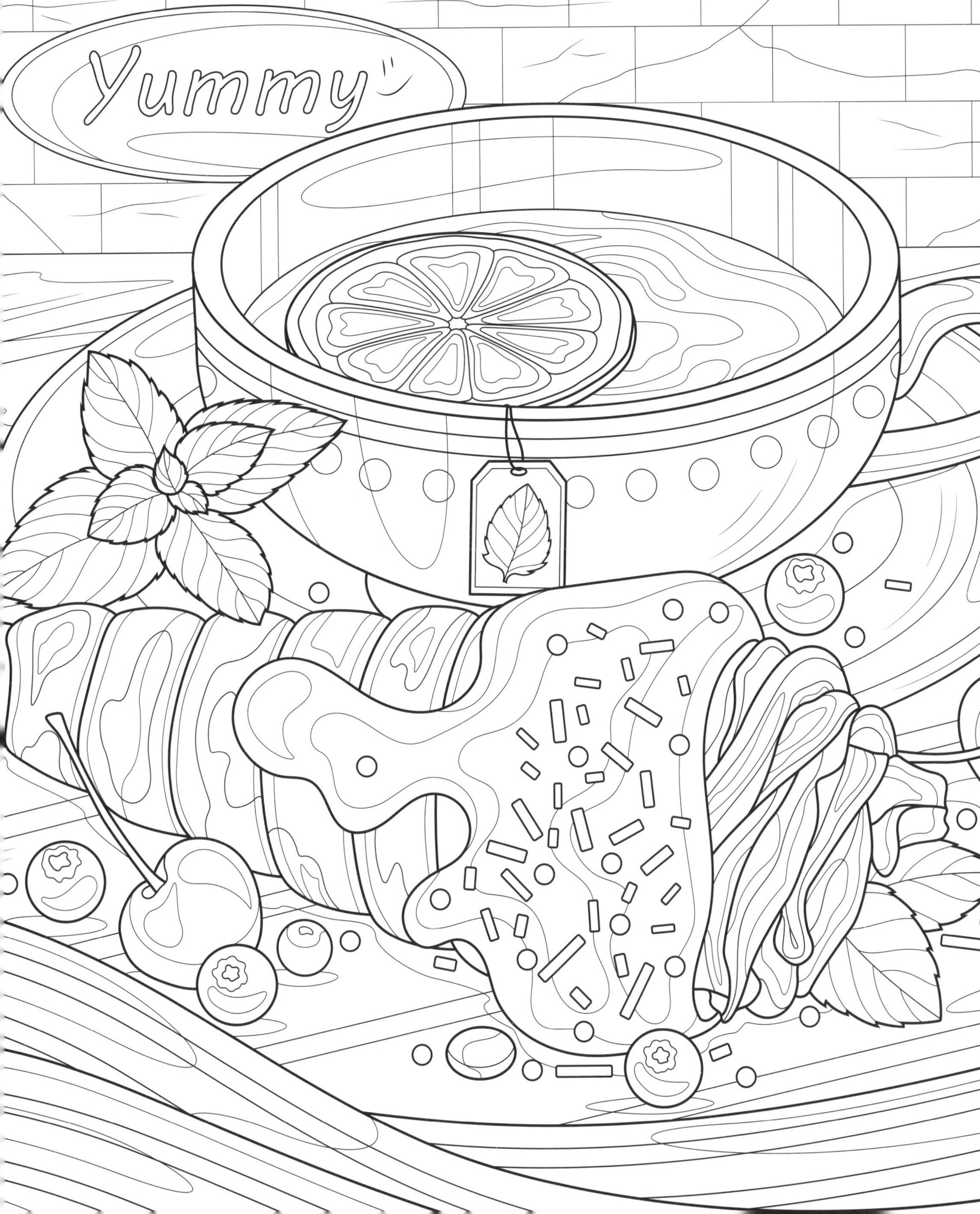
Yummy

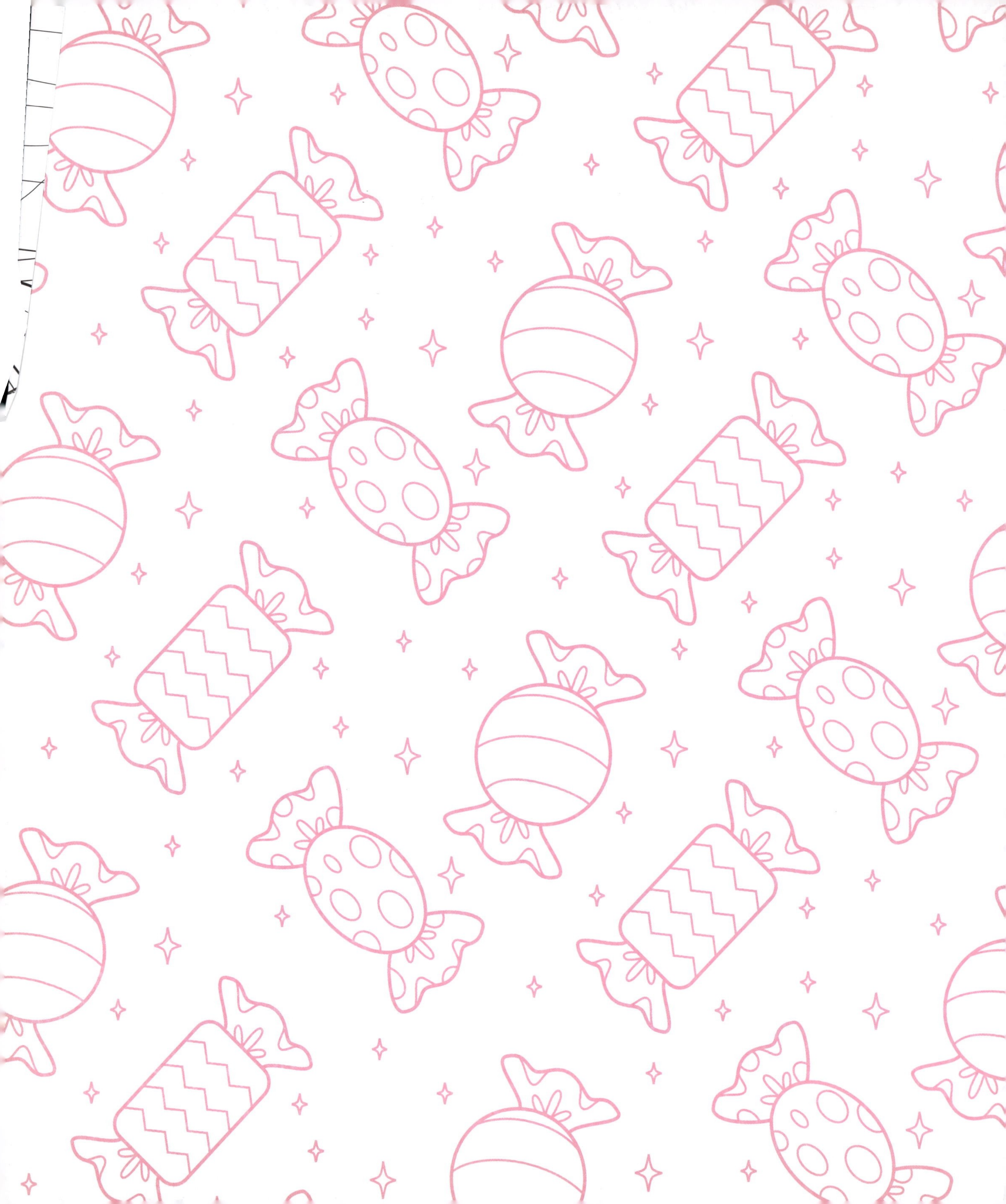

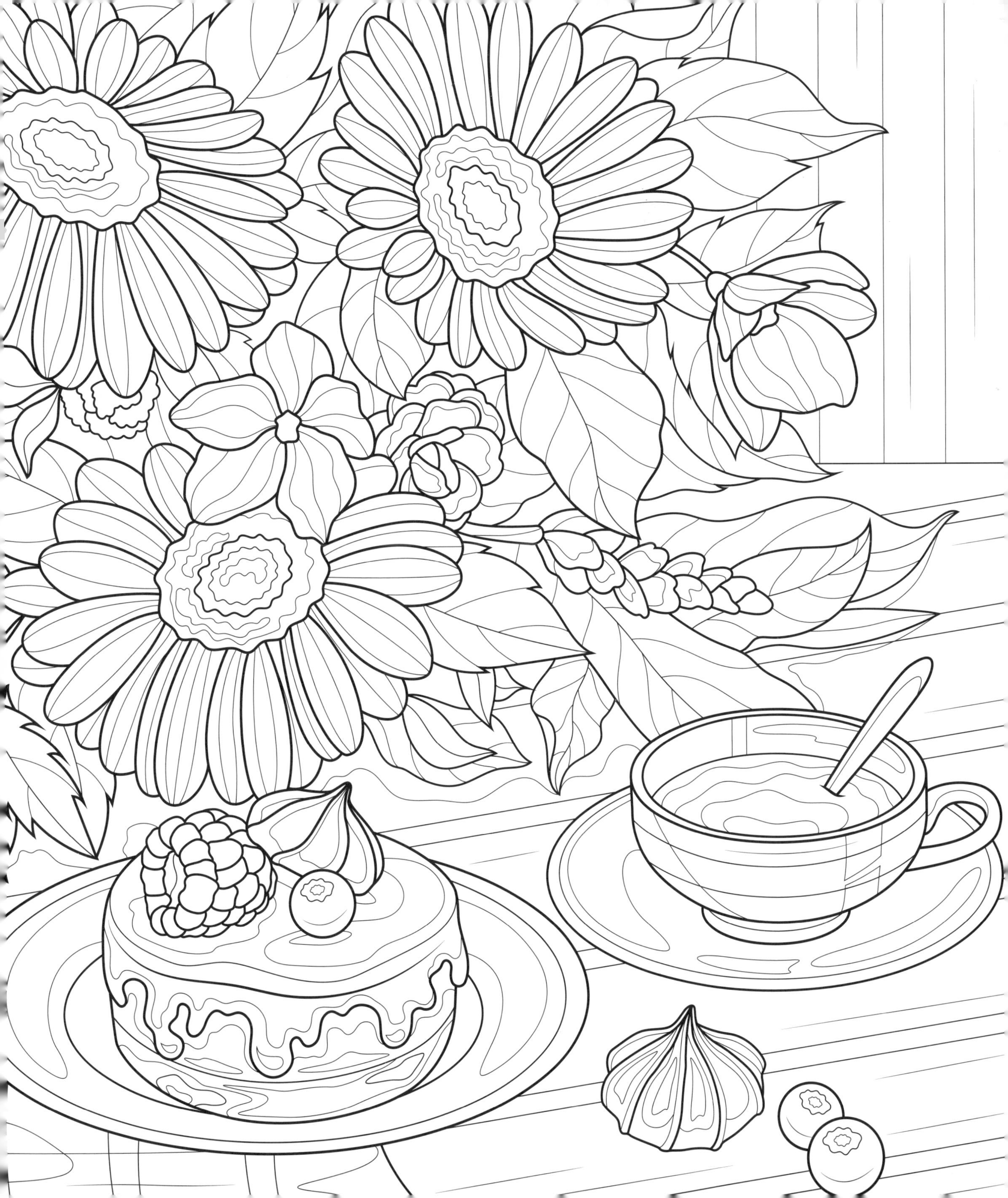

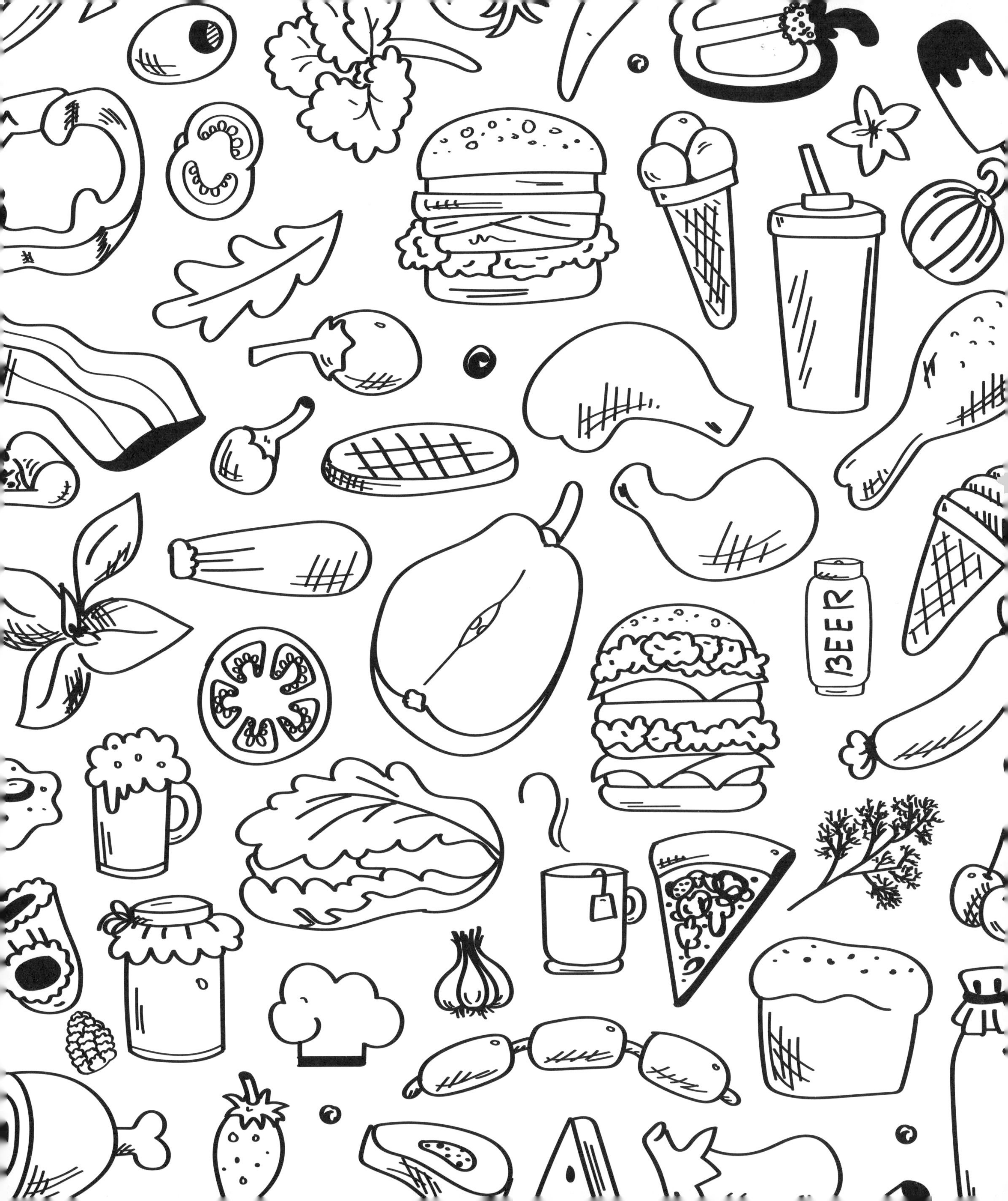
BEER

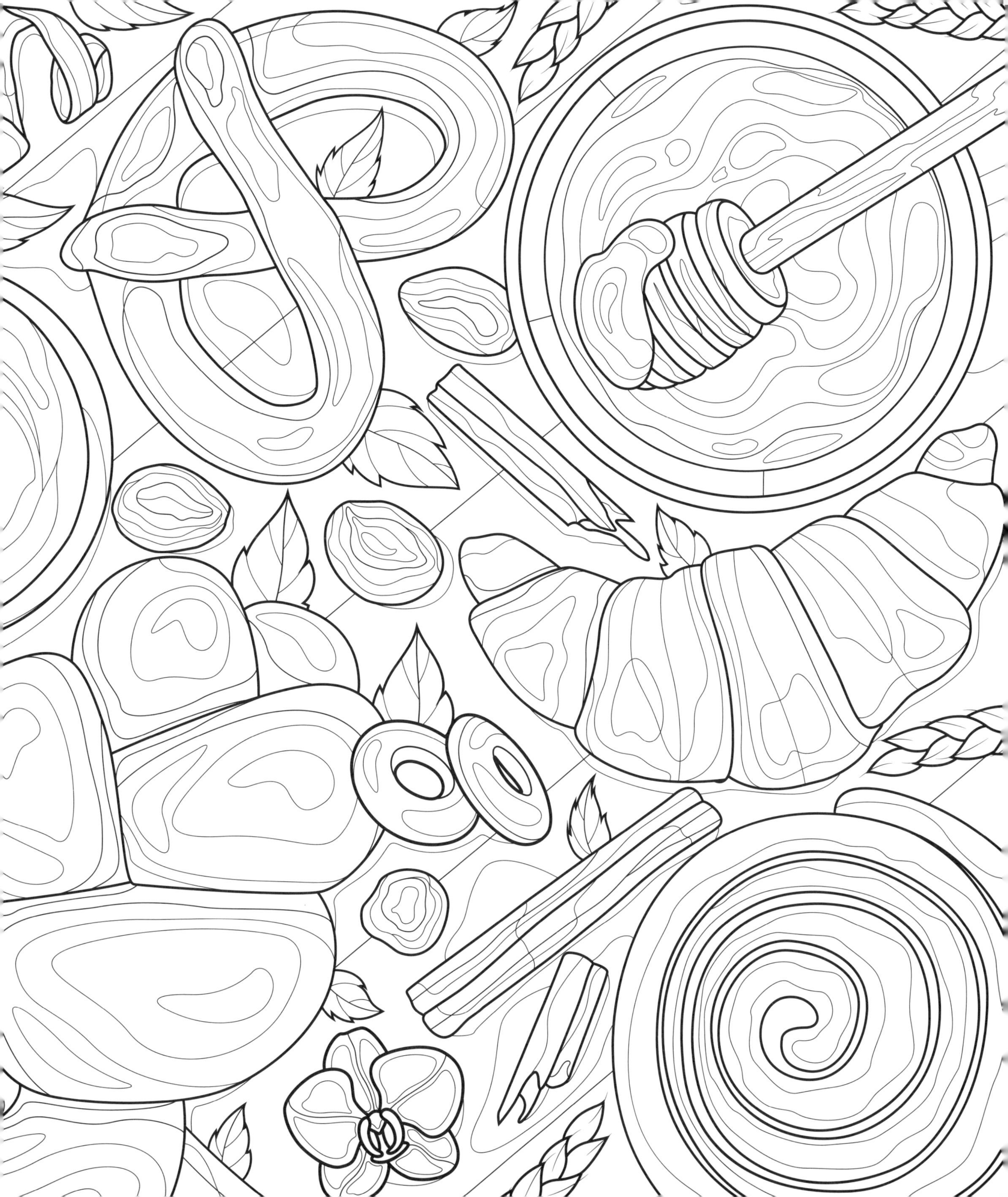

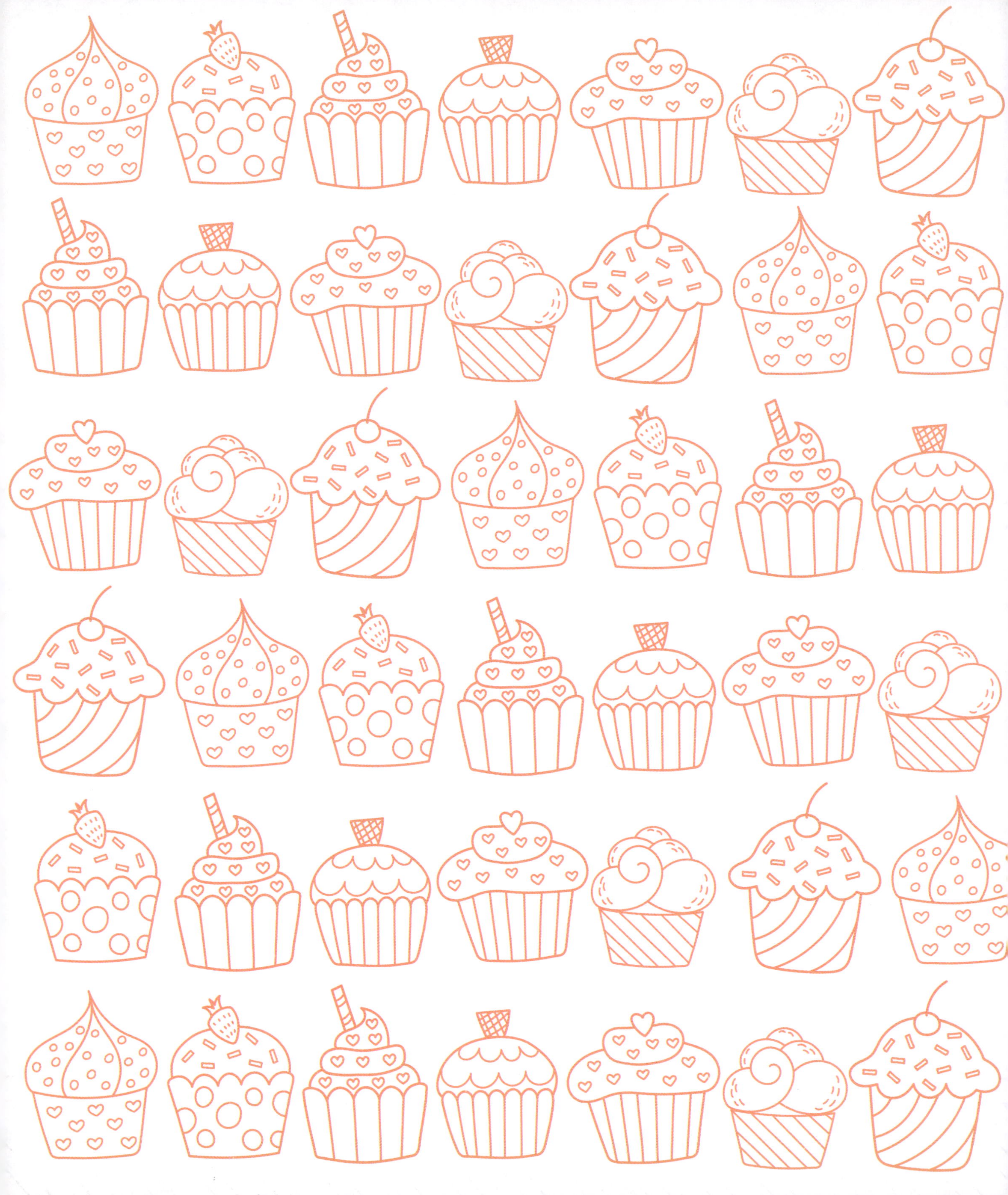

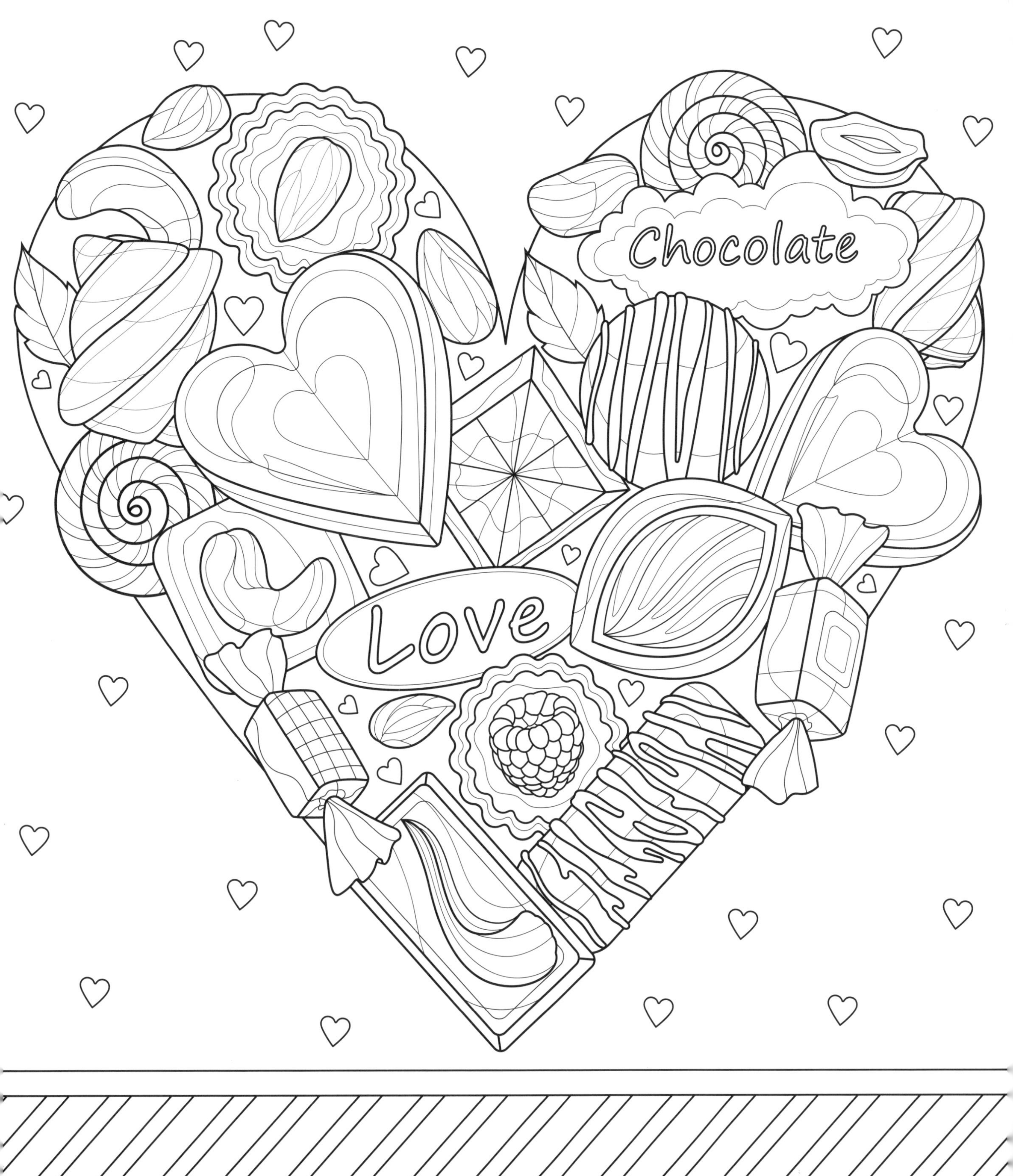

Chocolate
Love

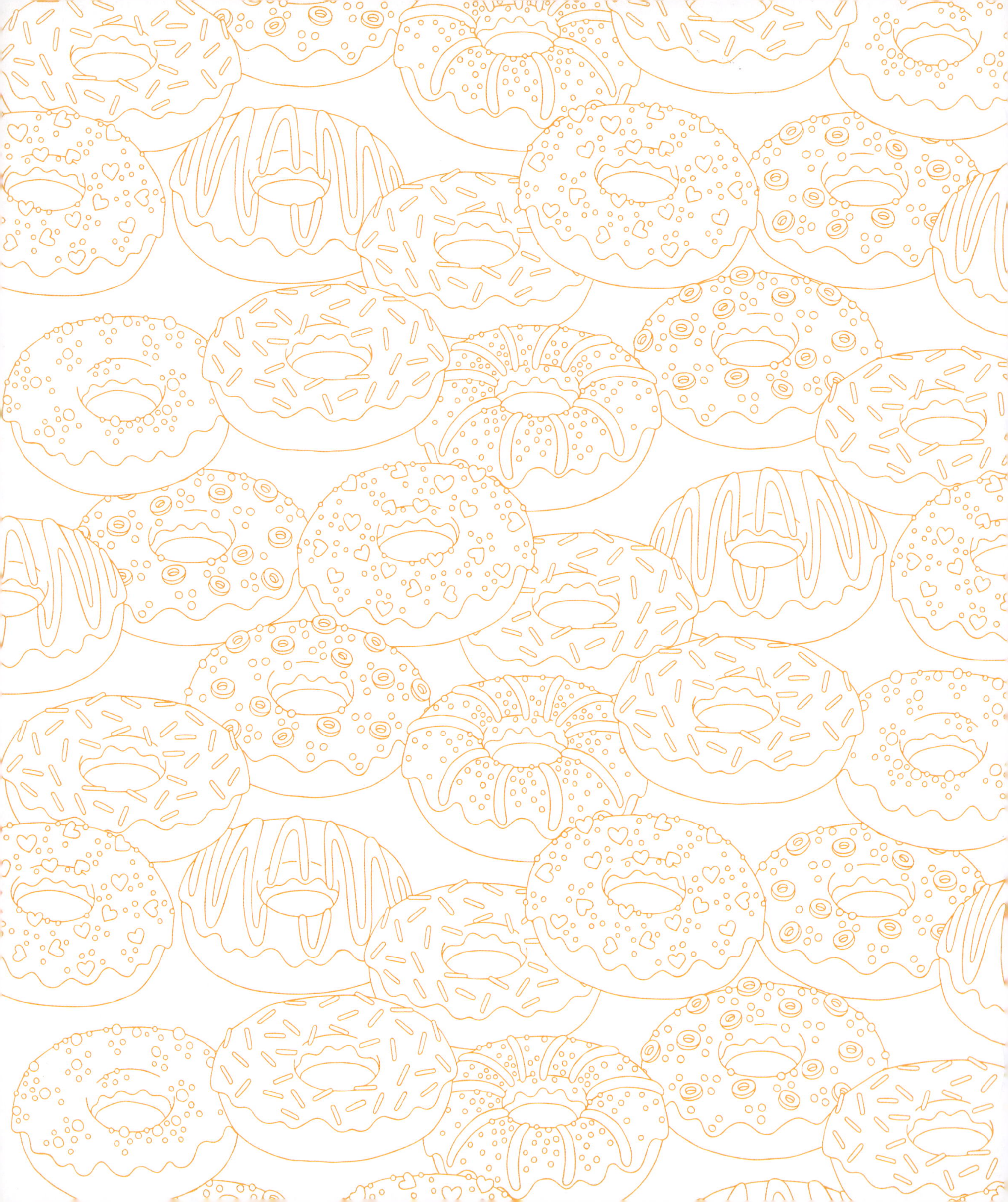

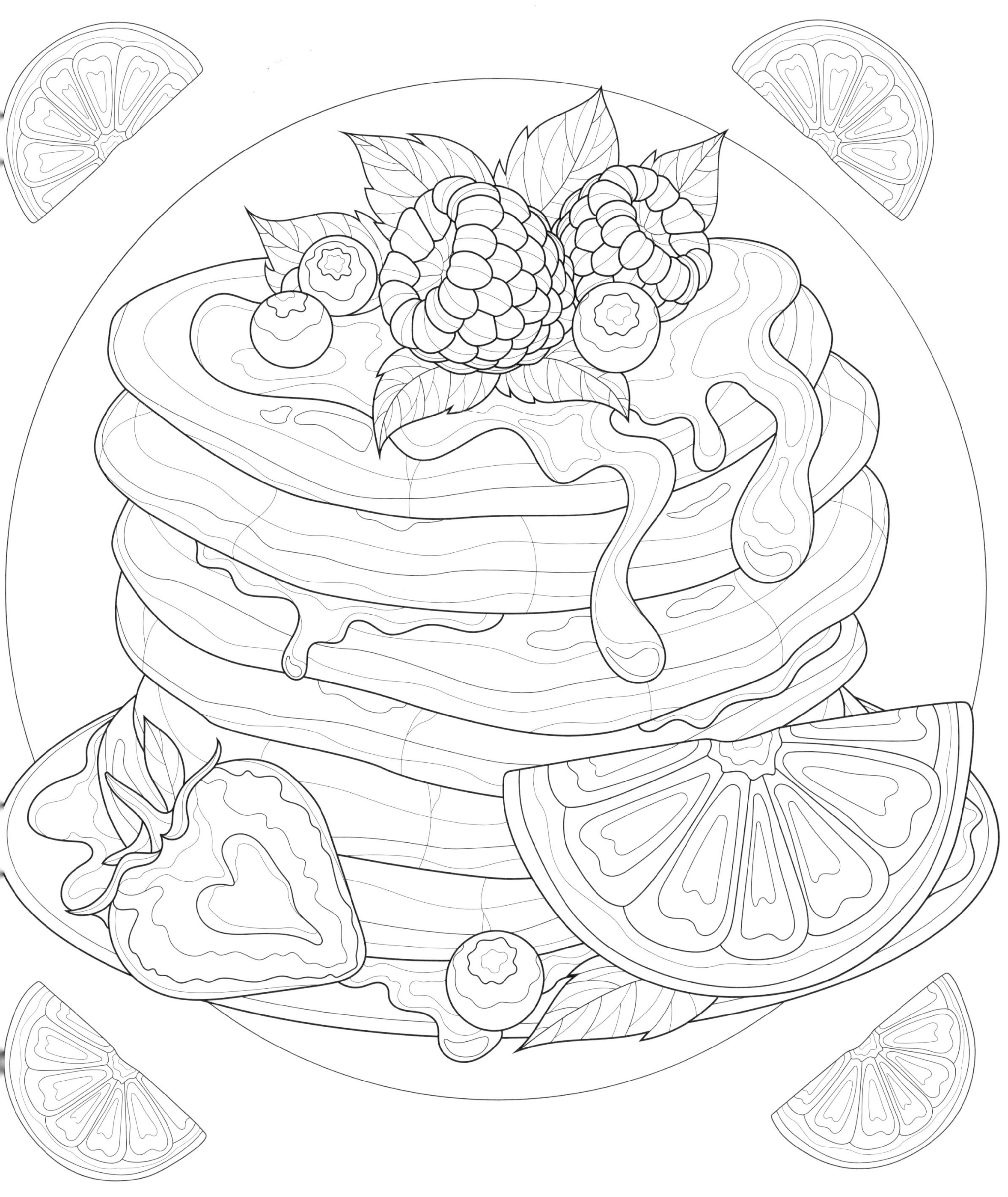

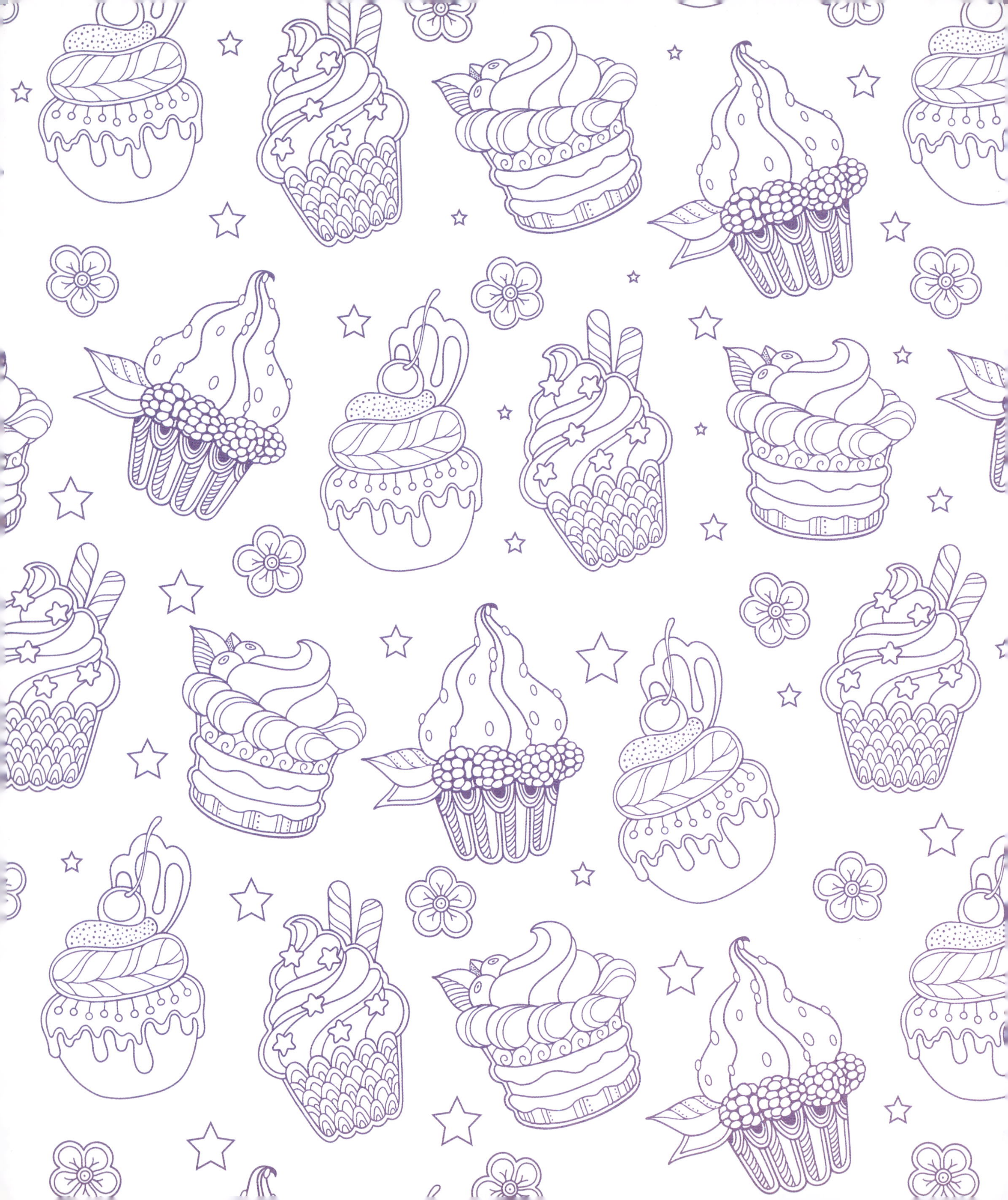

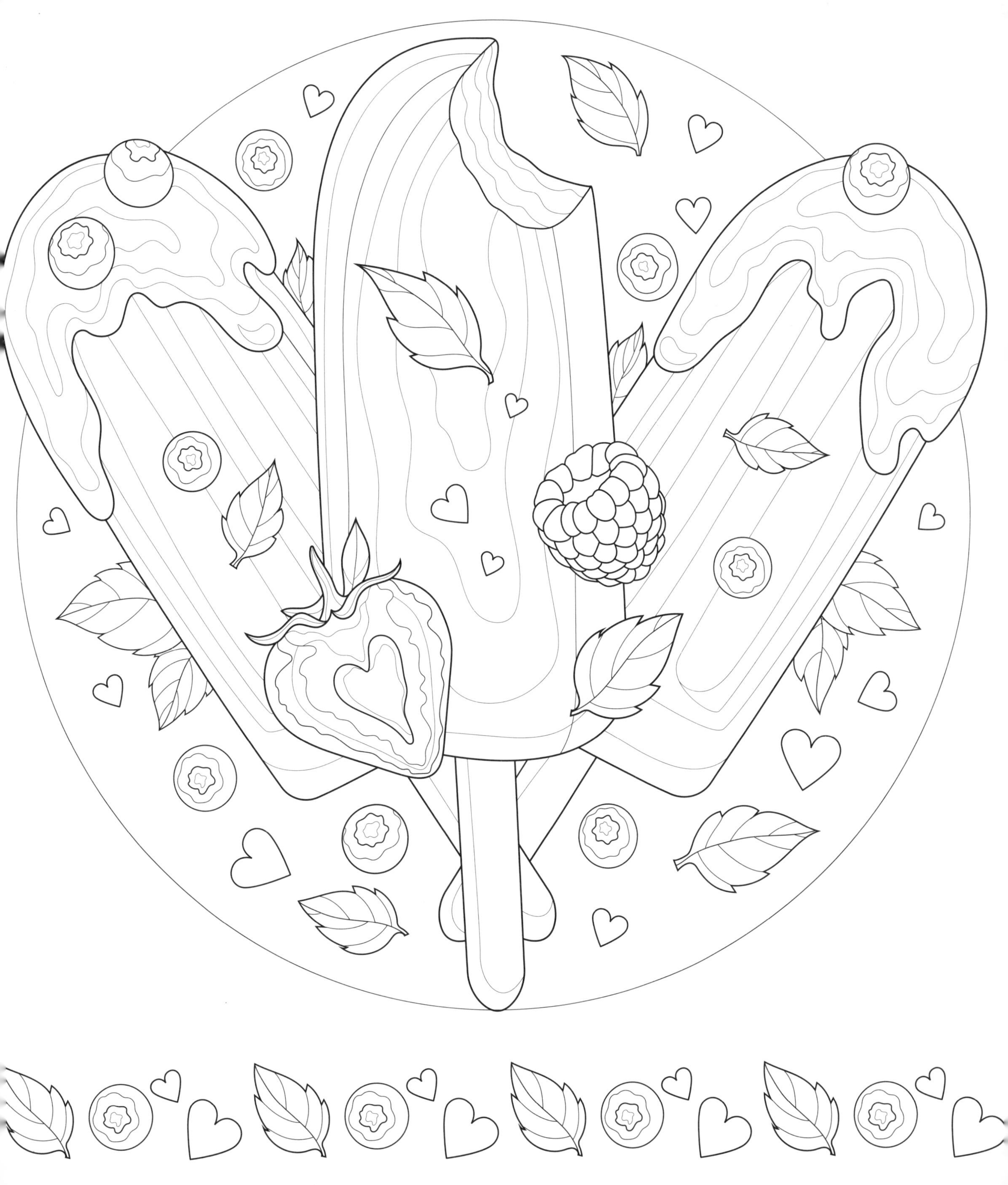

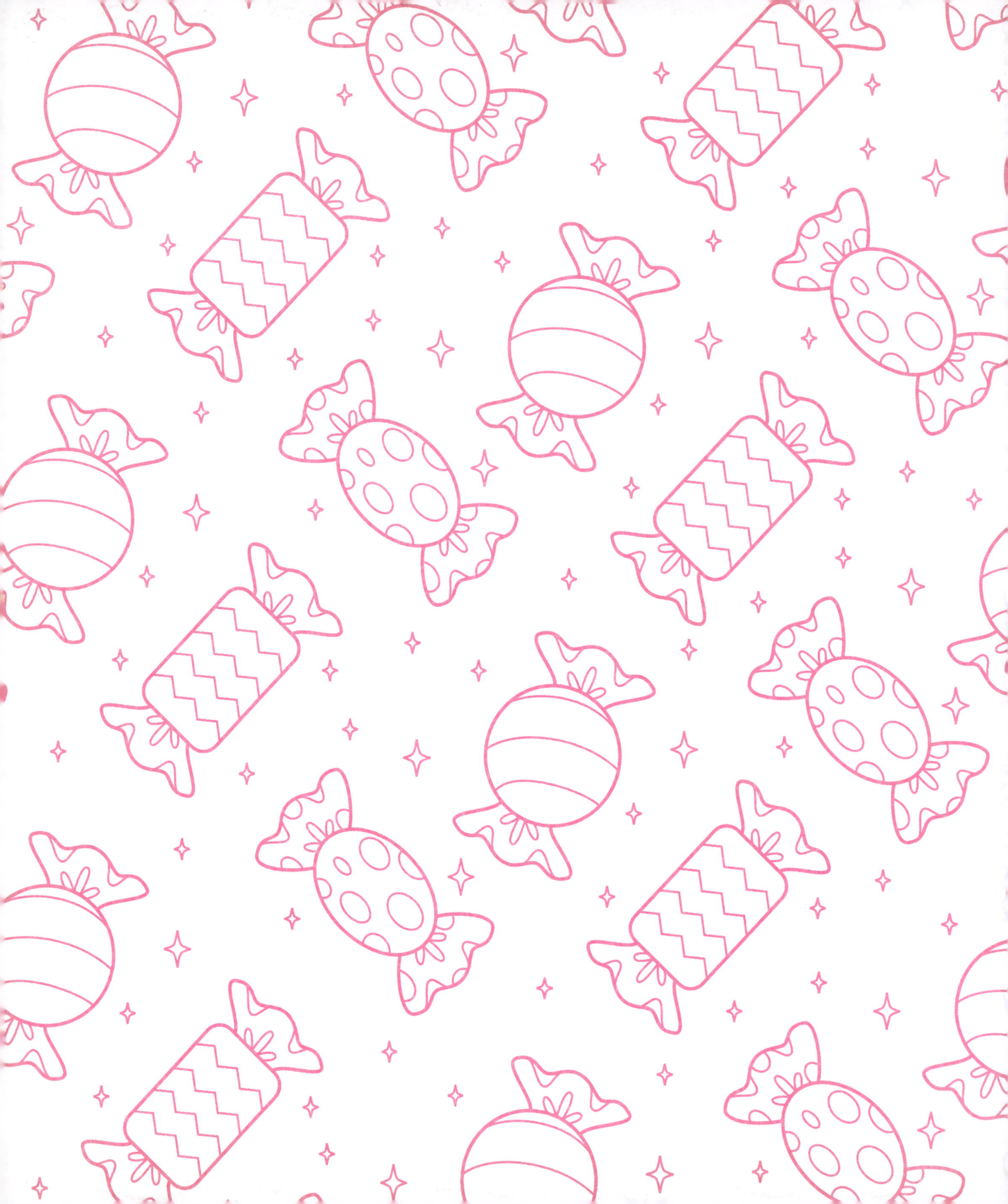

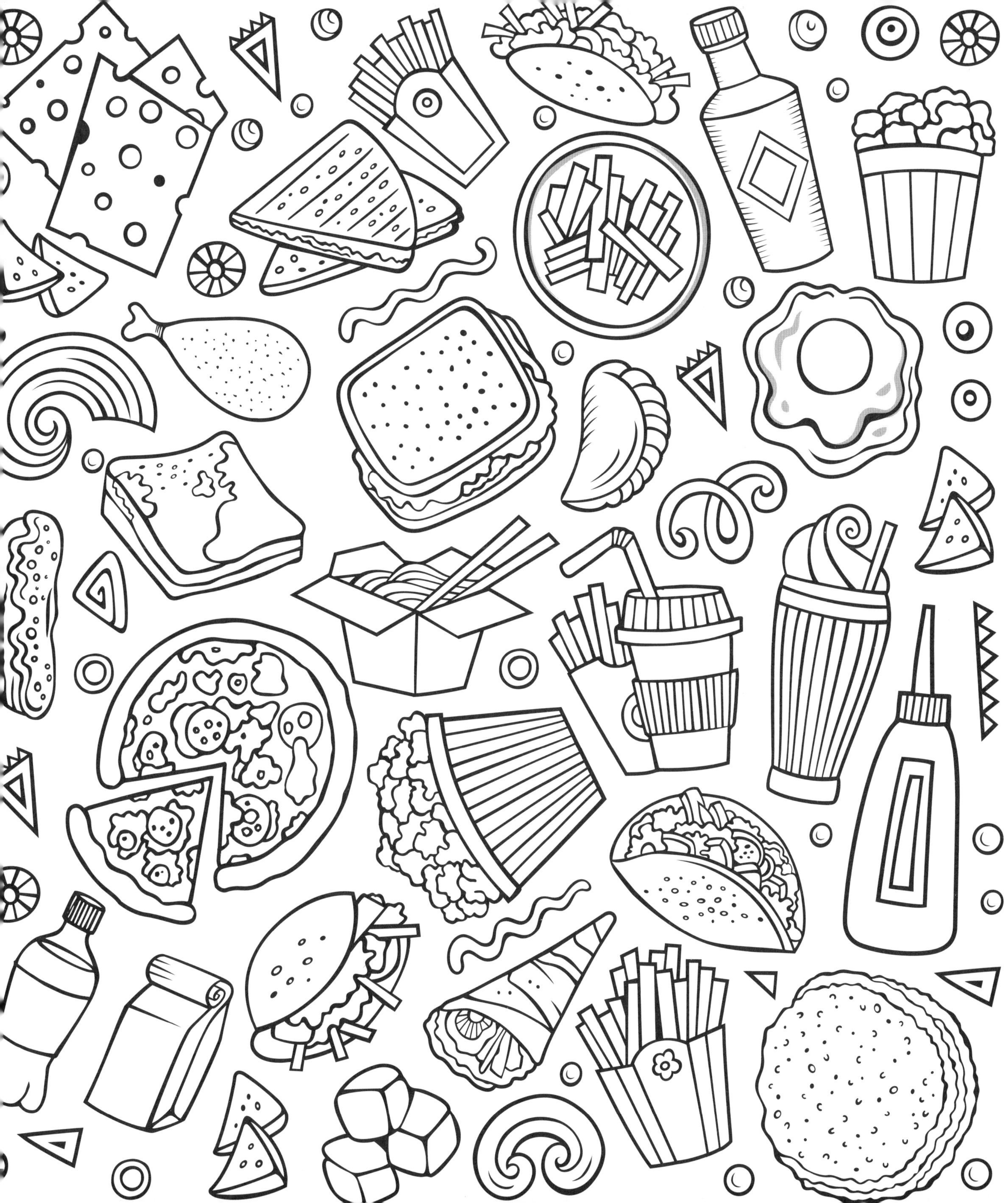

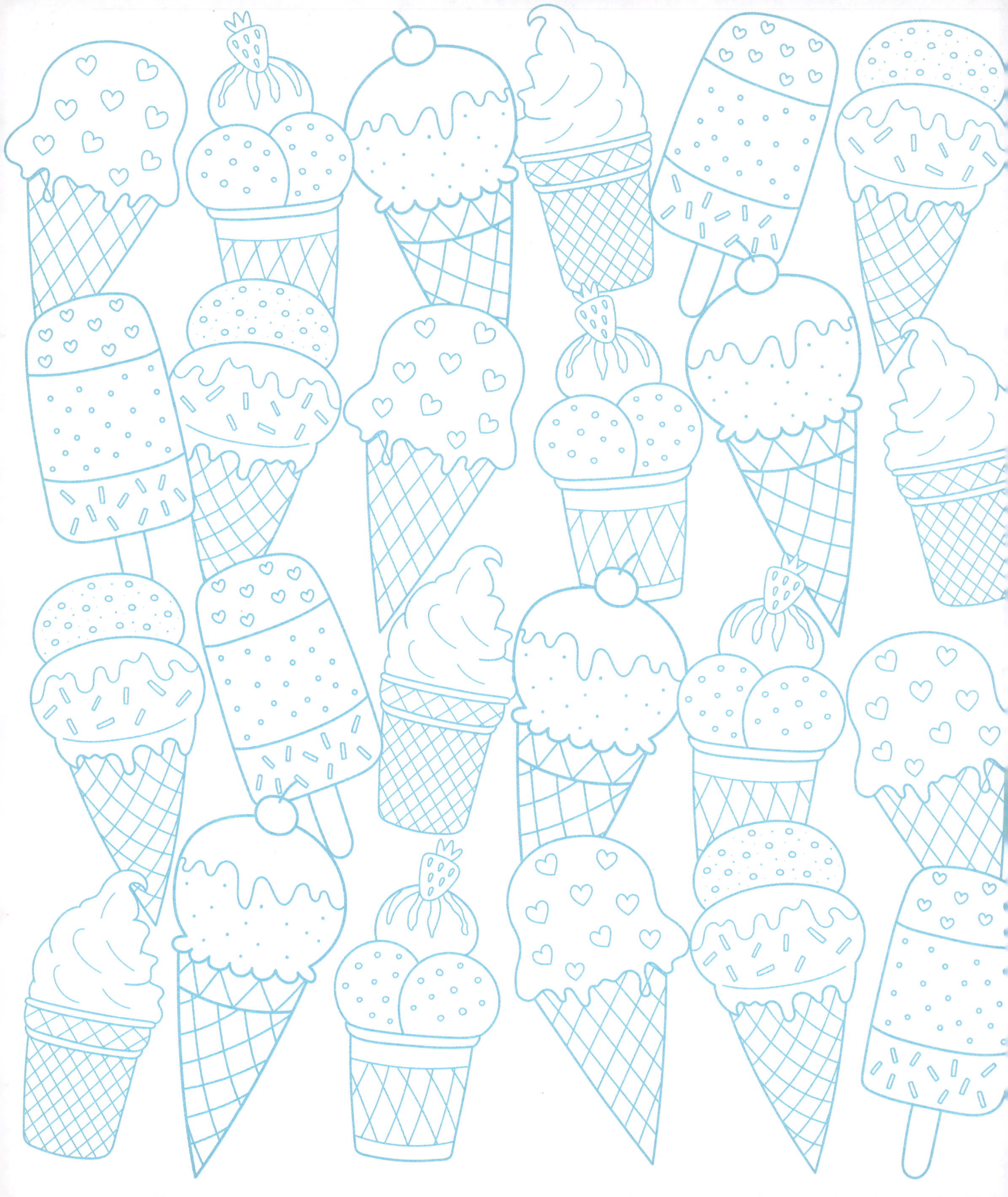

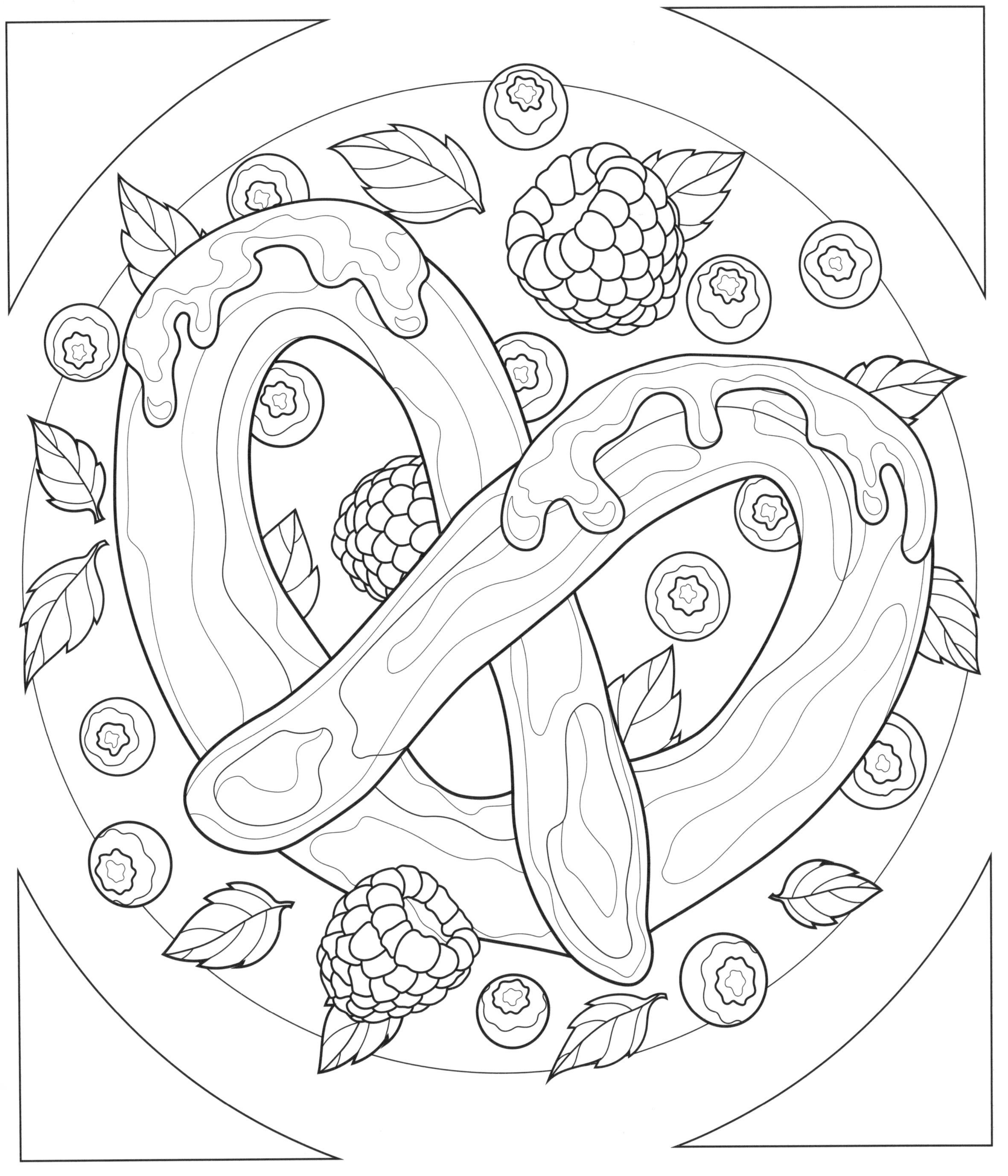

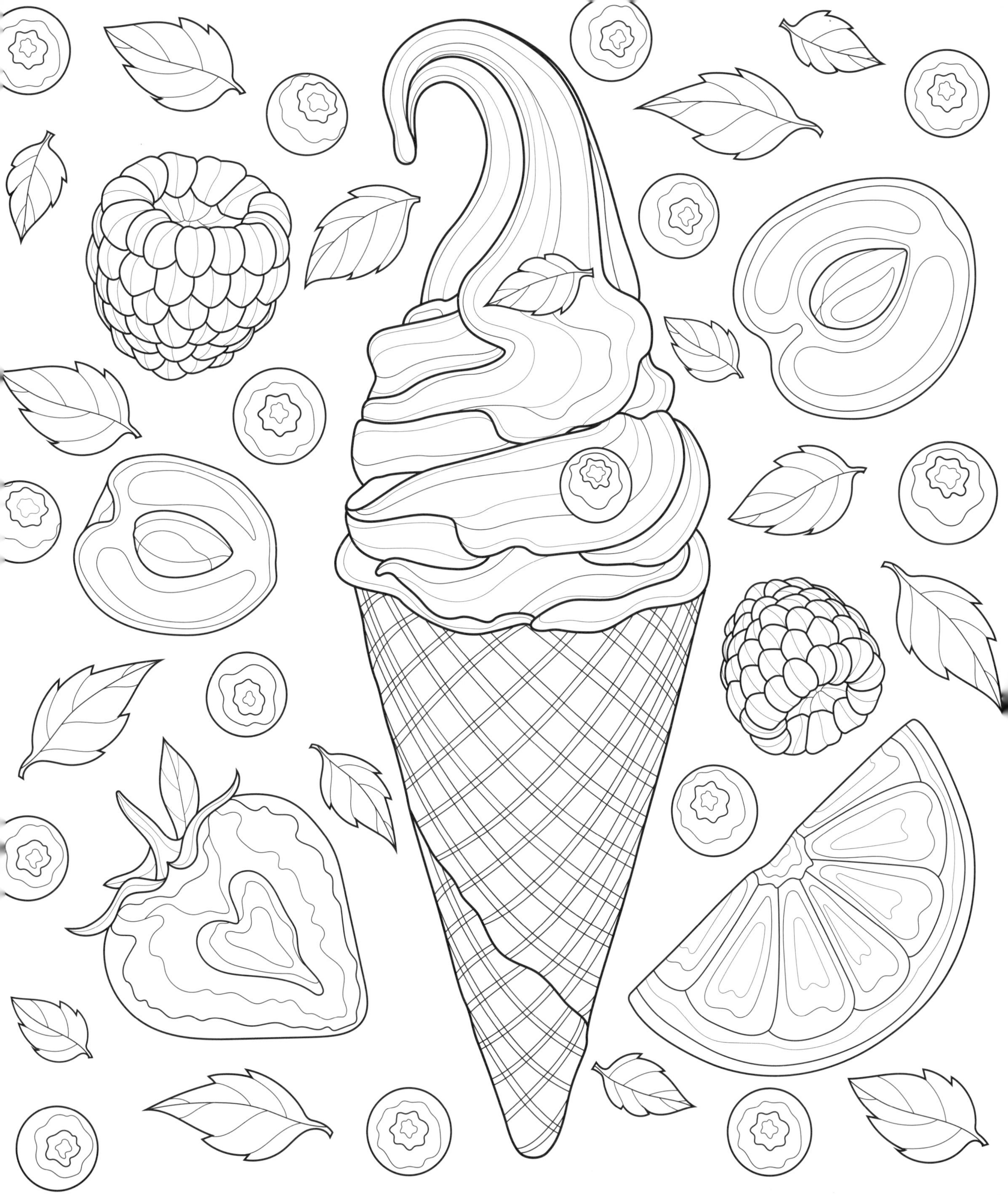

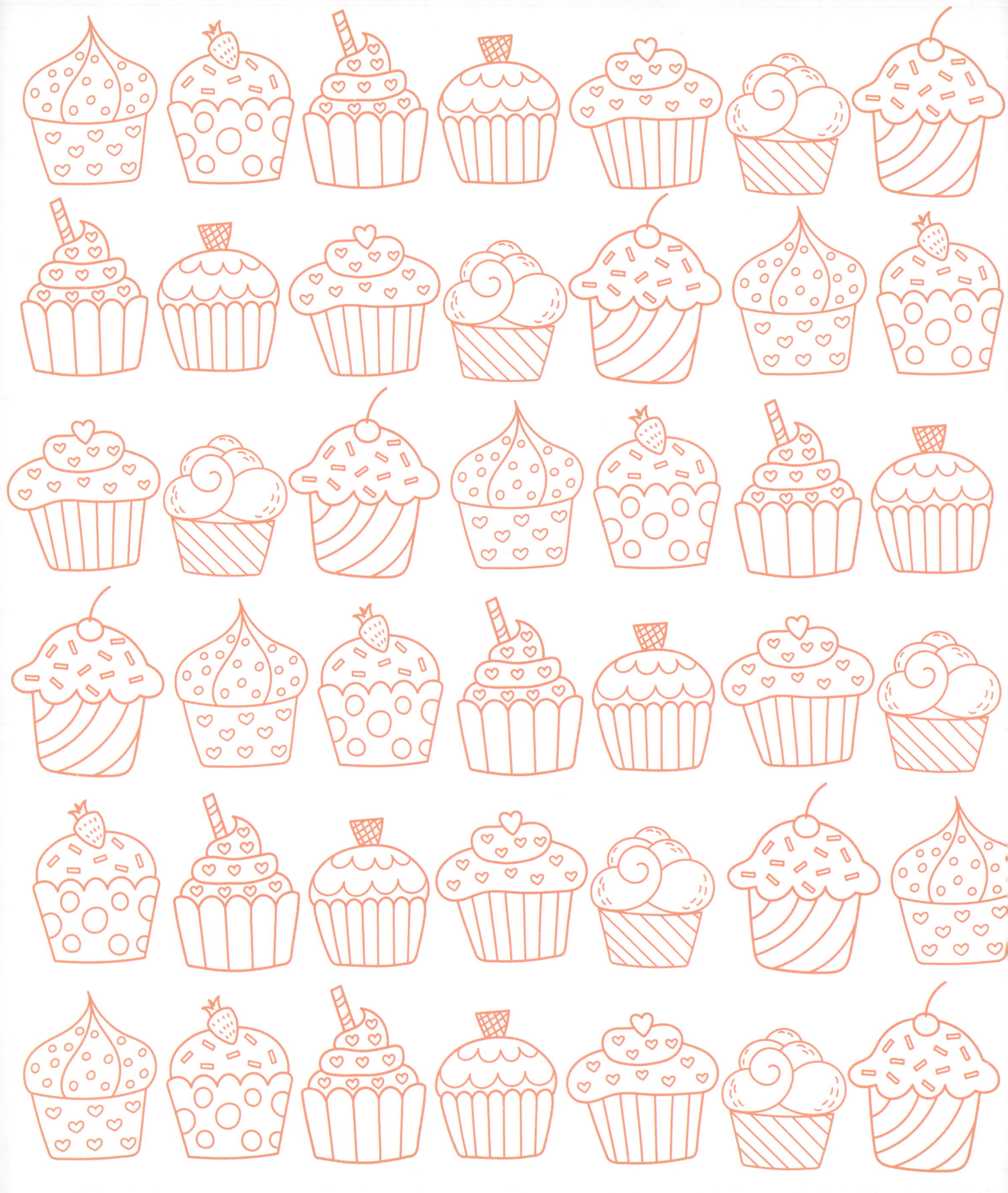

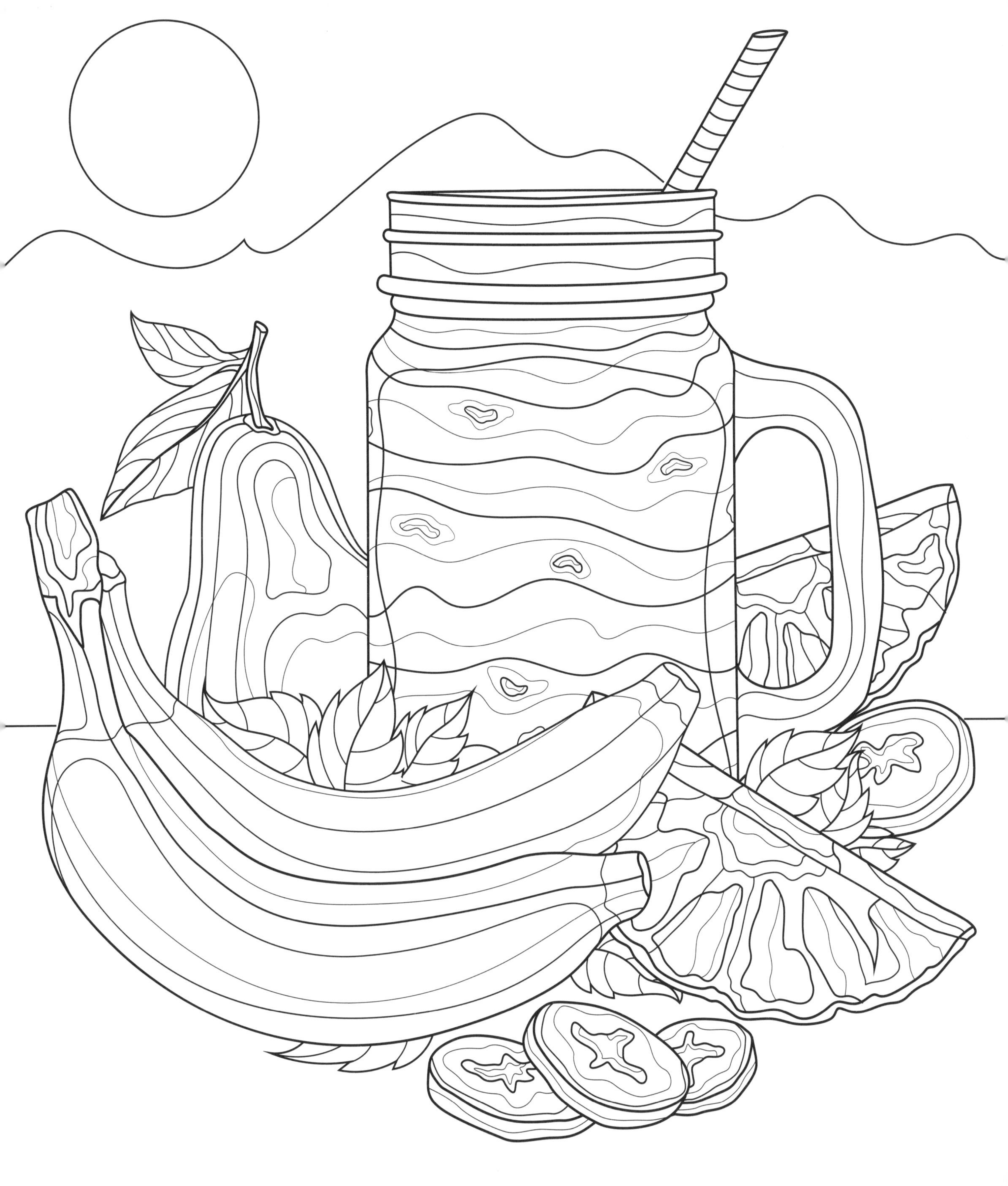

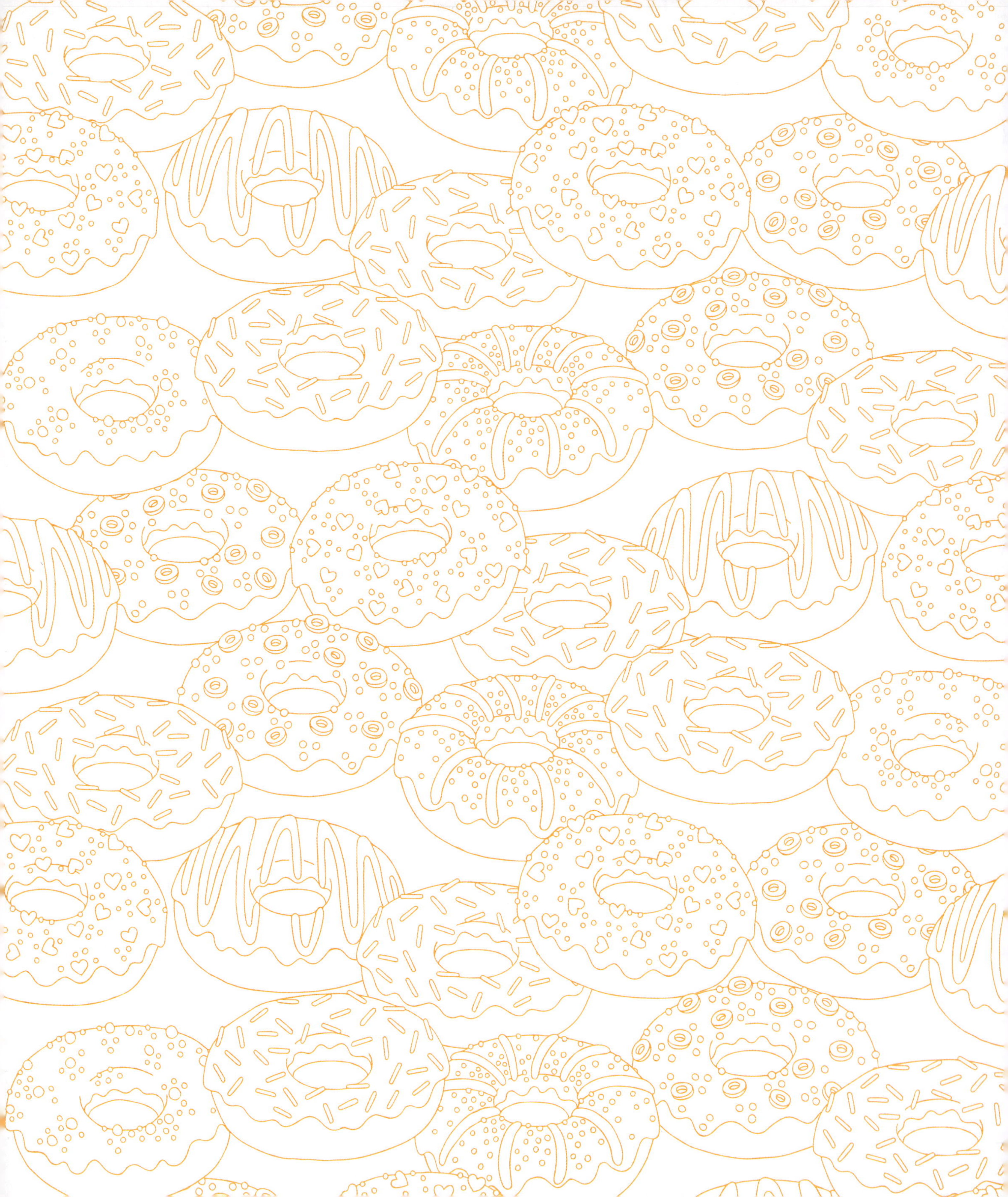

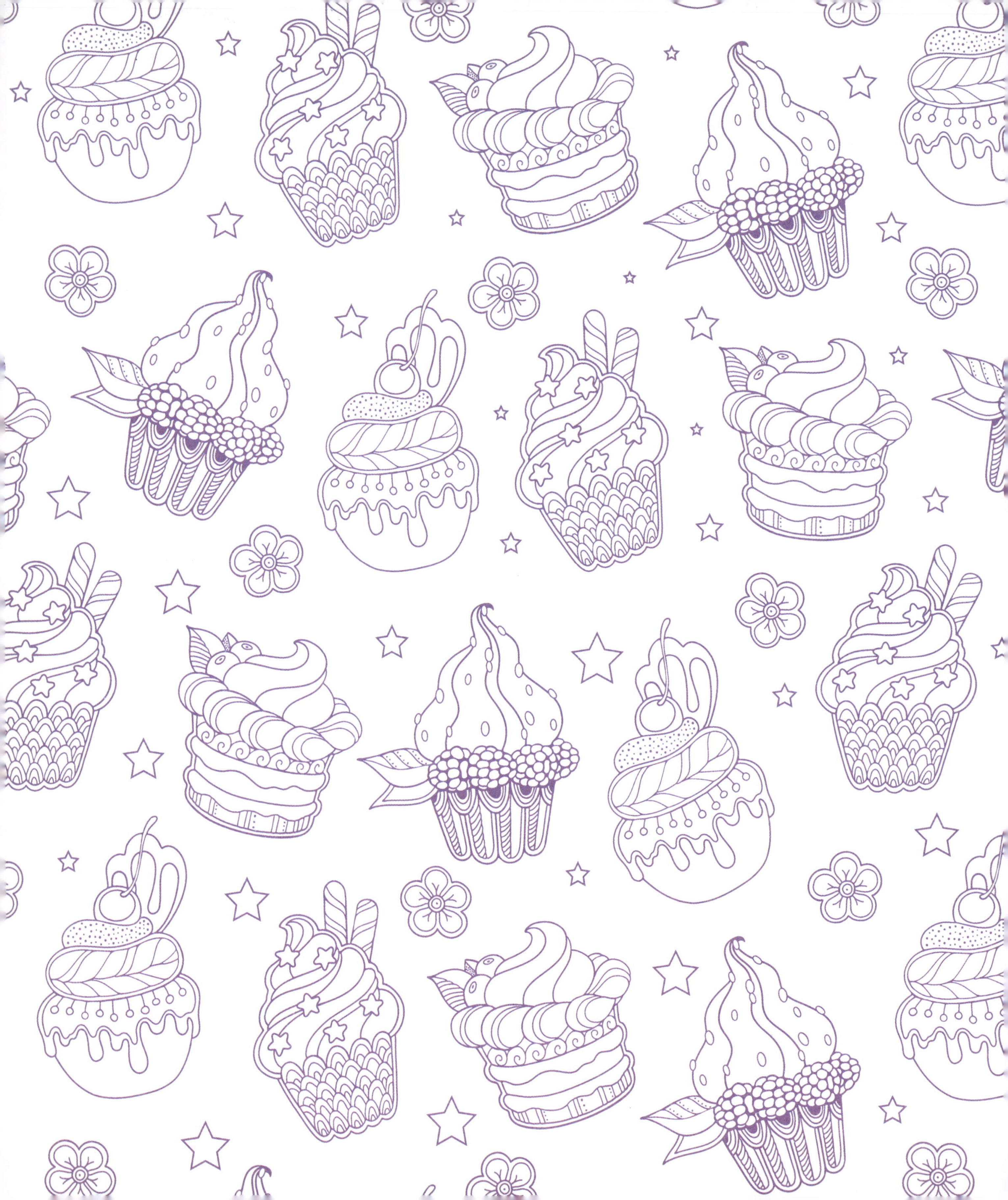

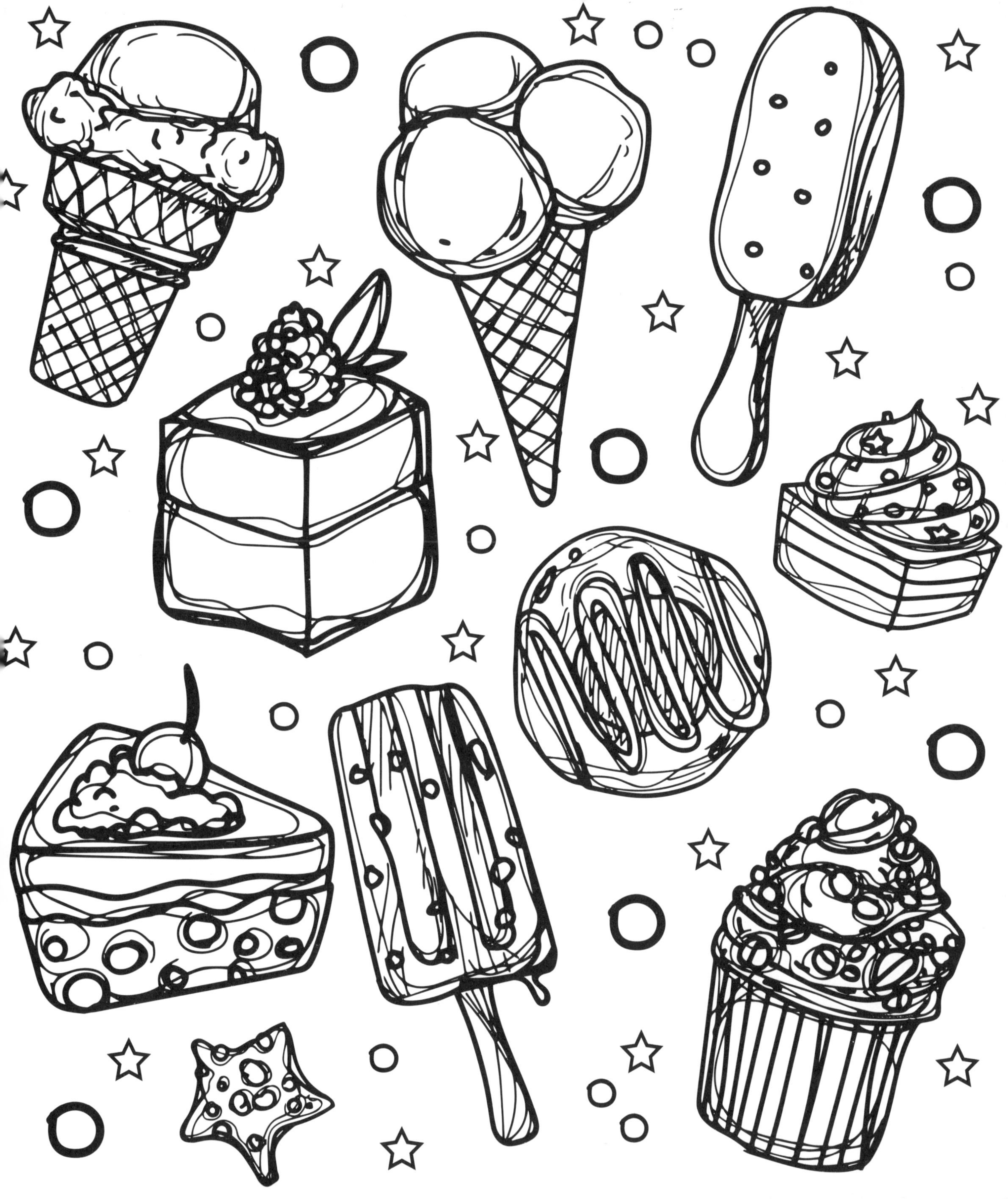

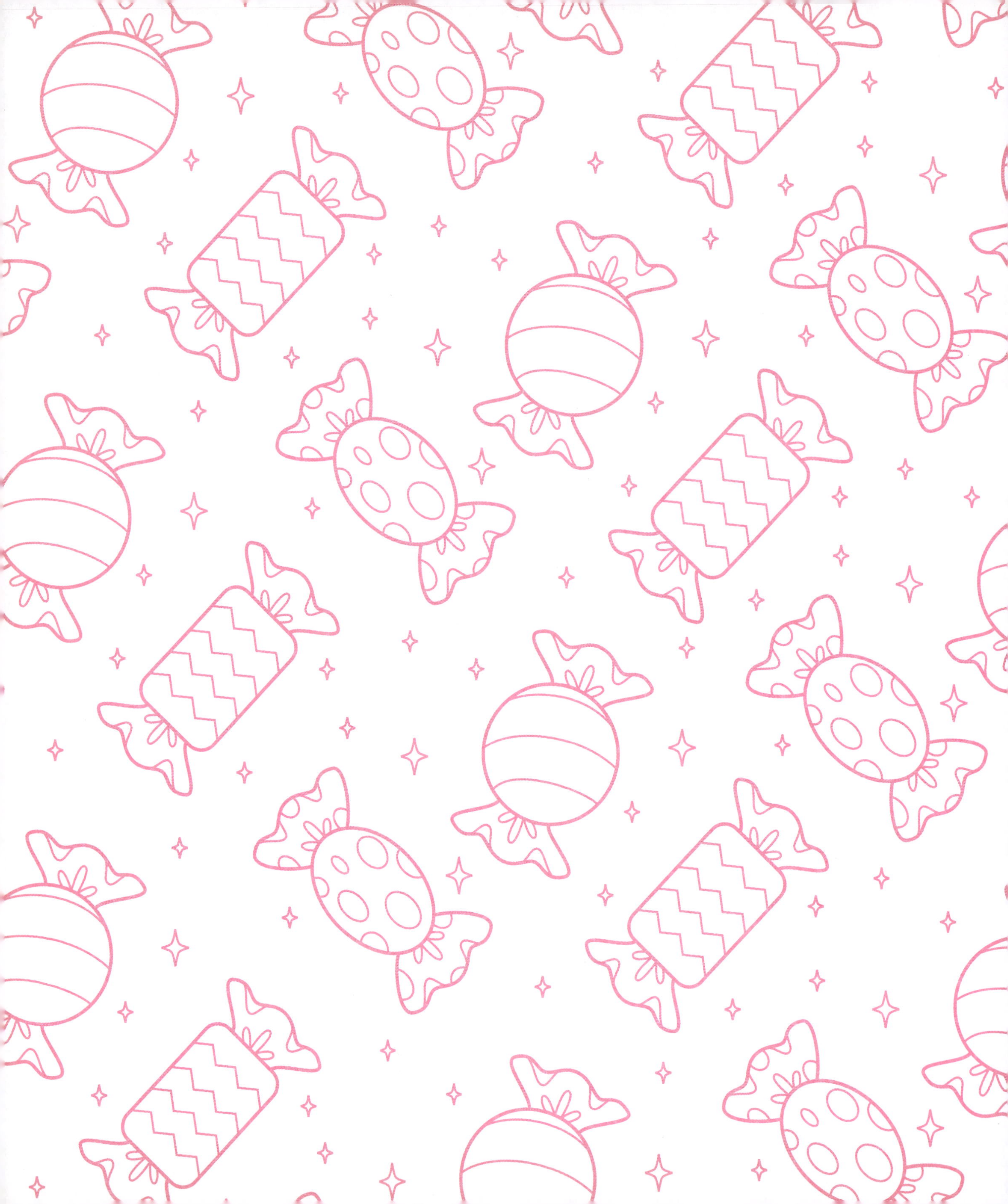

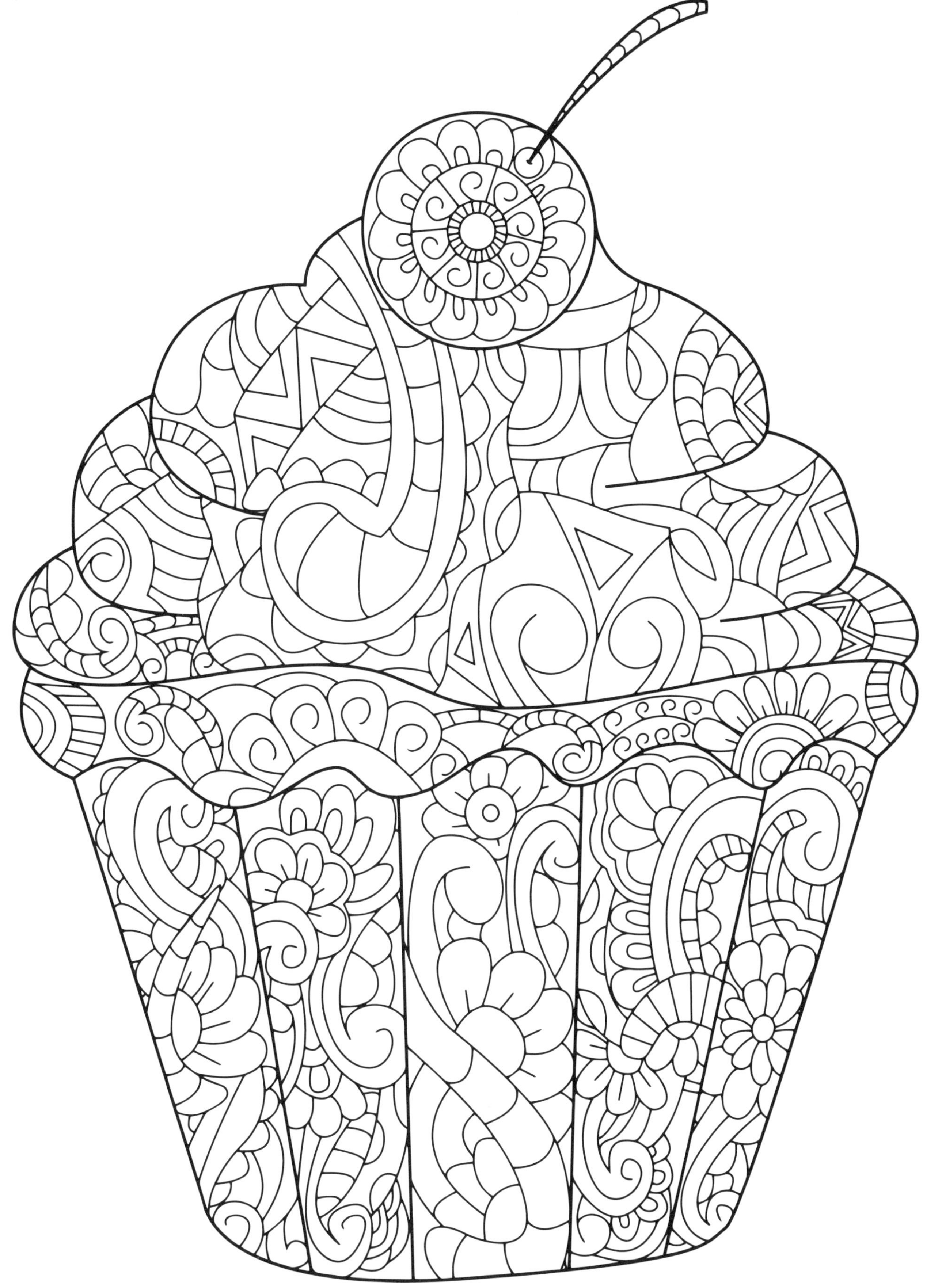

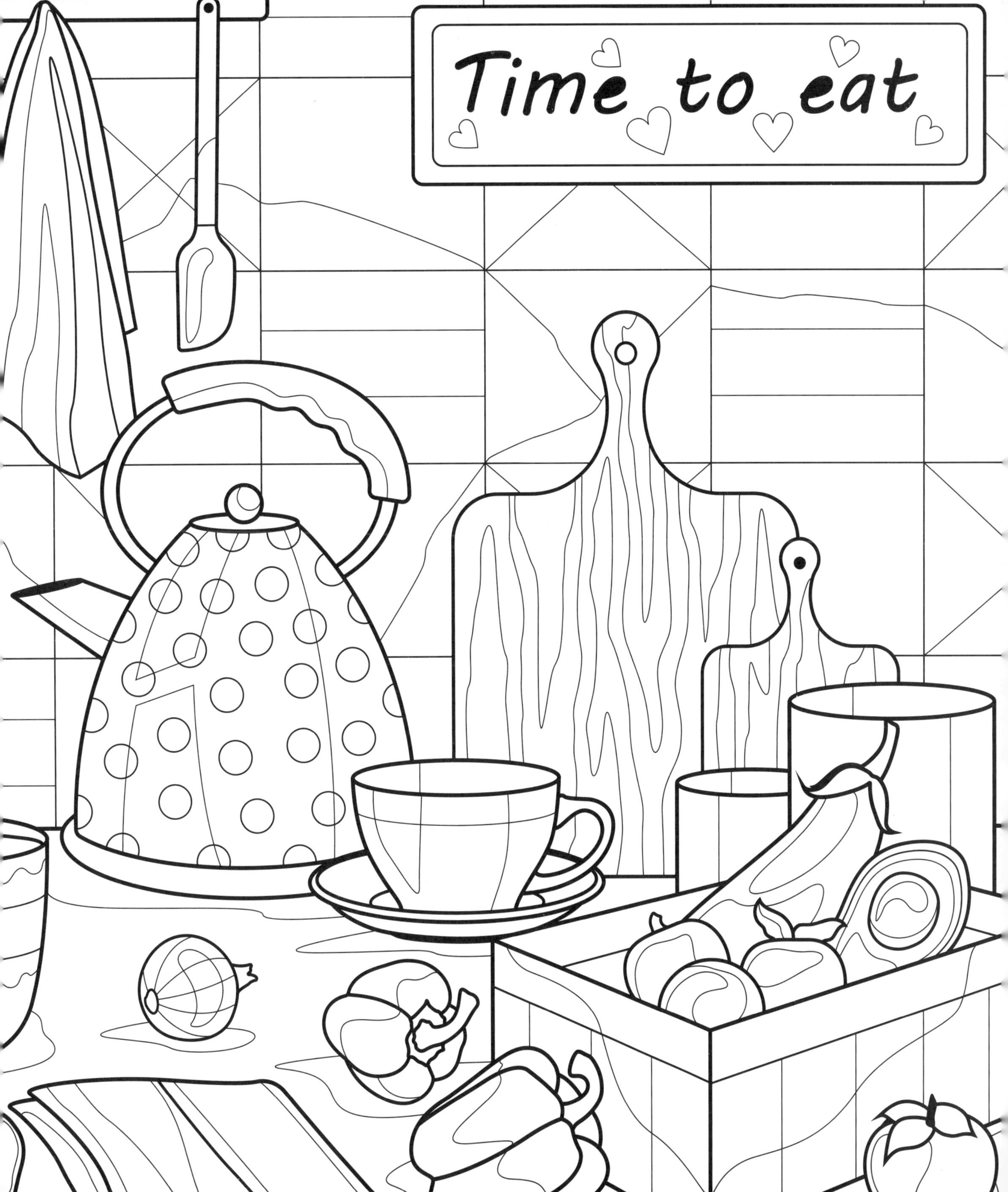
Time to eat

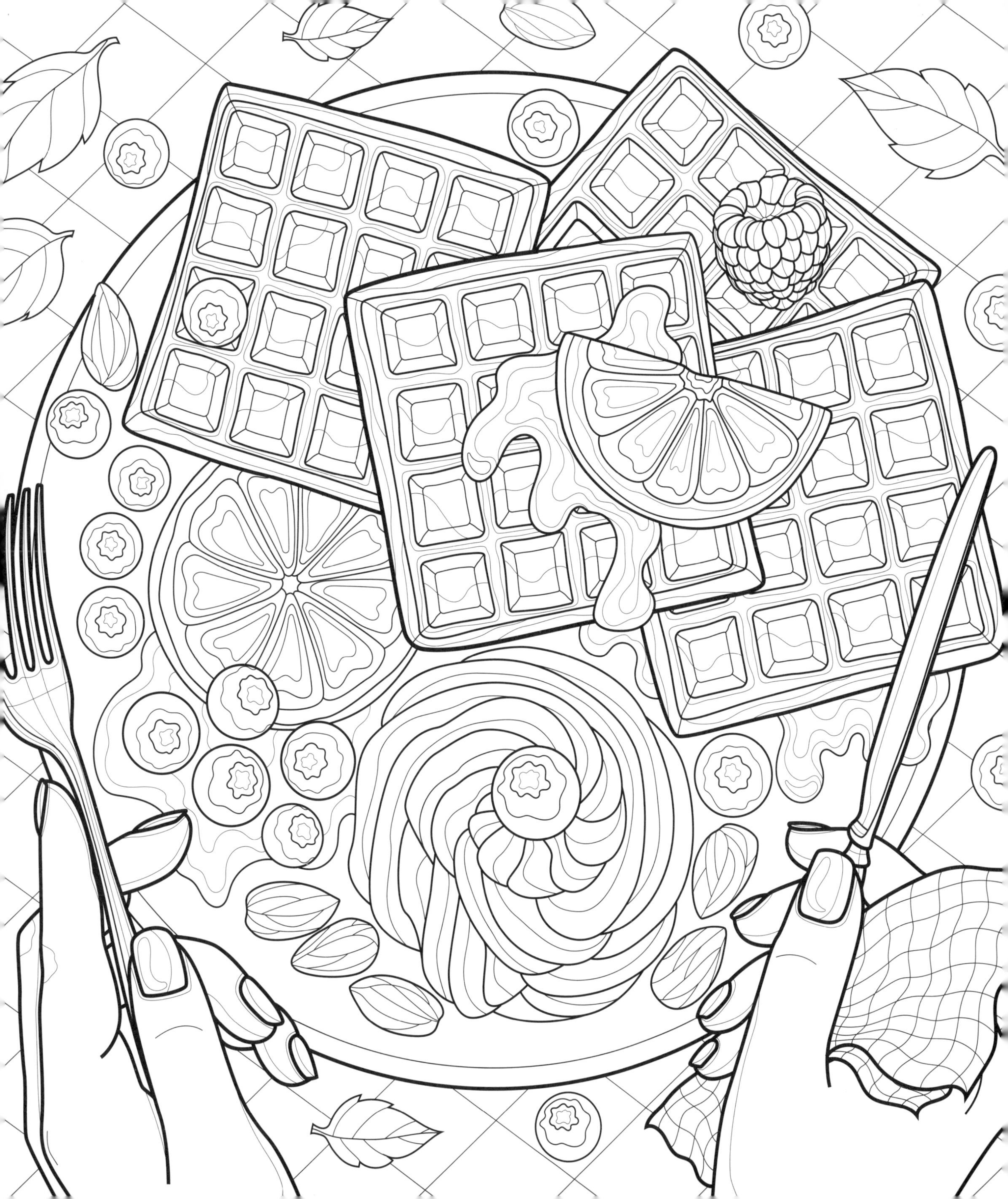

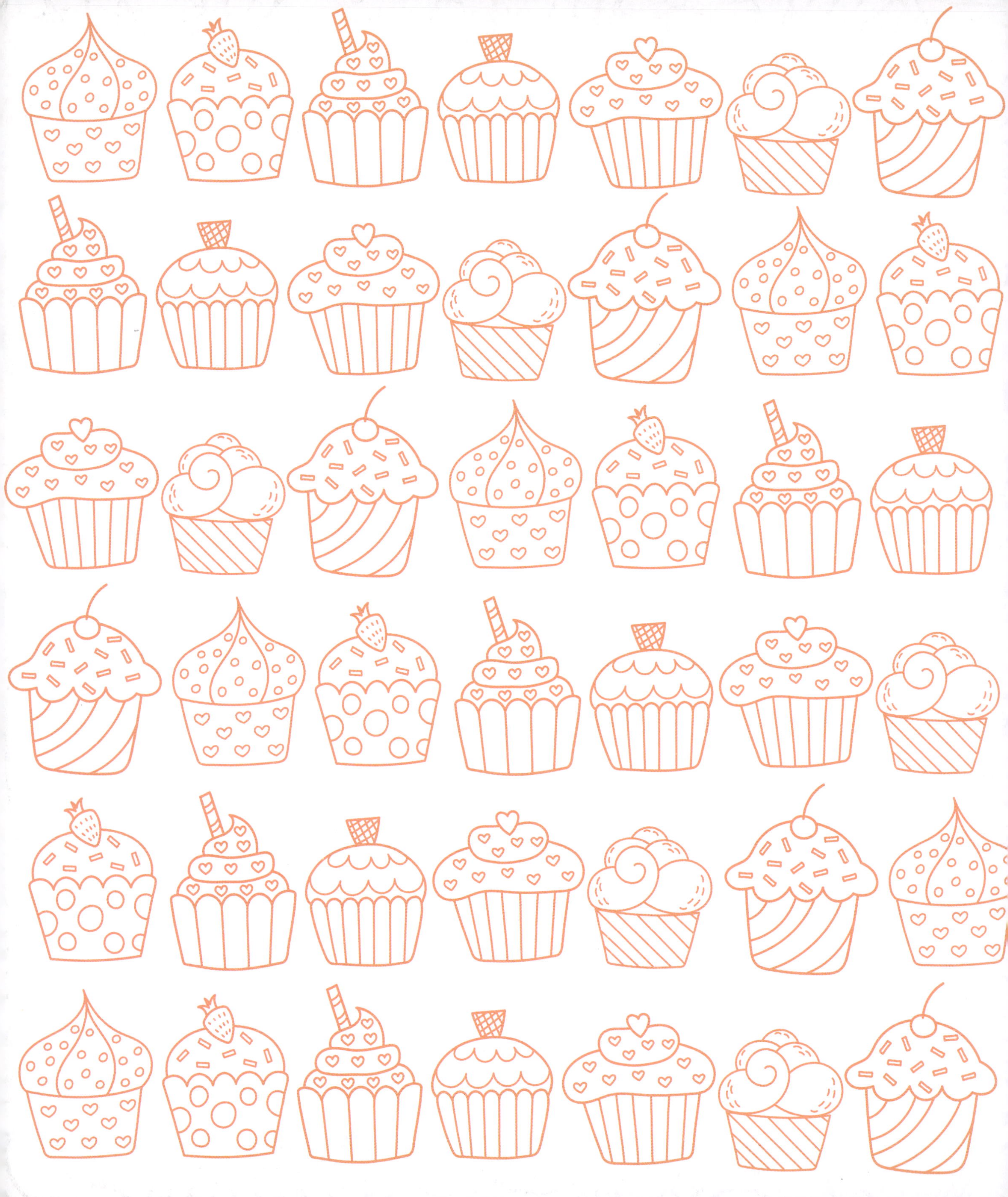

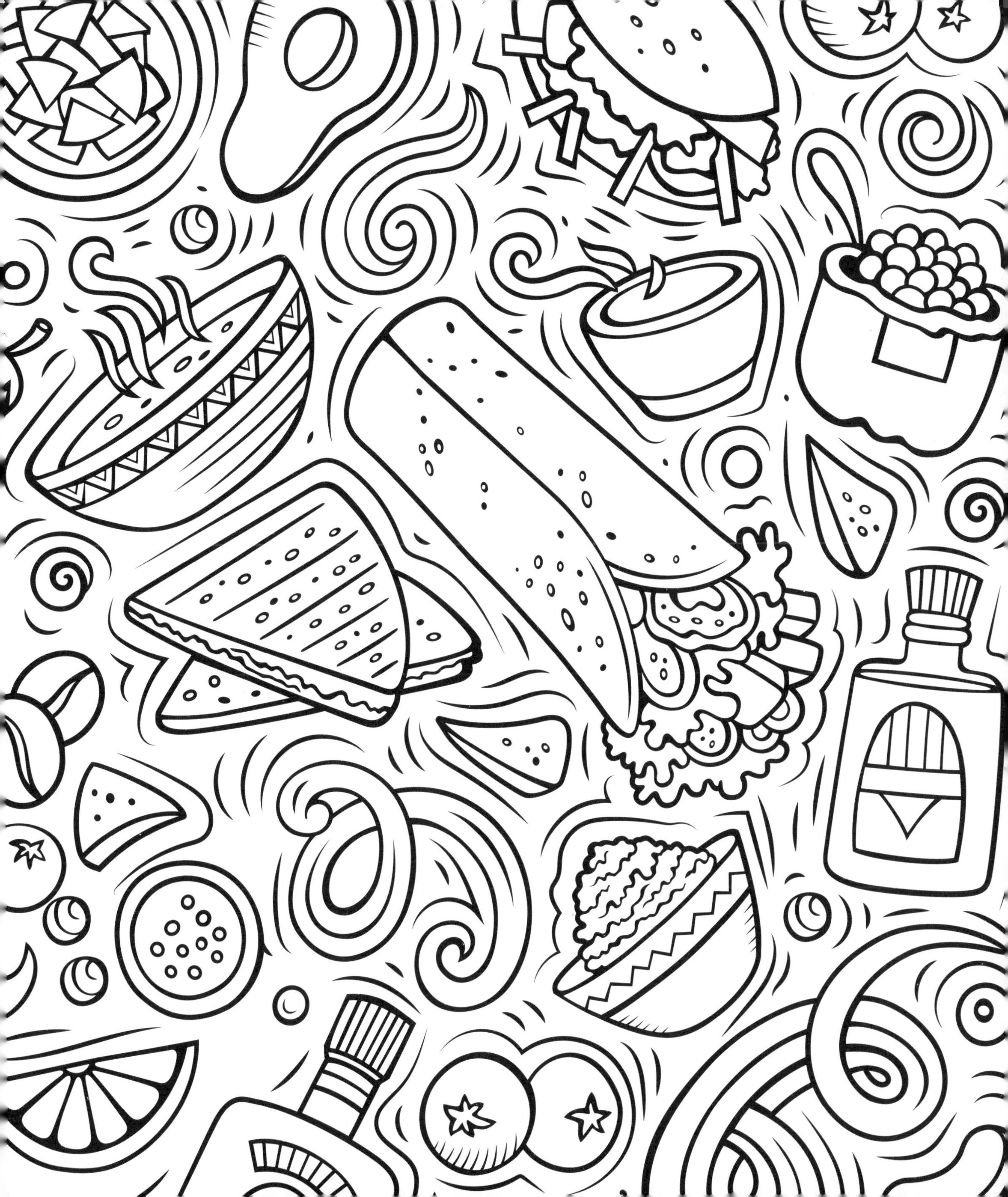

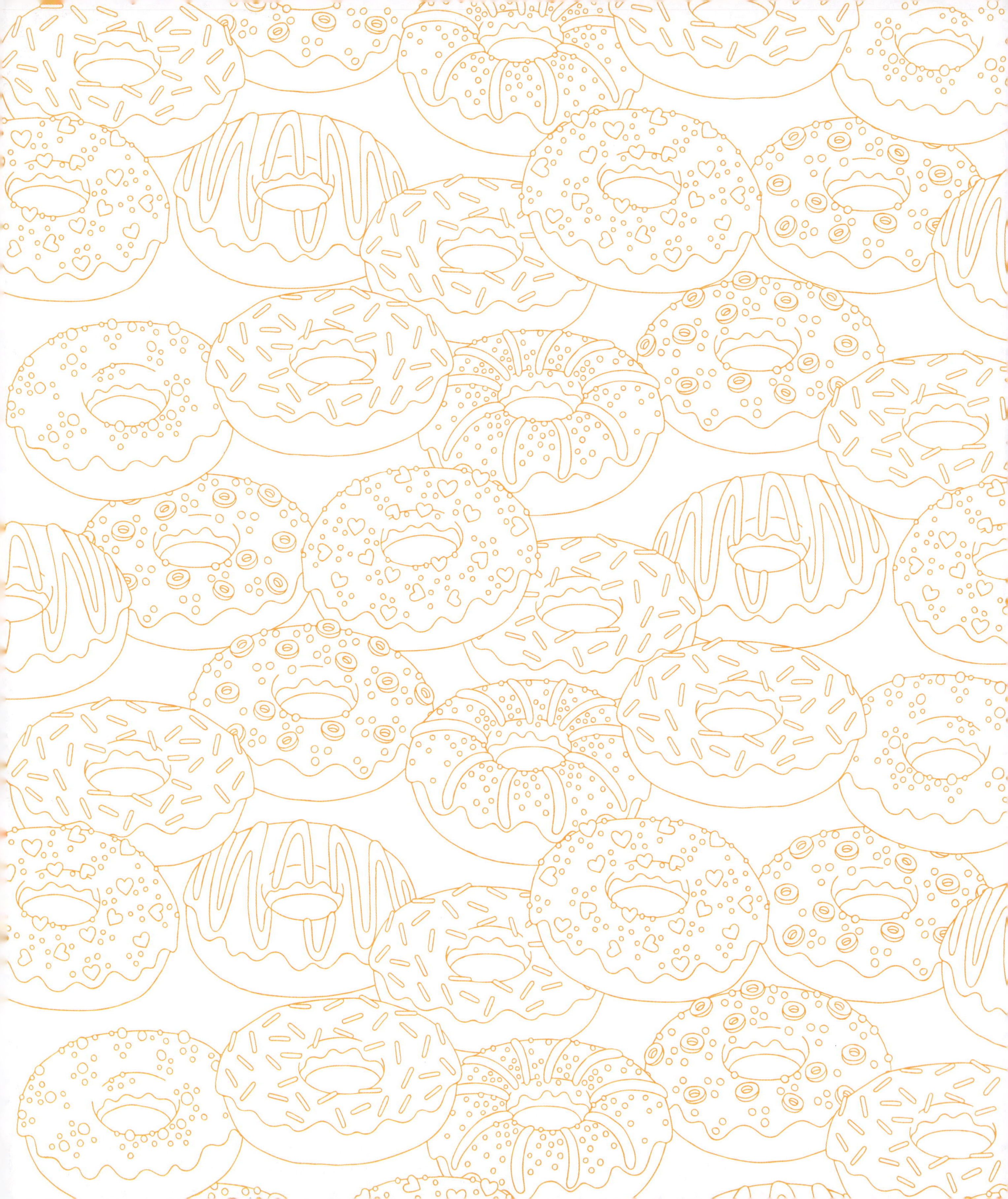

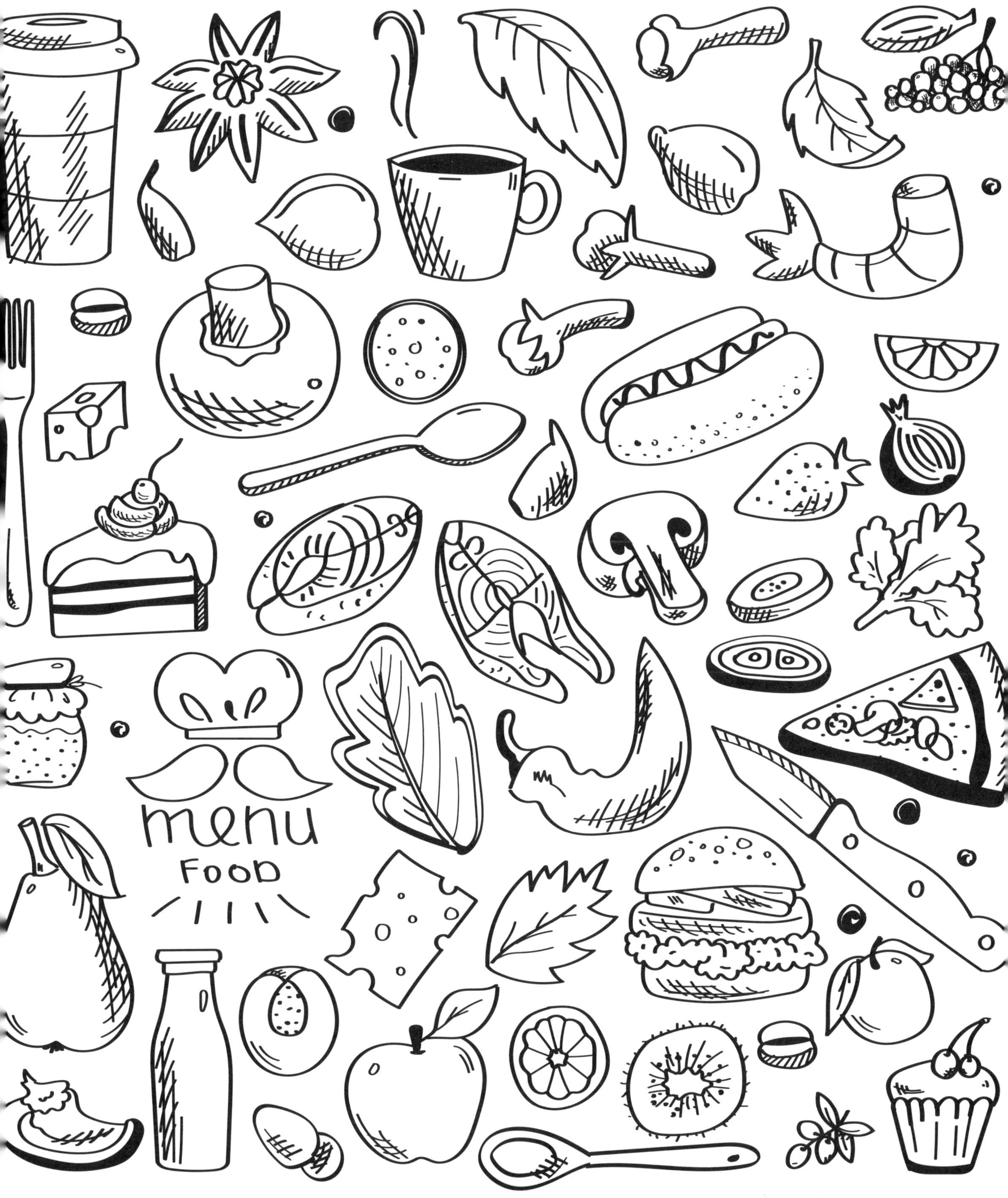

menu
Food

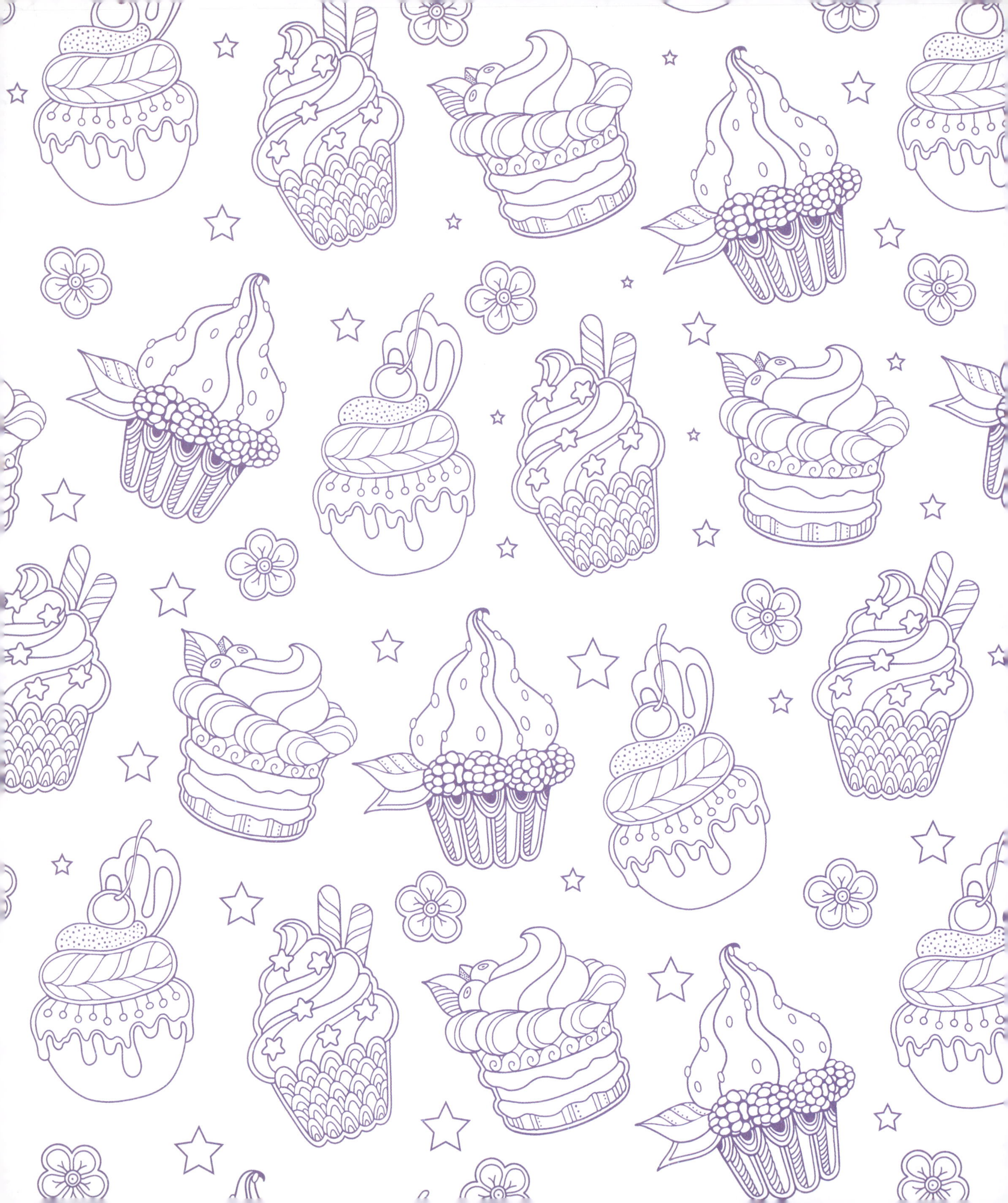

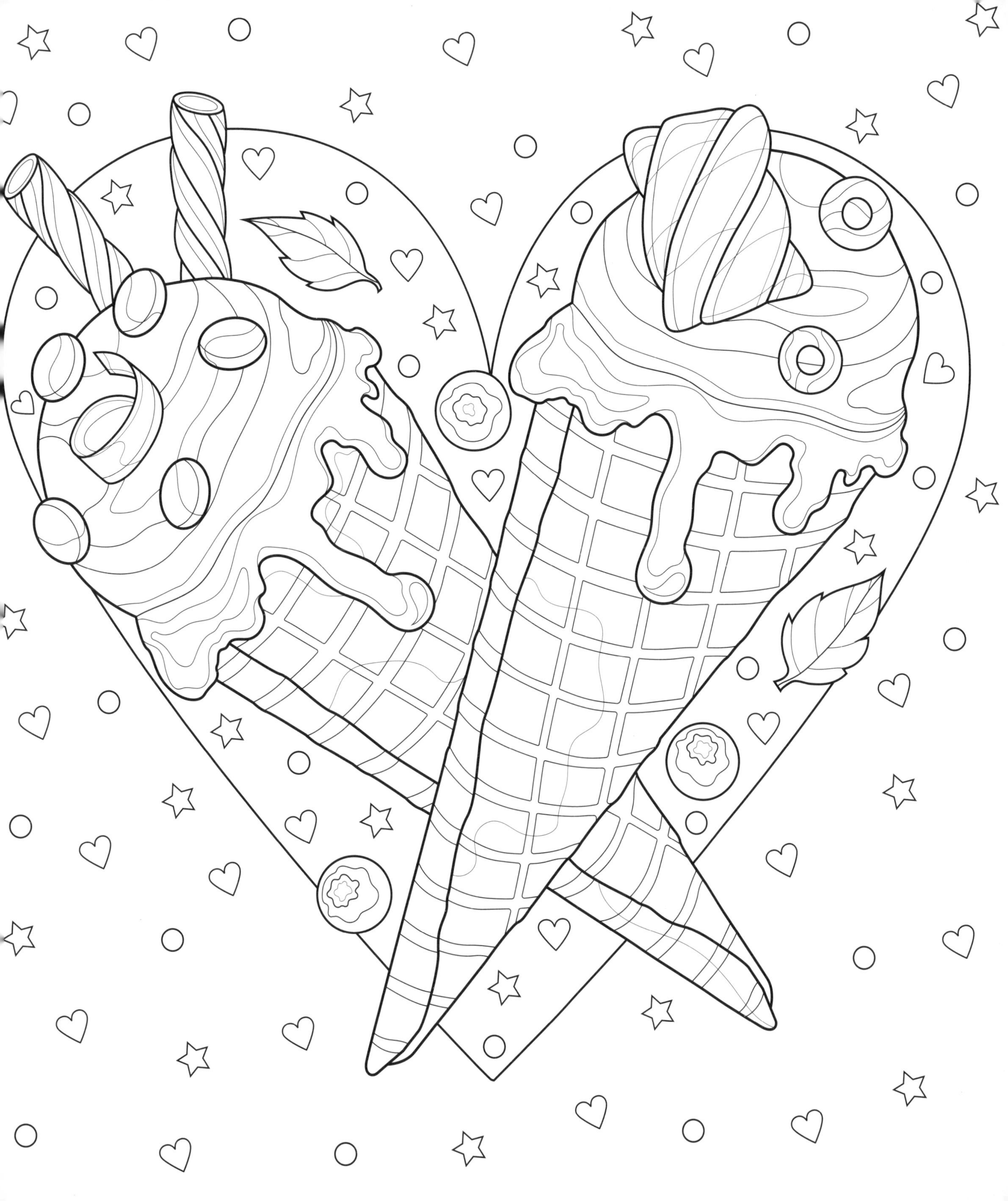

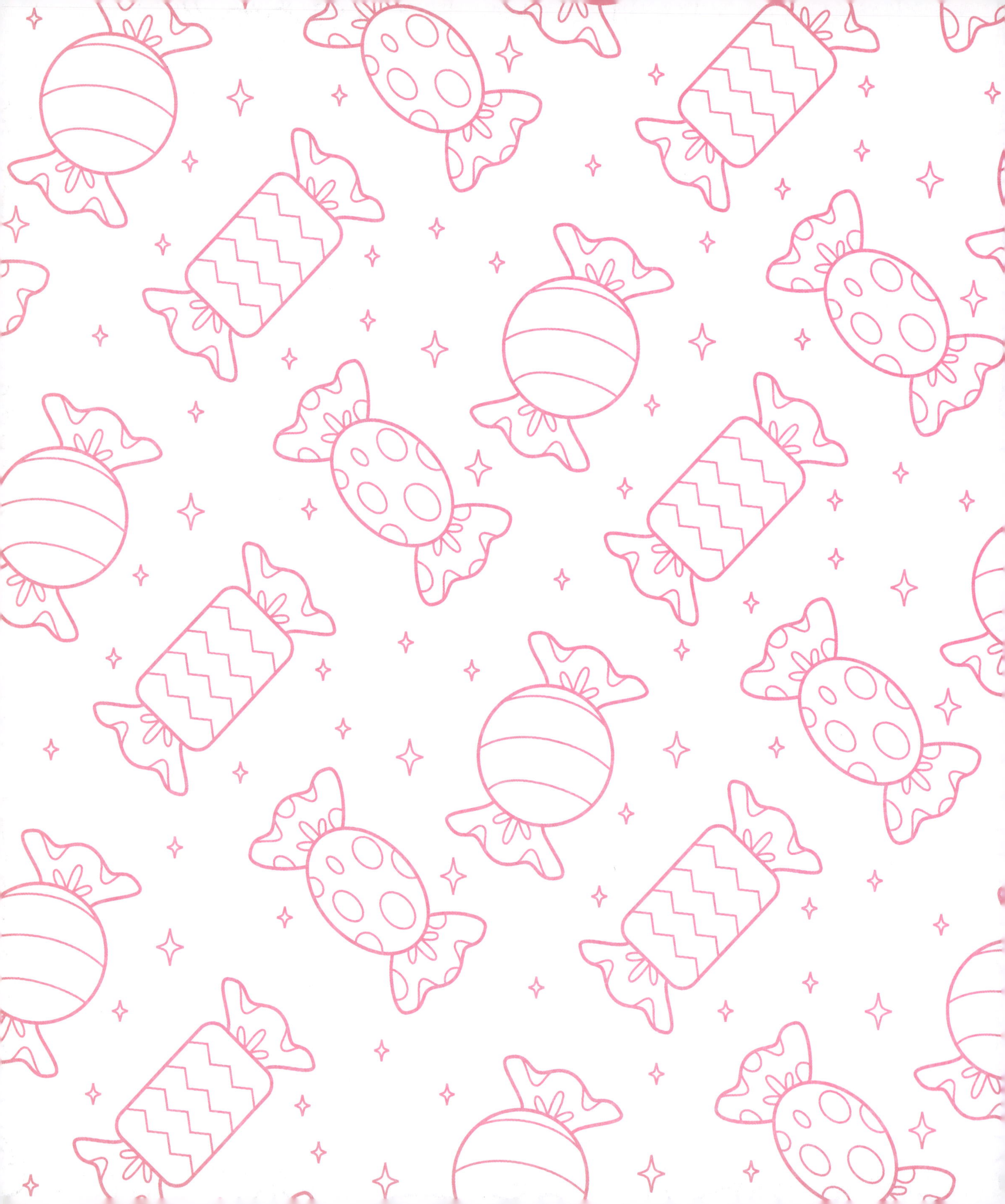

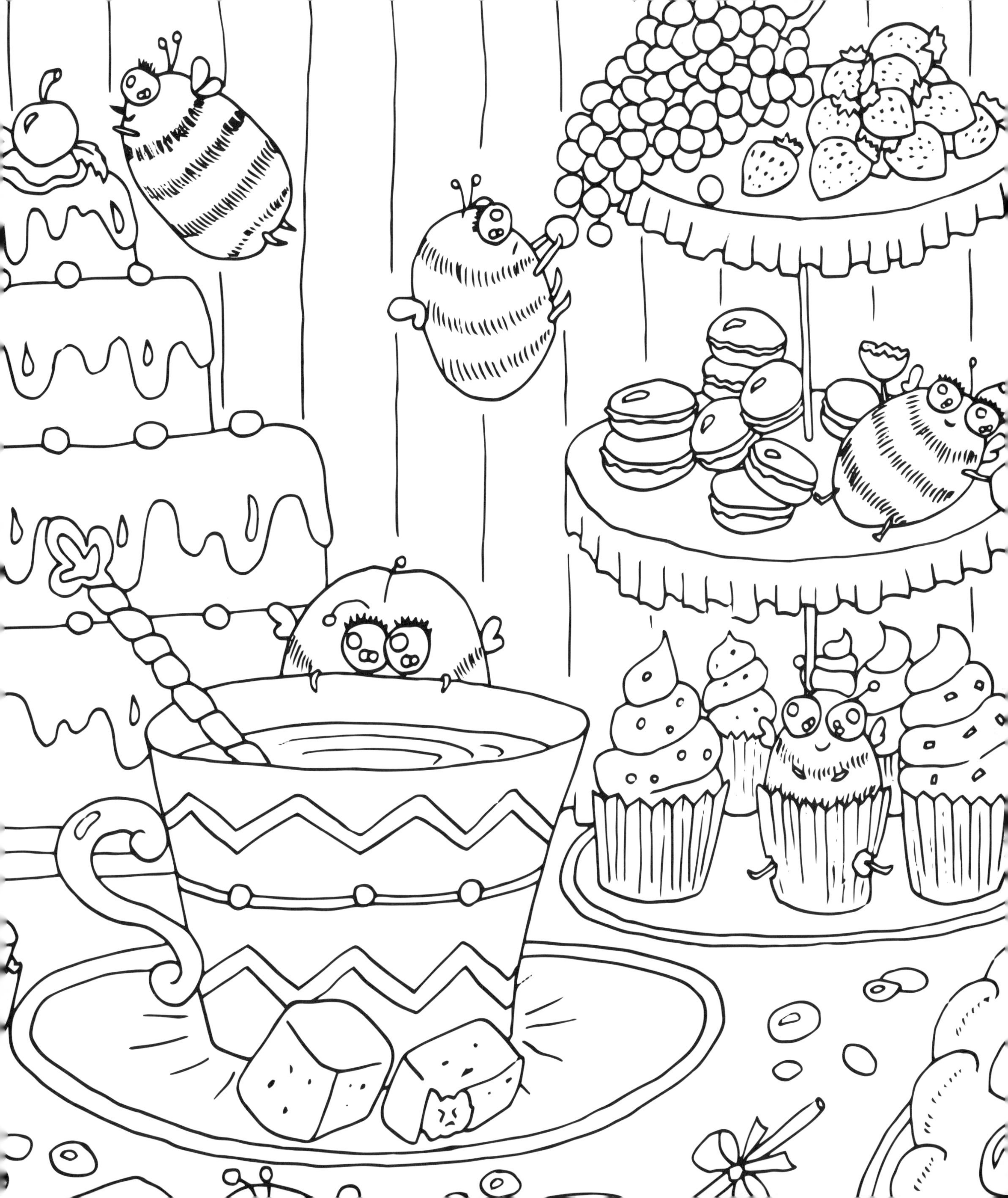

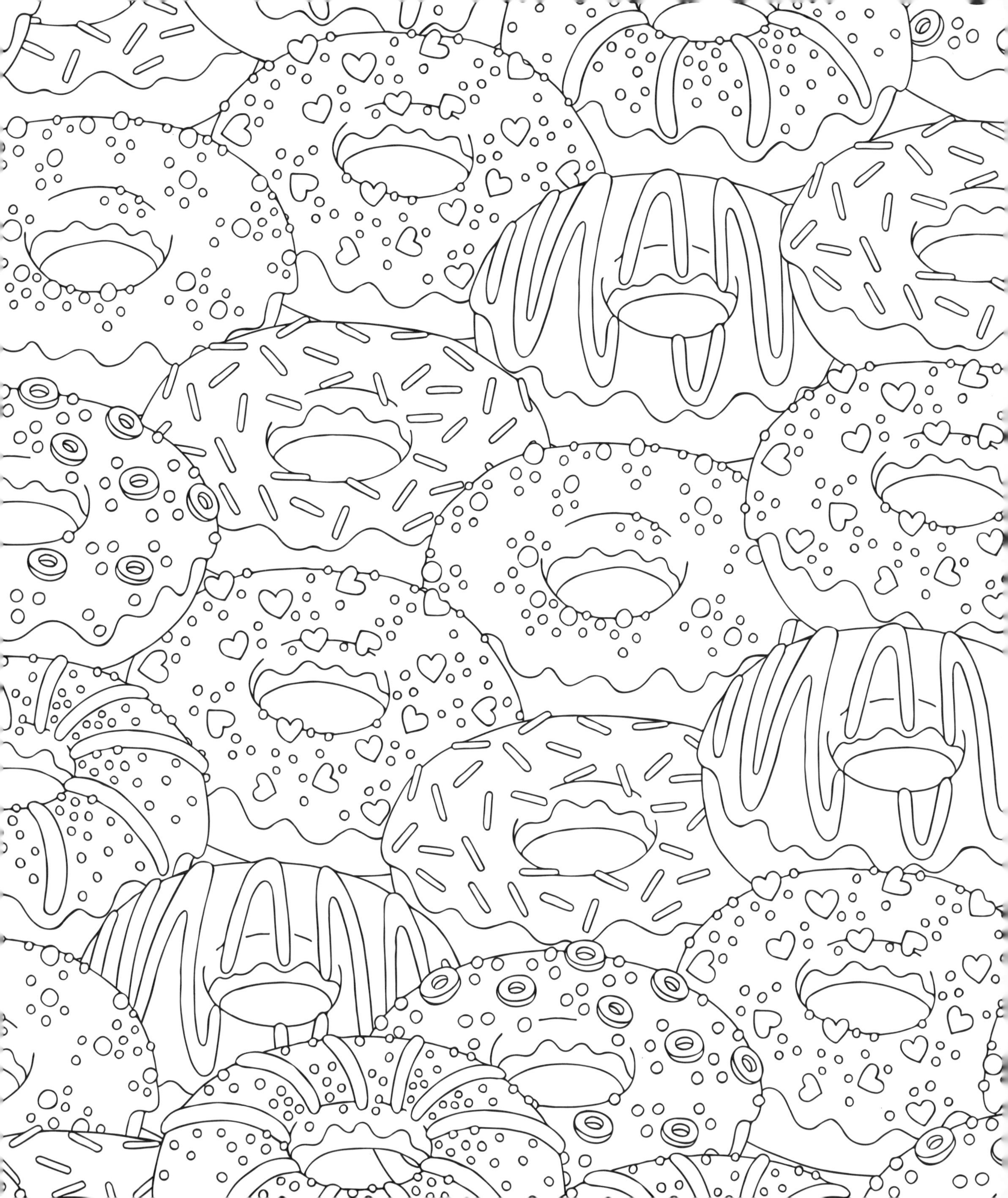

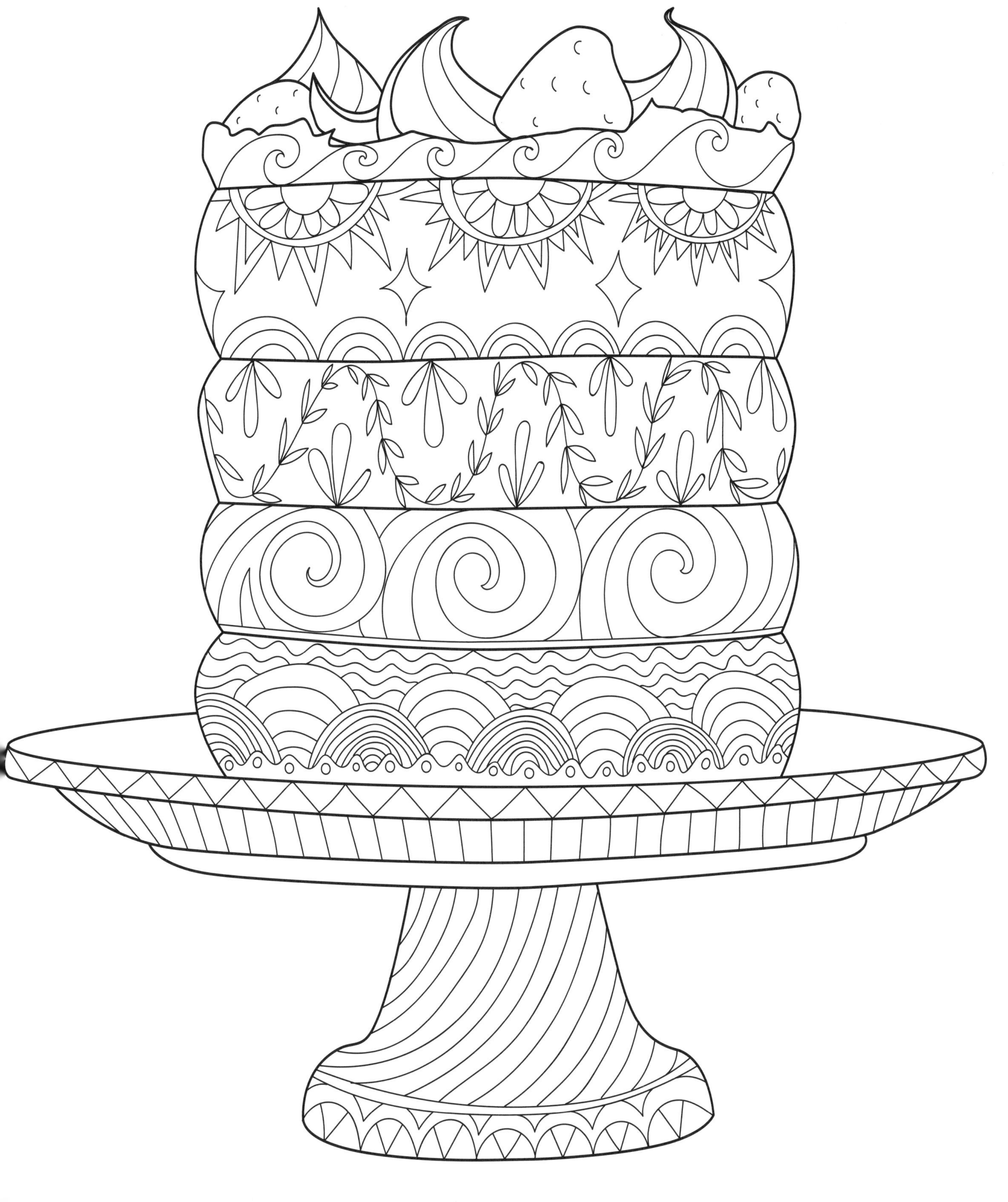

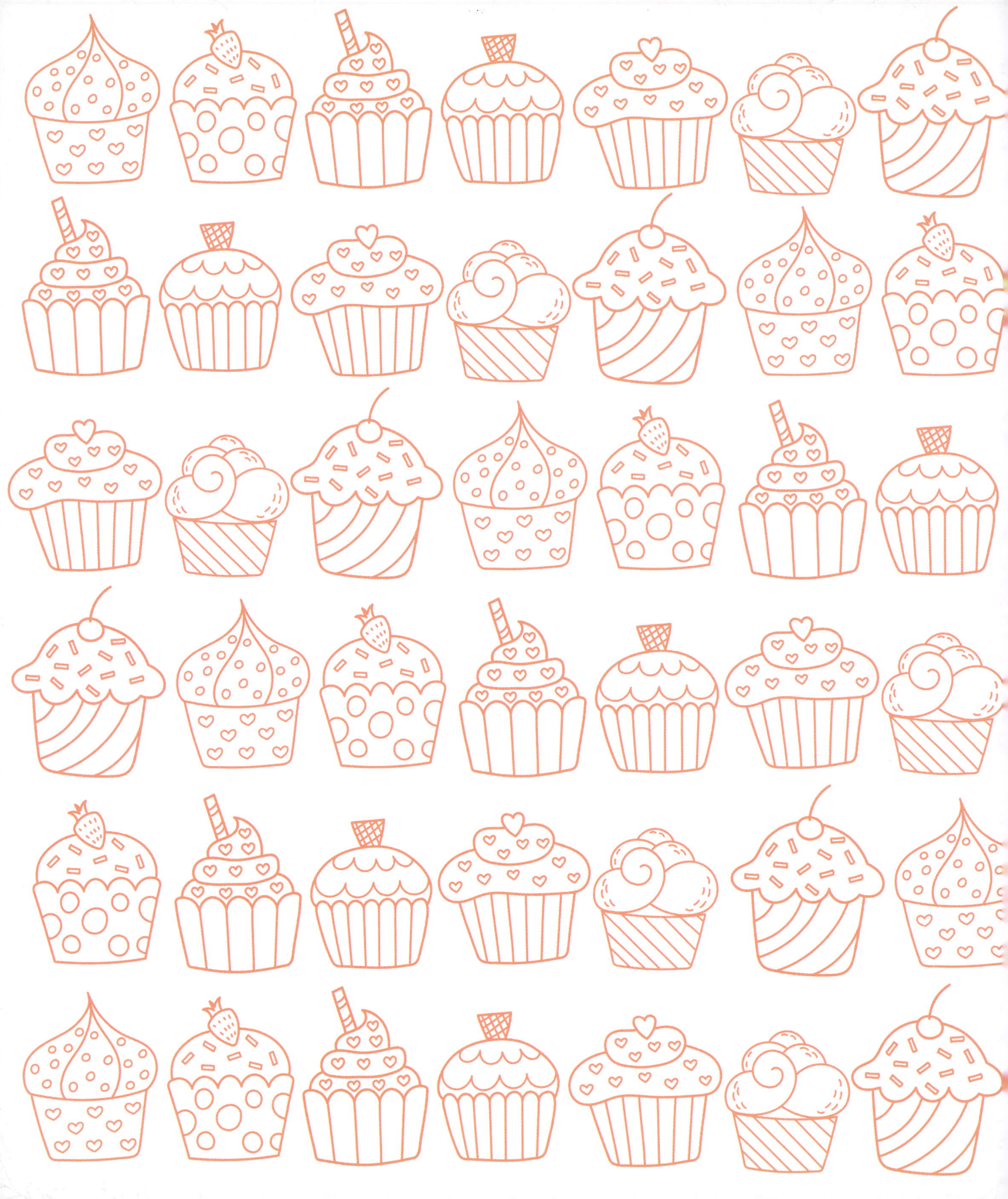

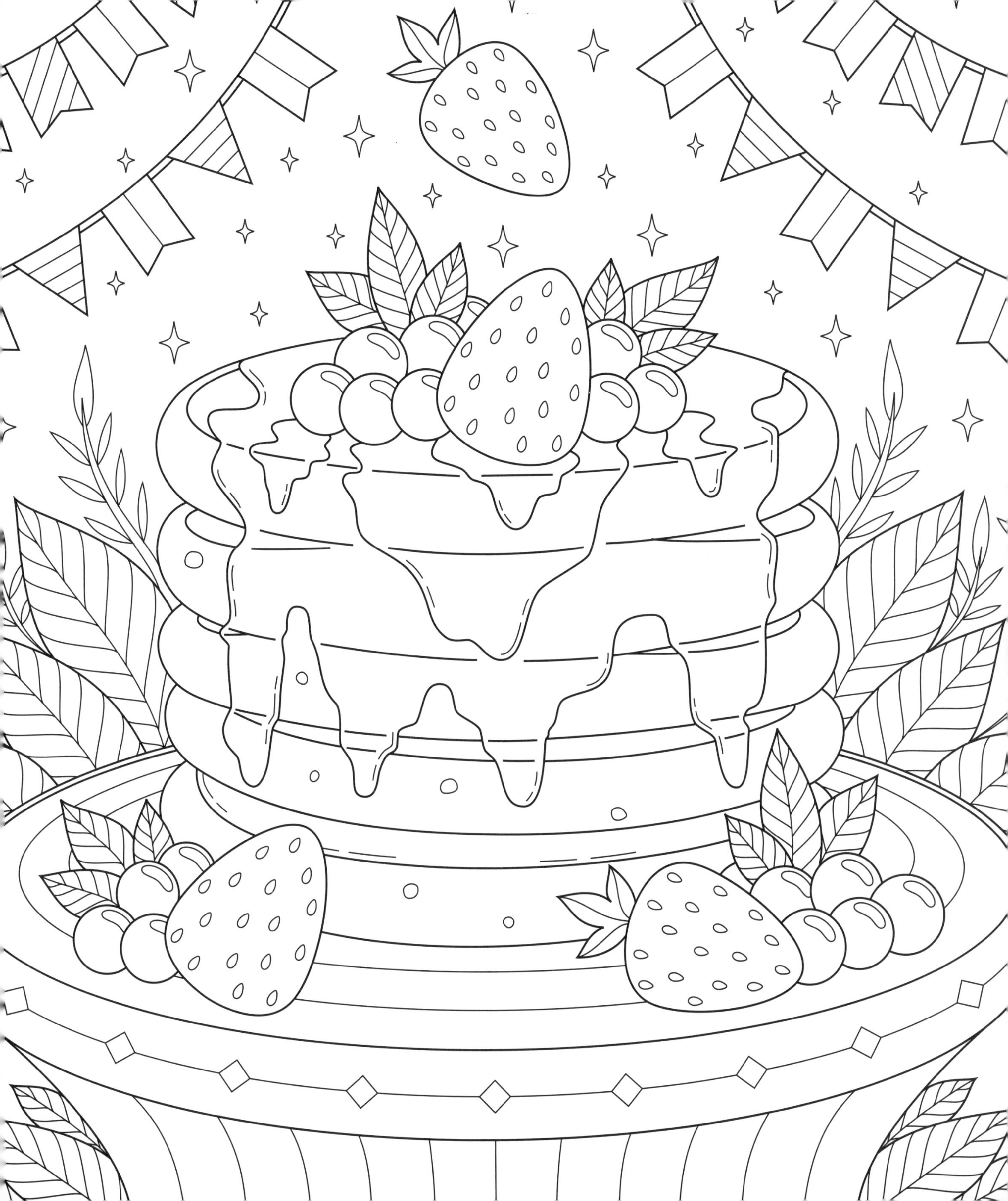

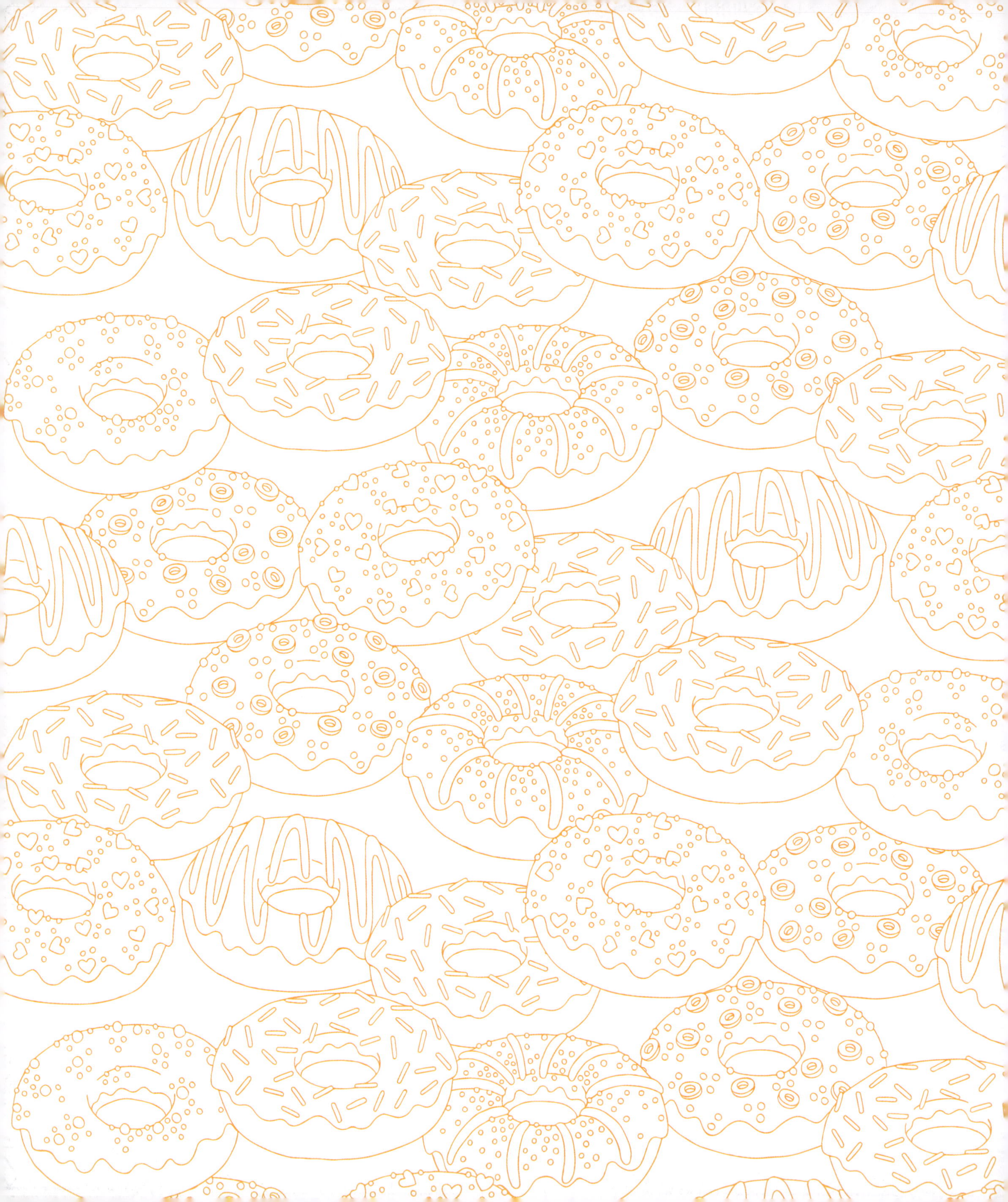

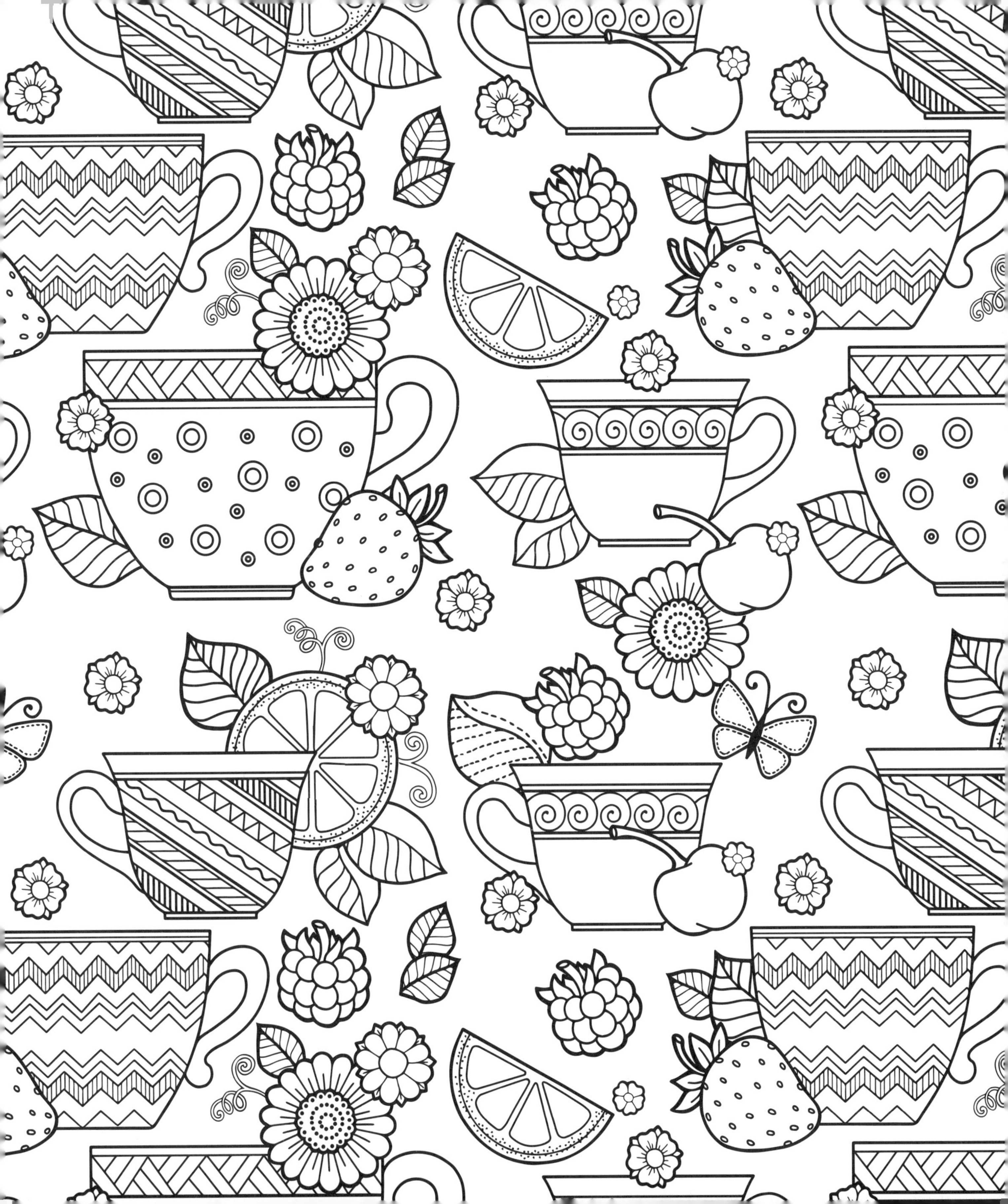

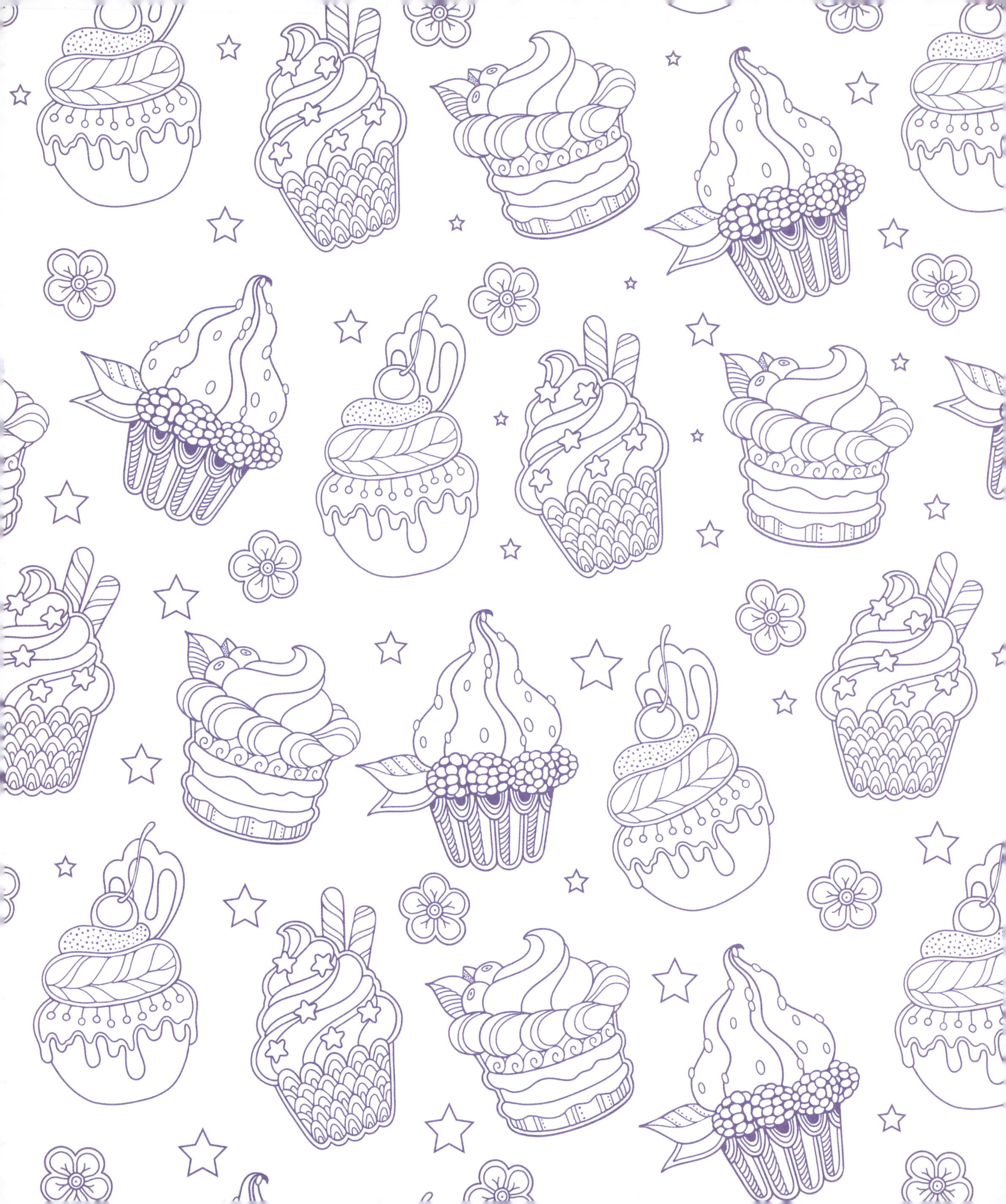

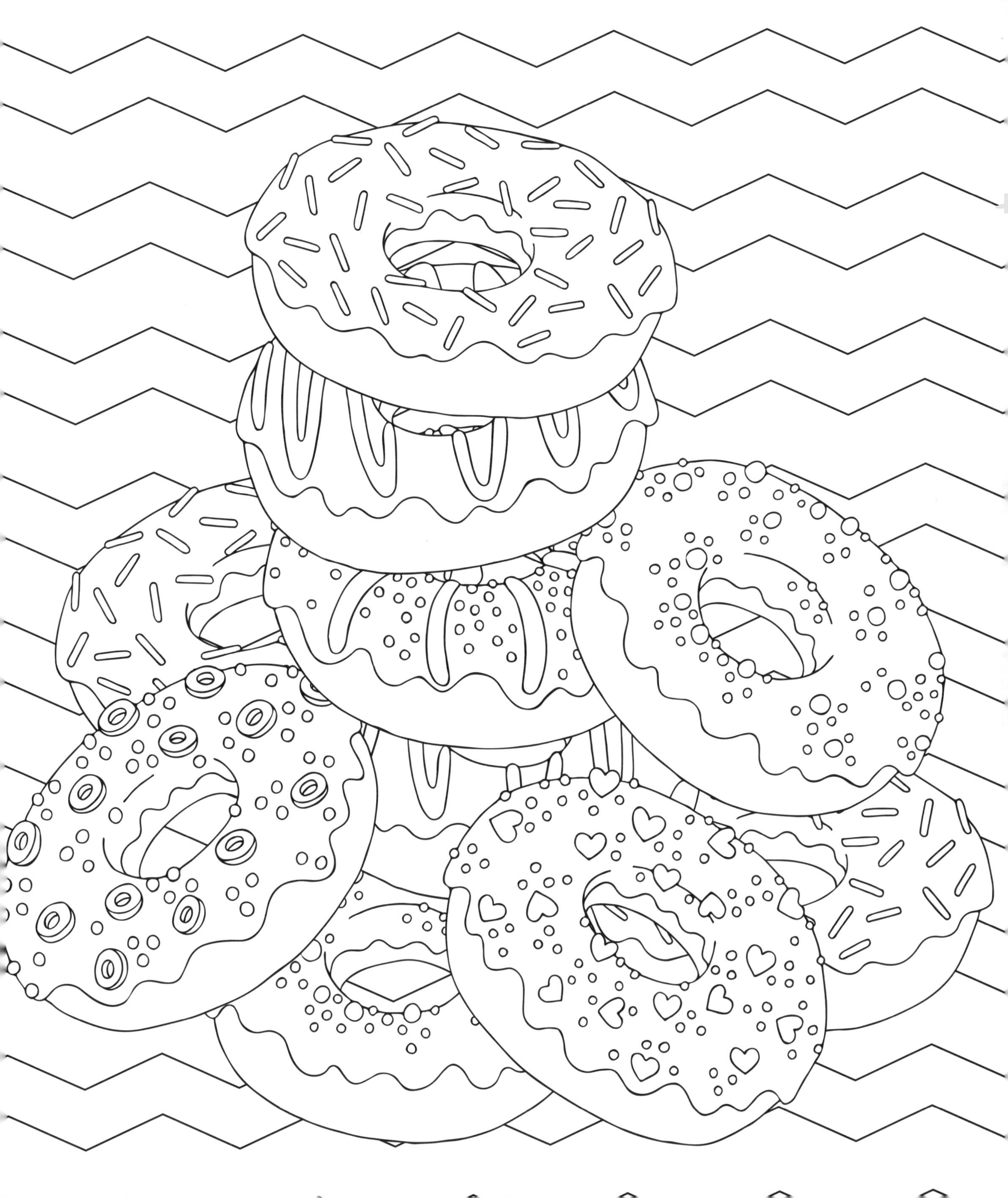

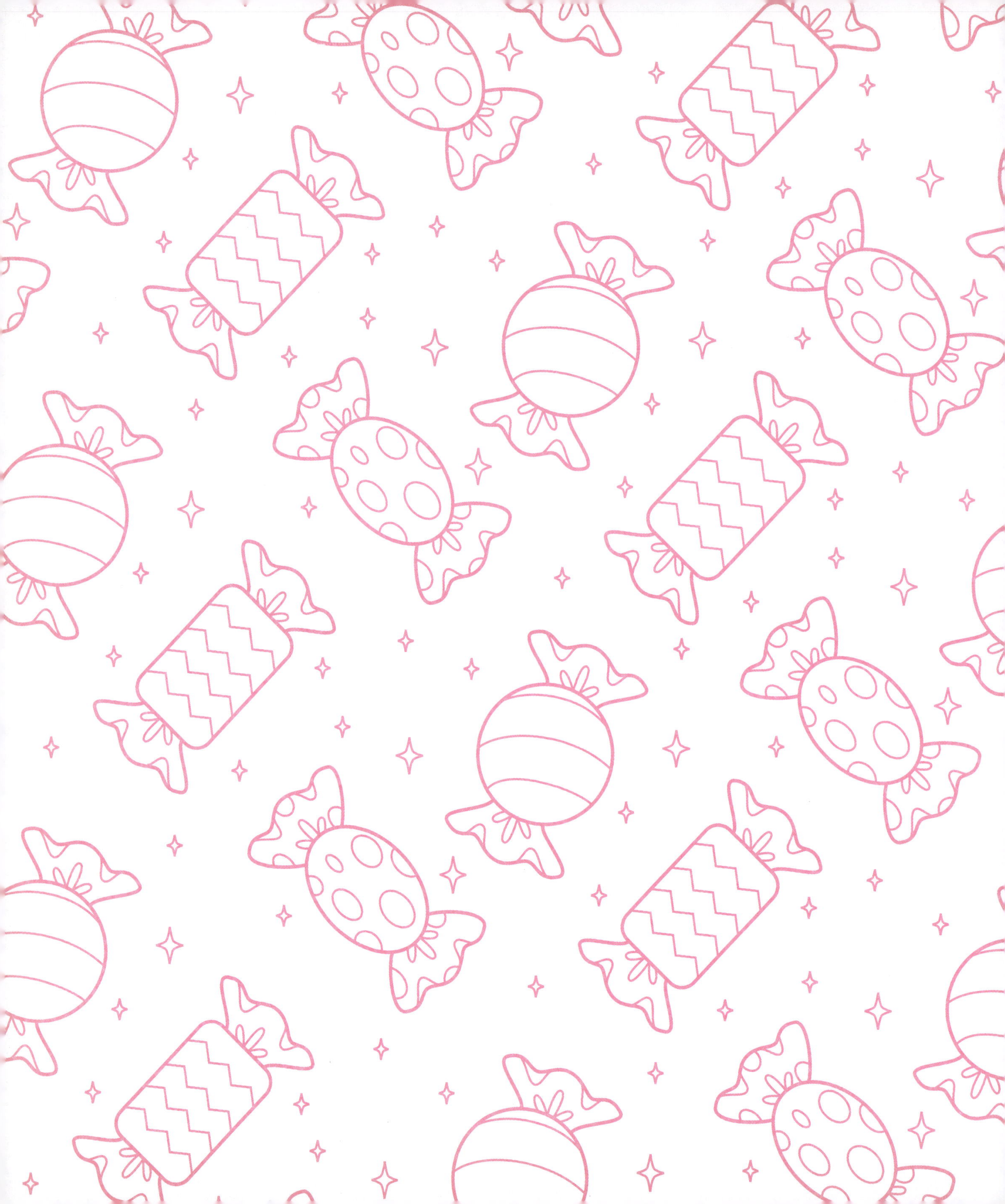

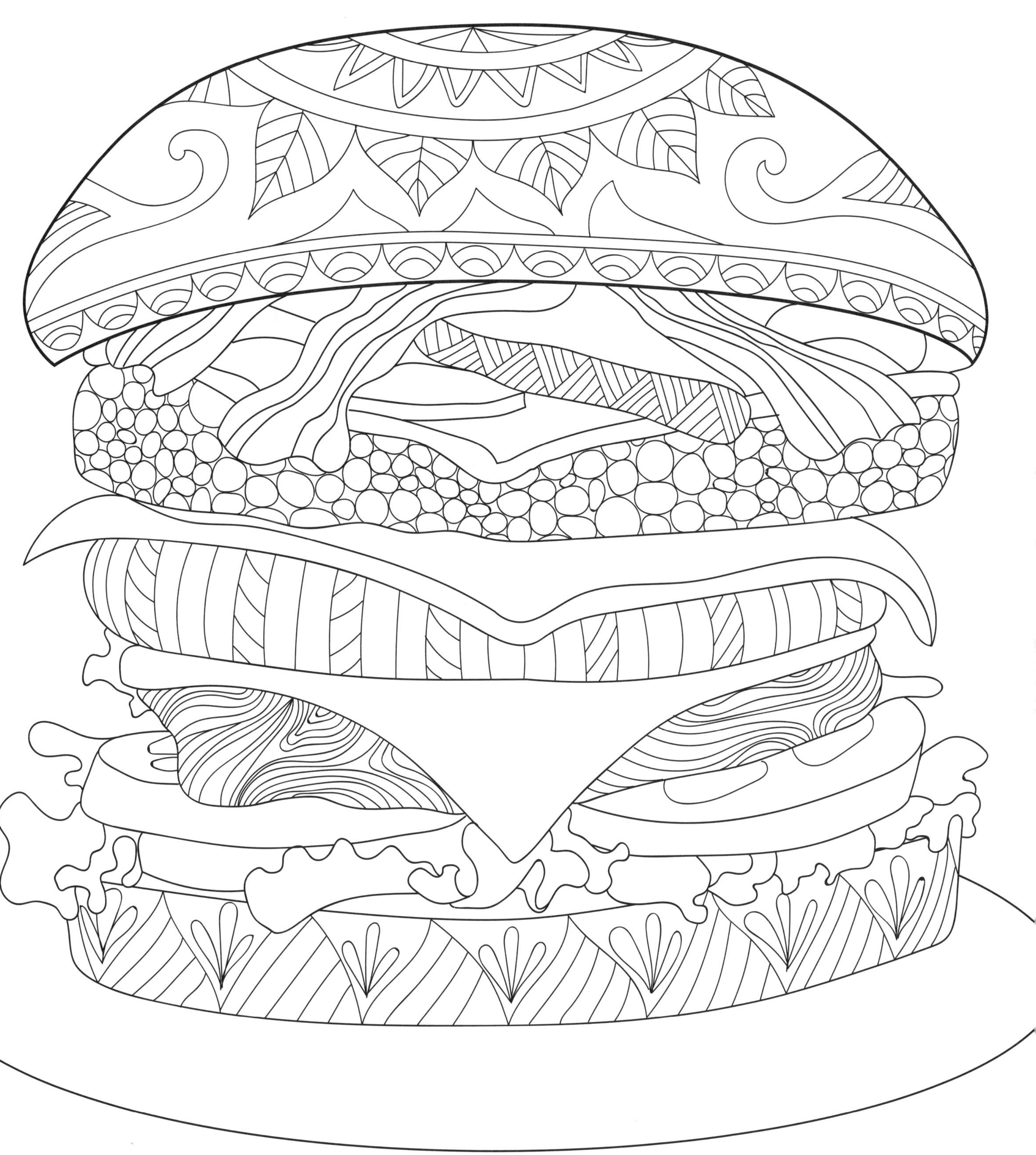

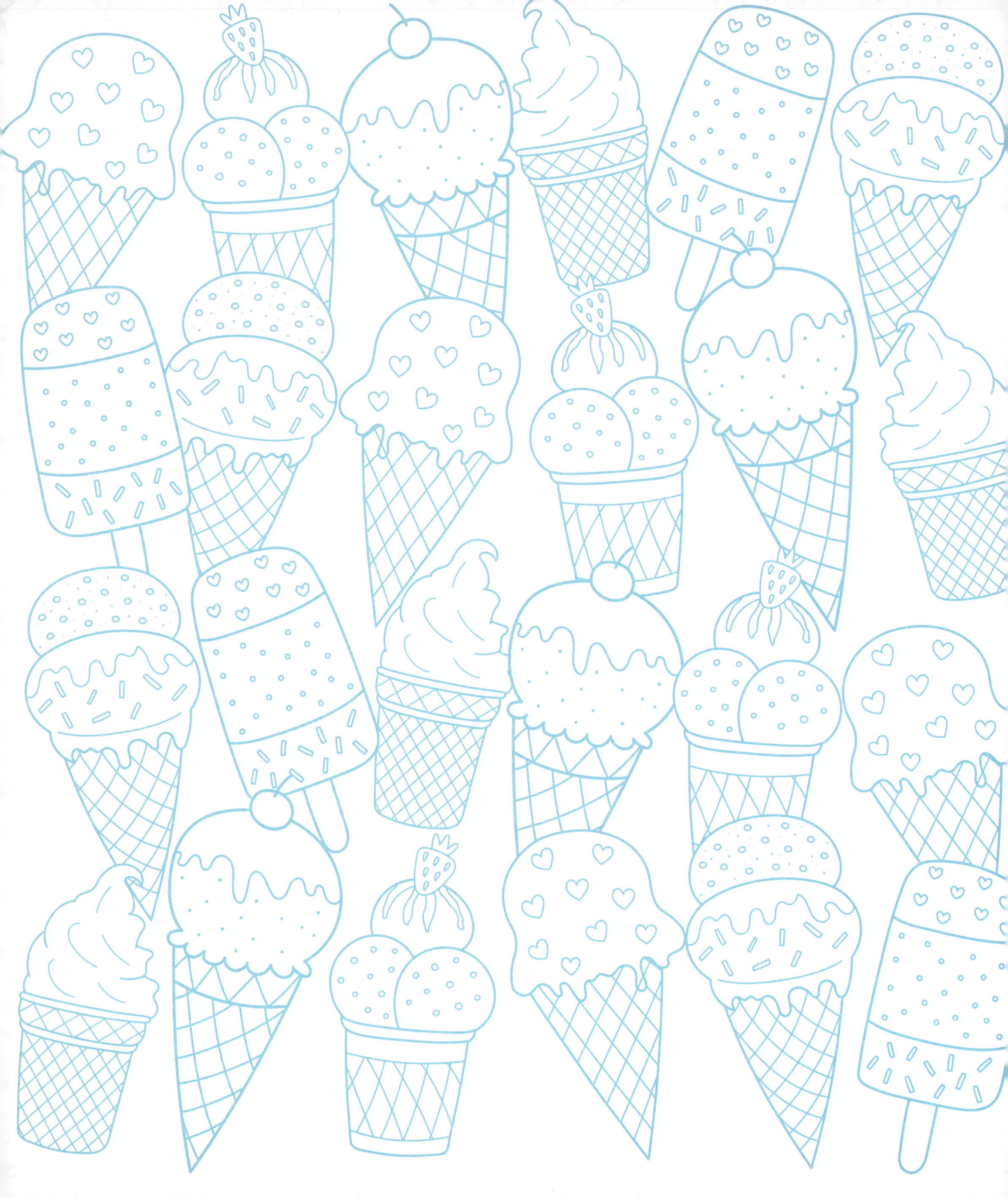

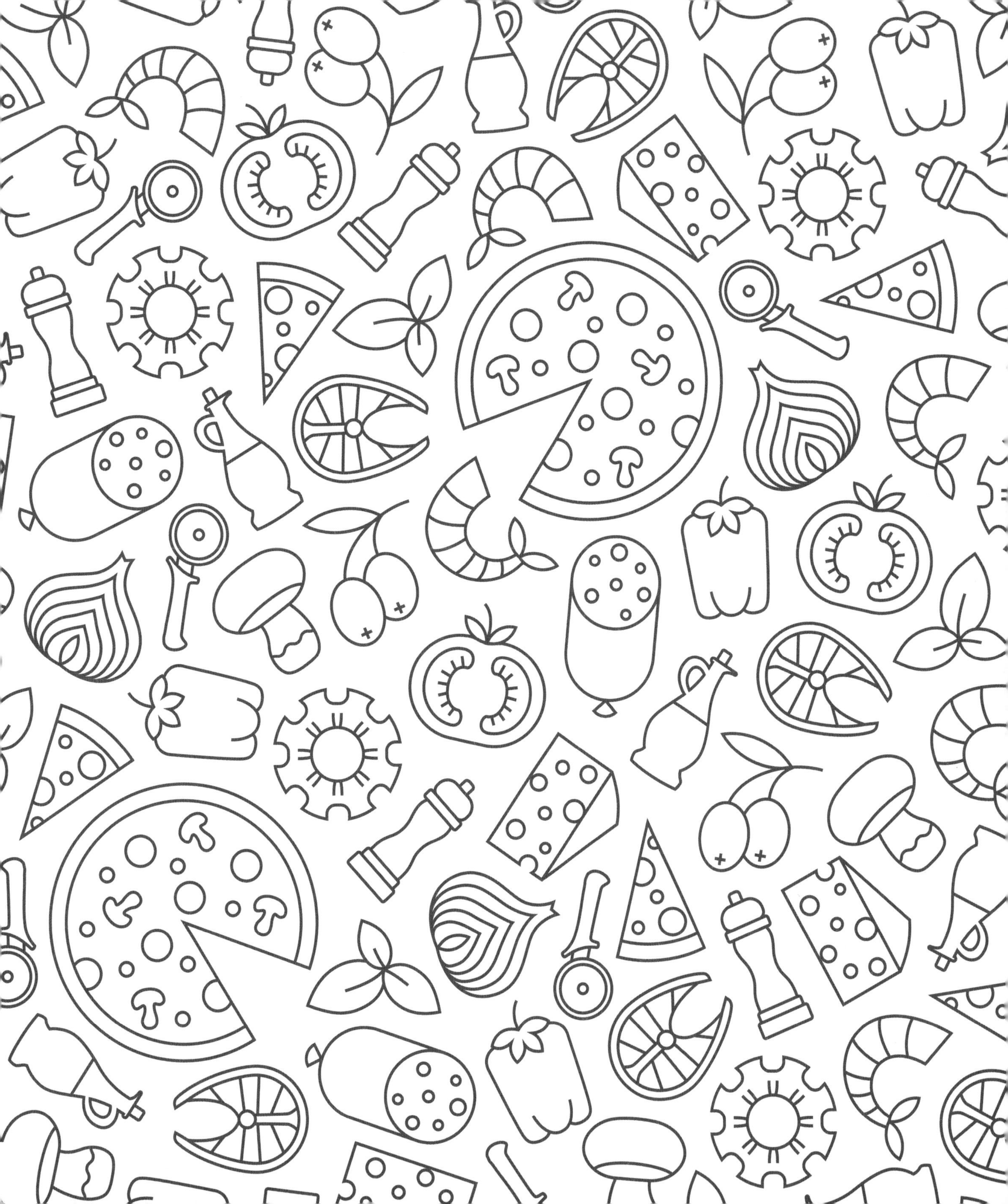

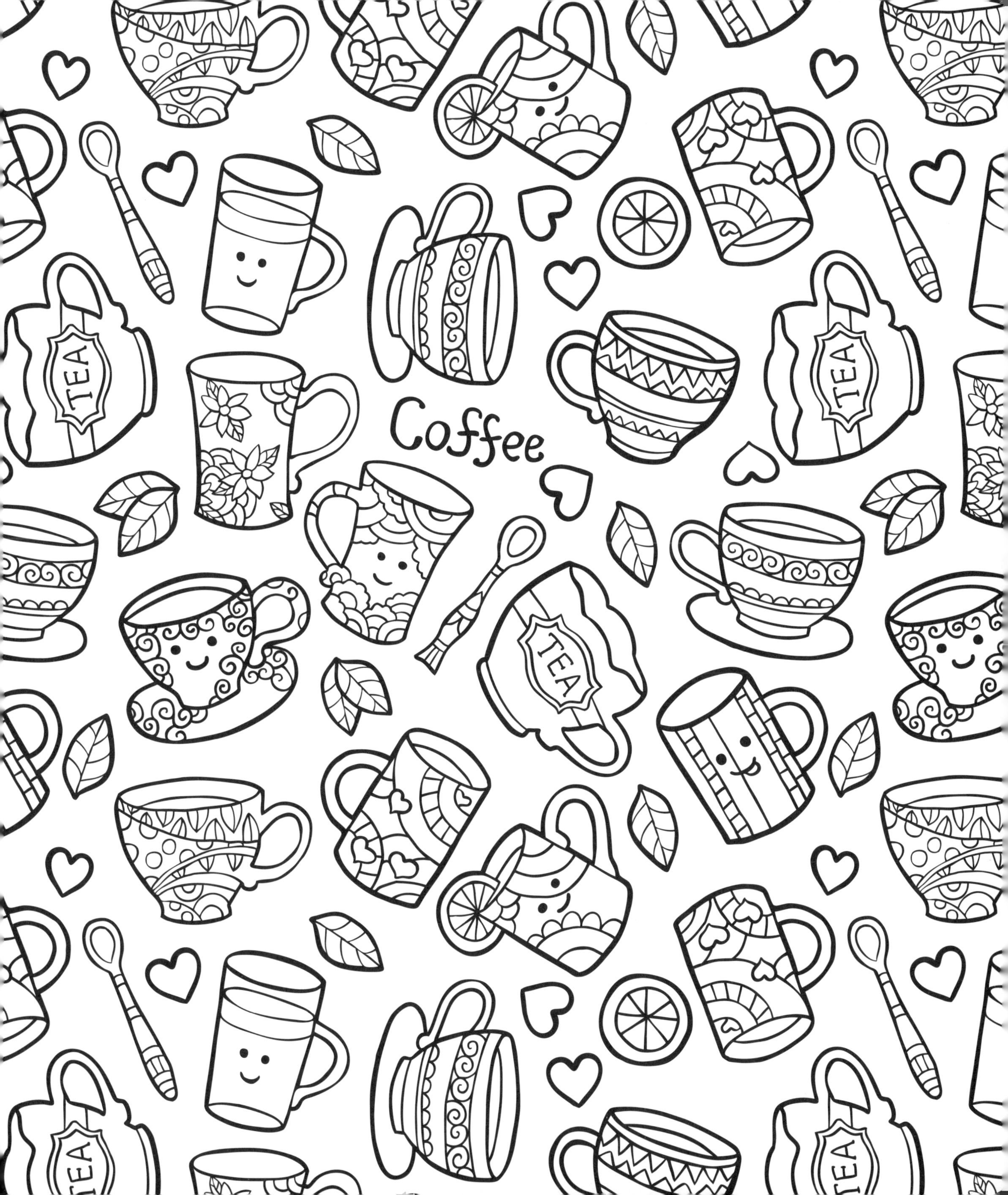

TEA
Coffee
TEA
TEA

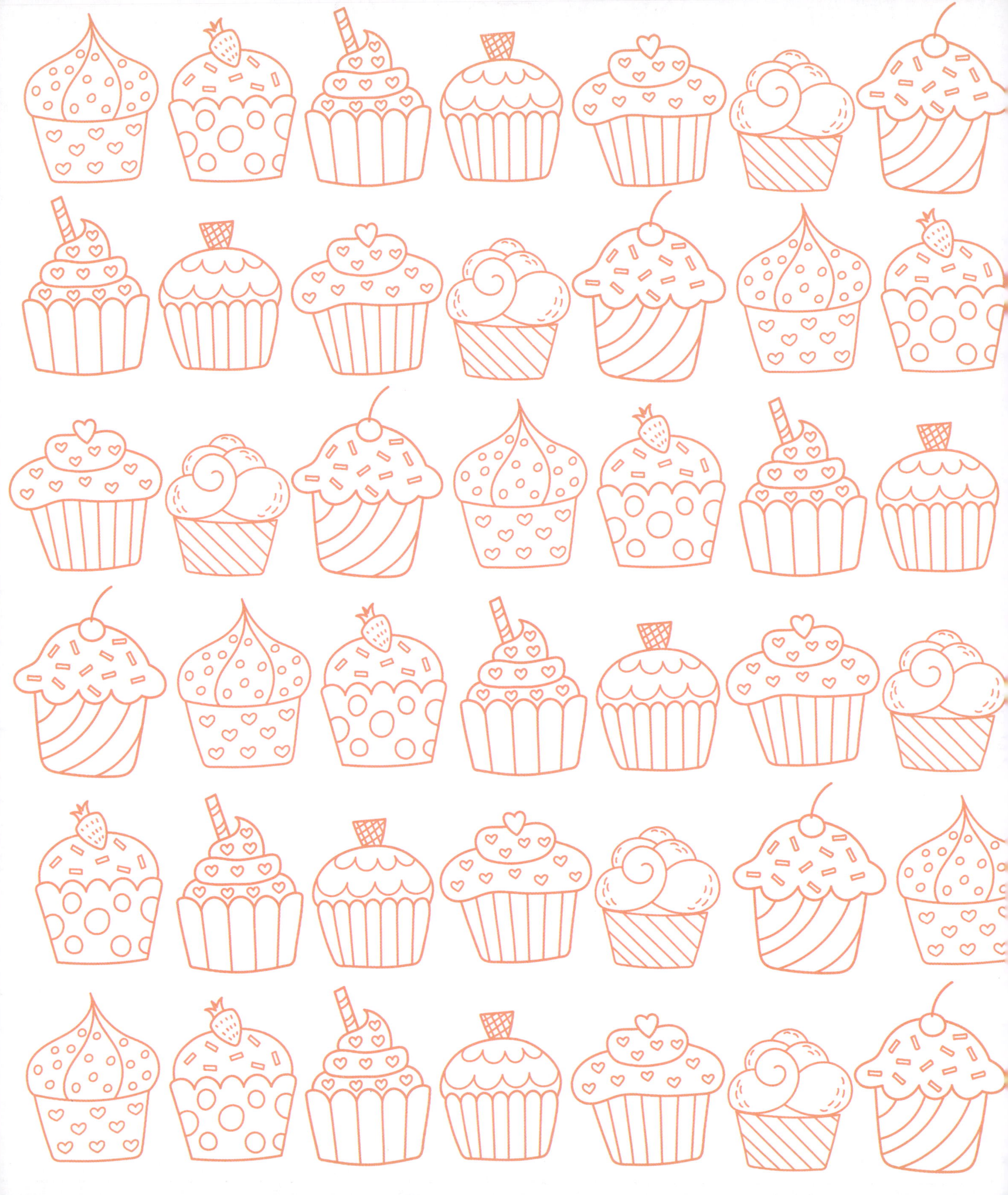

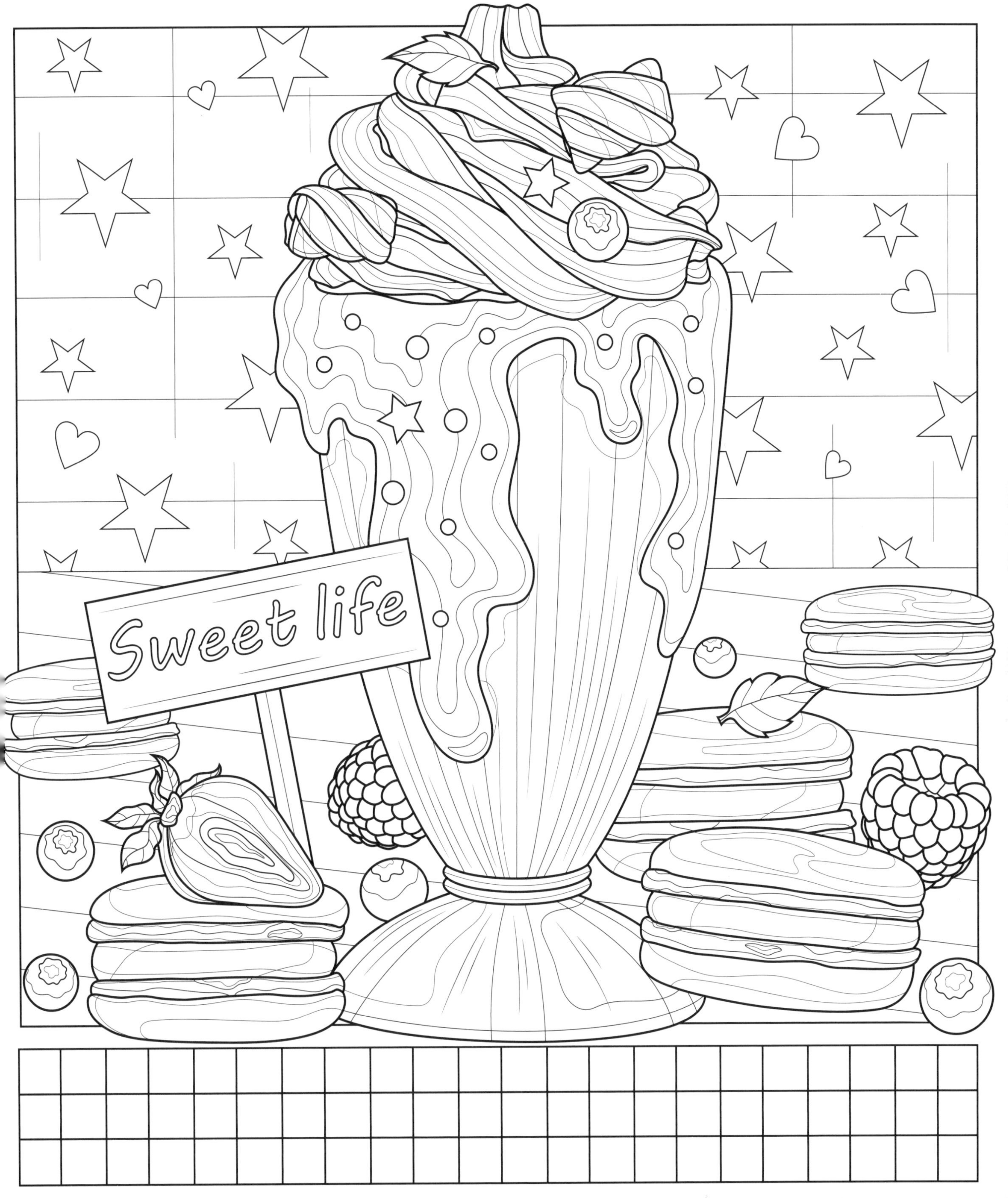
Sweet life

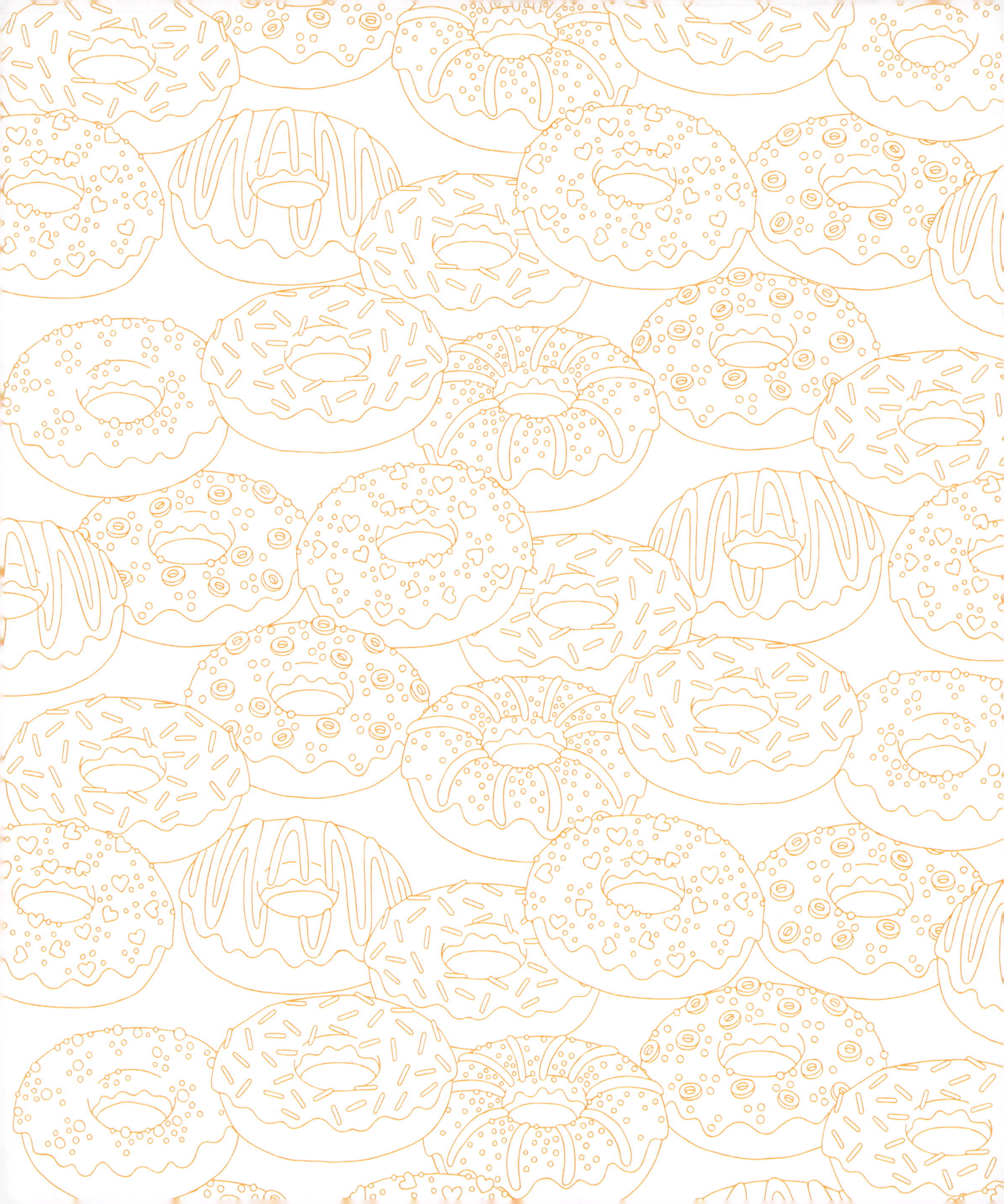

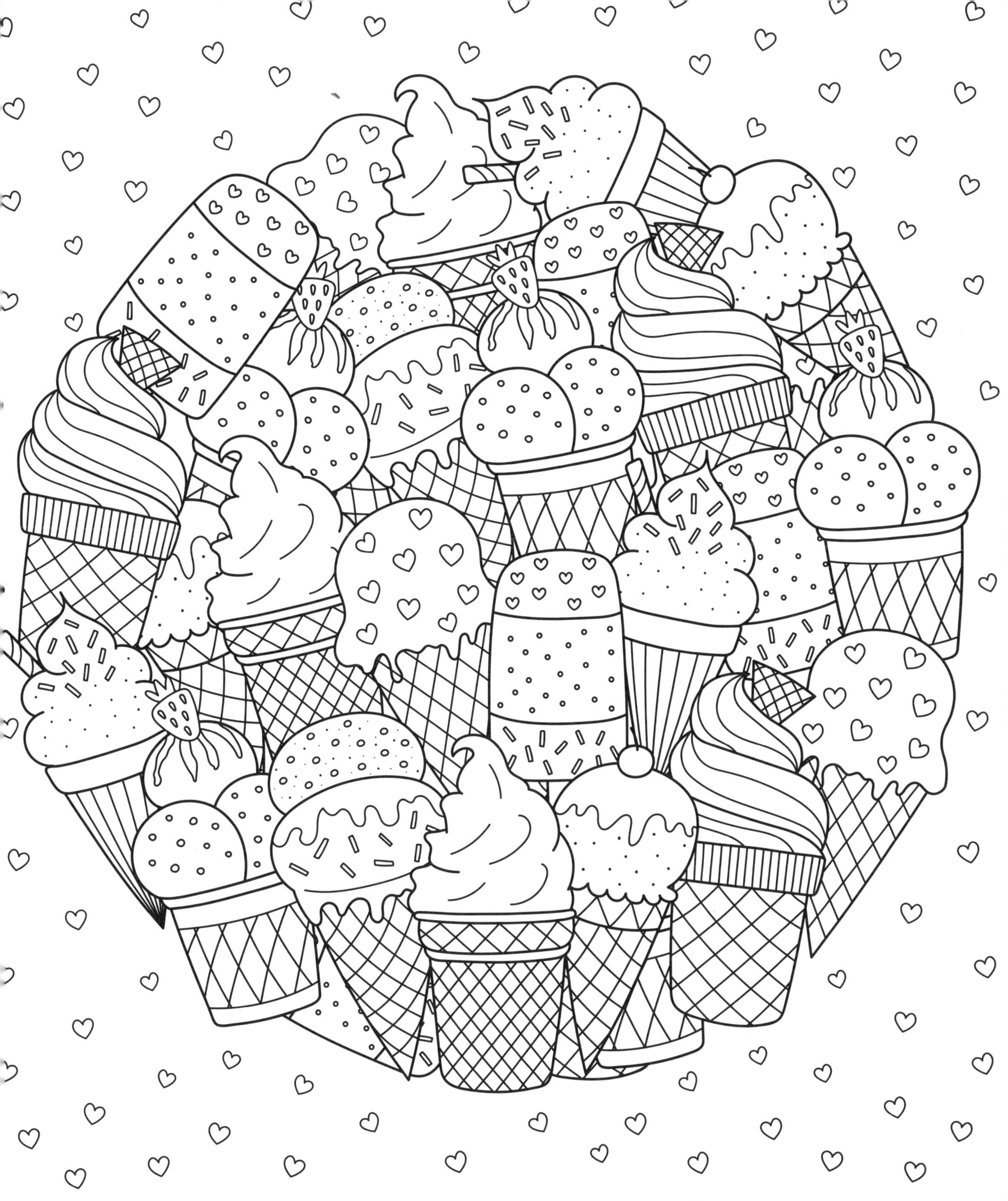

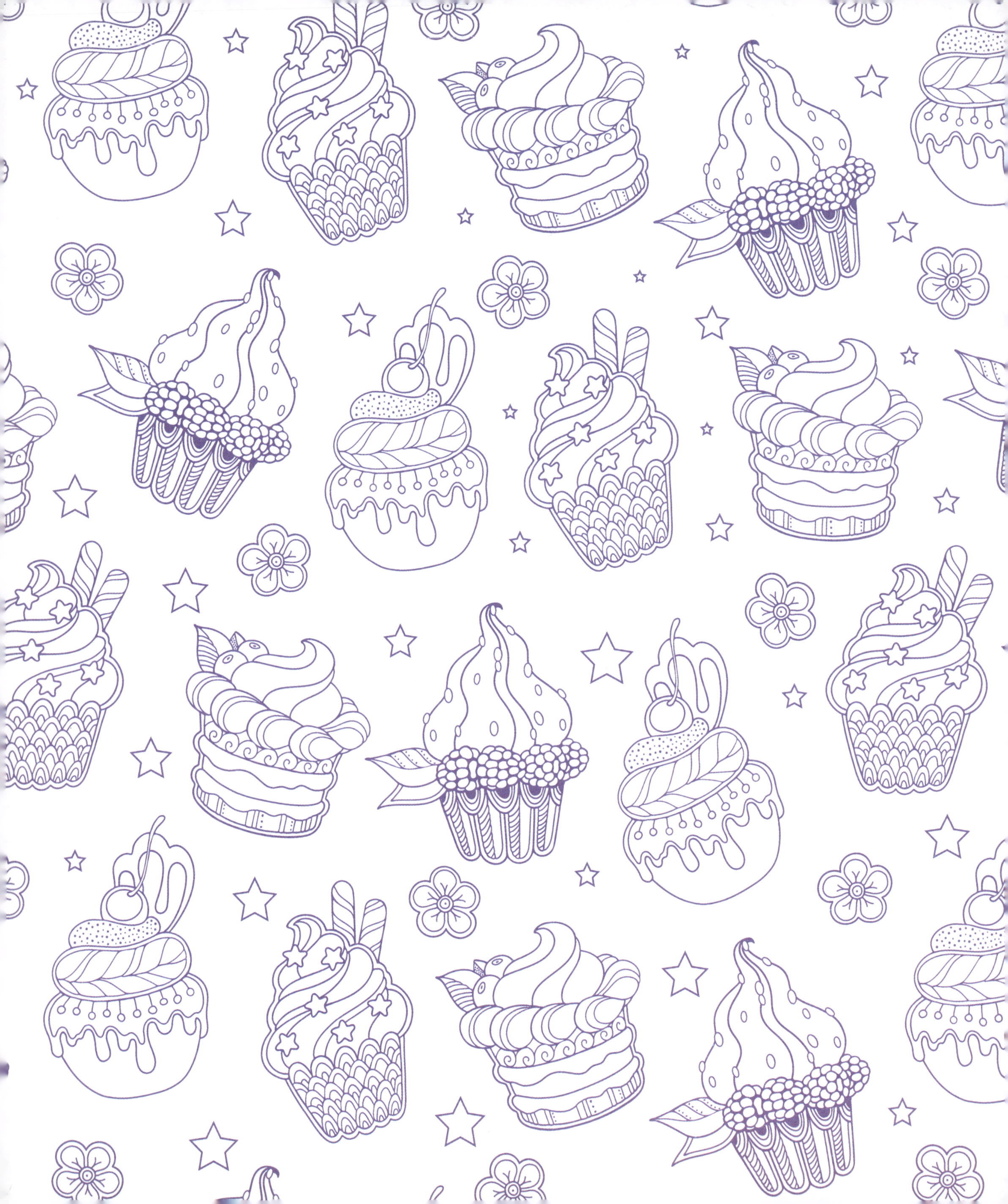

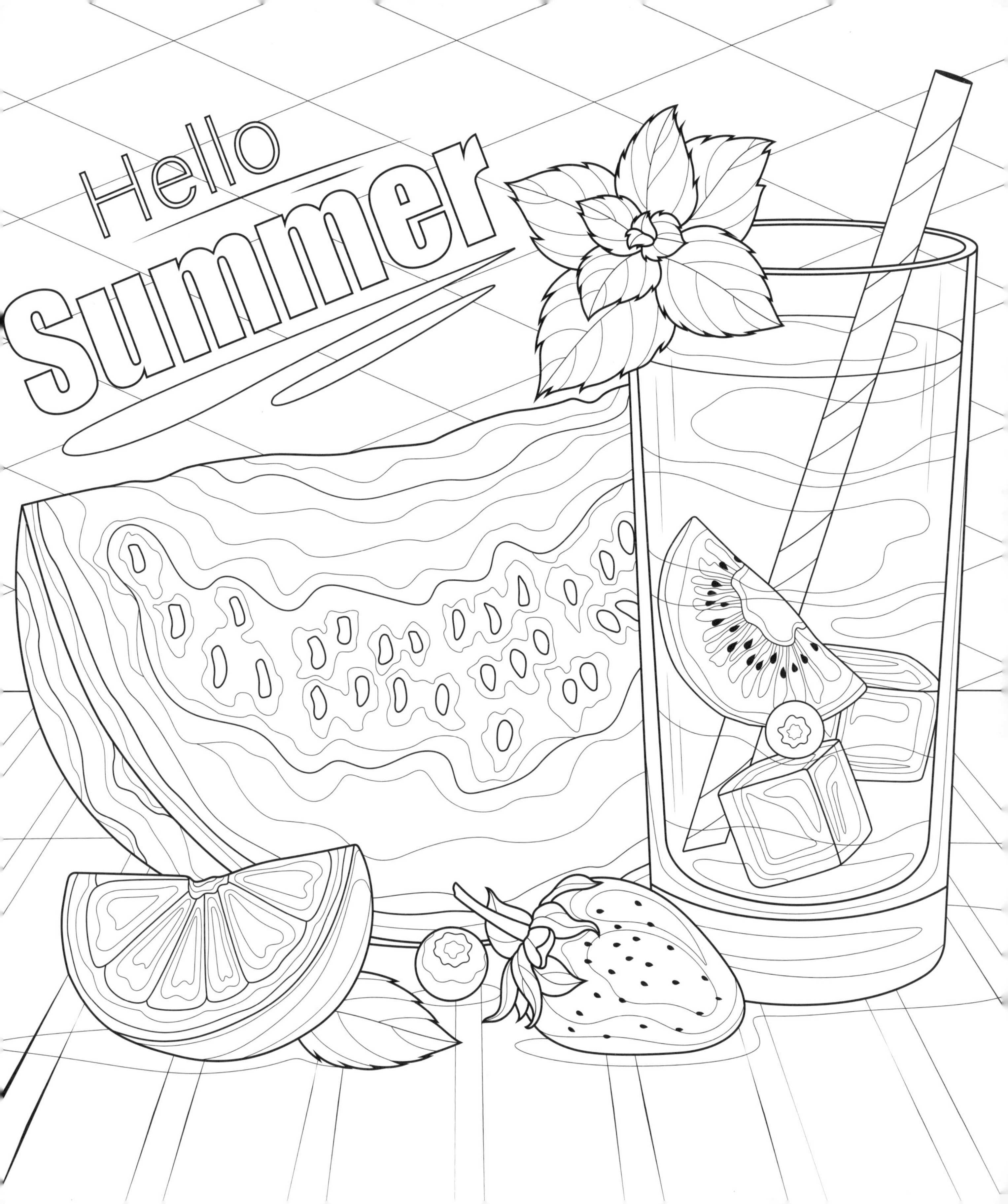

Hello
Summer

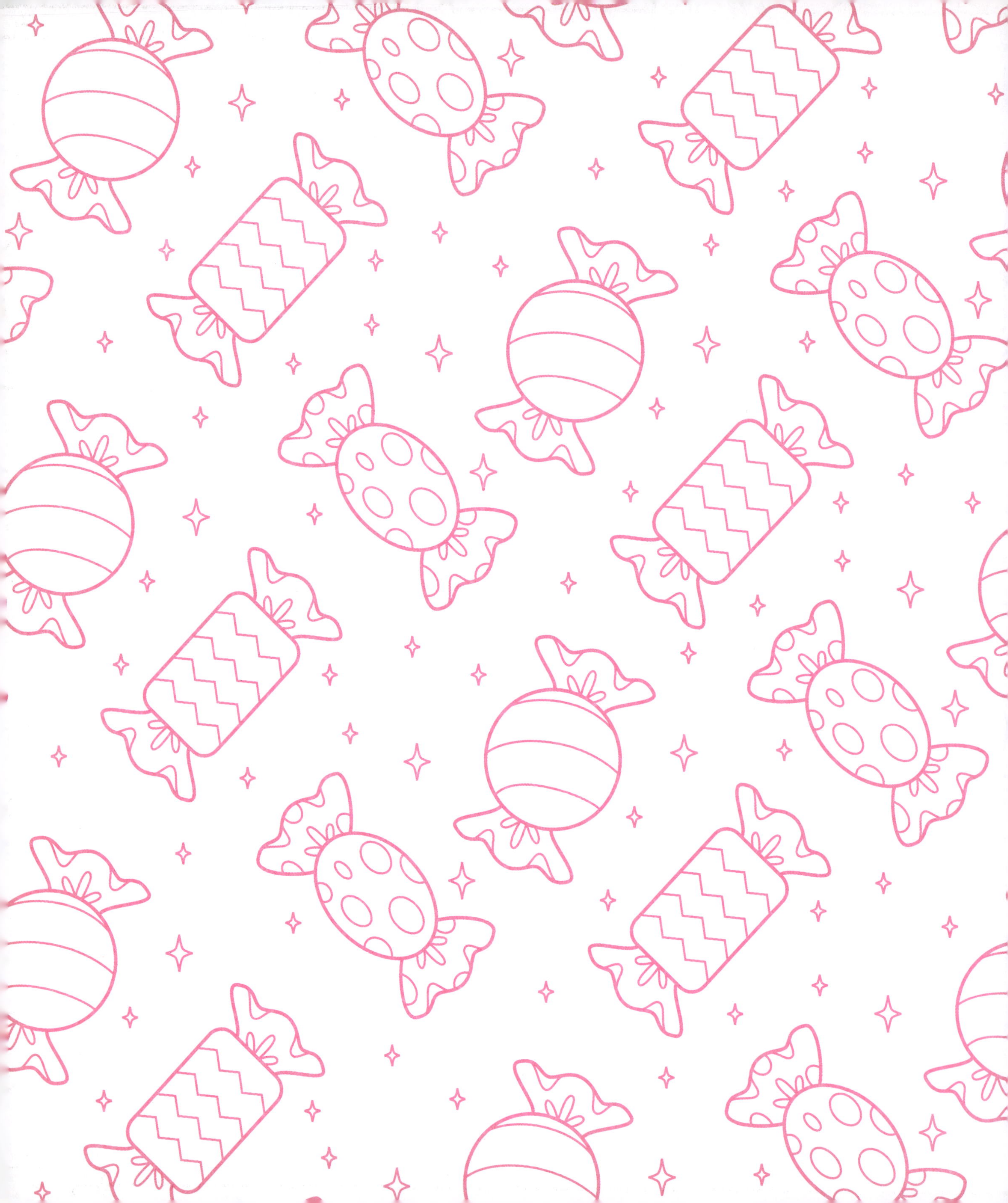

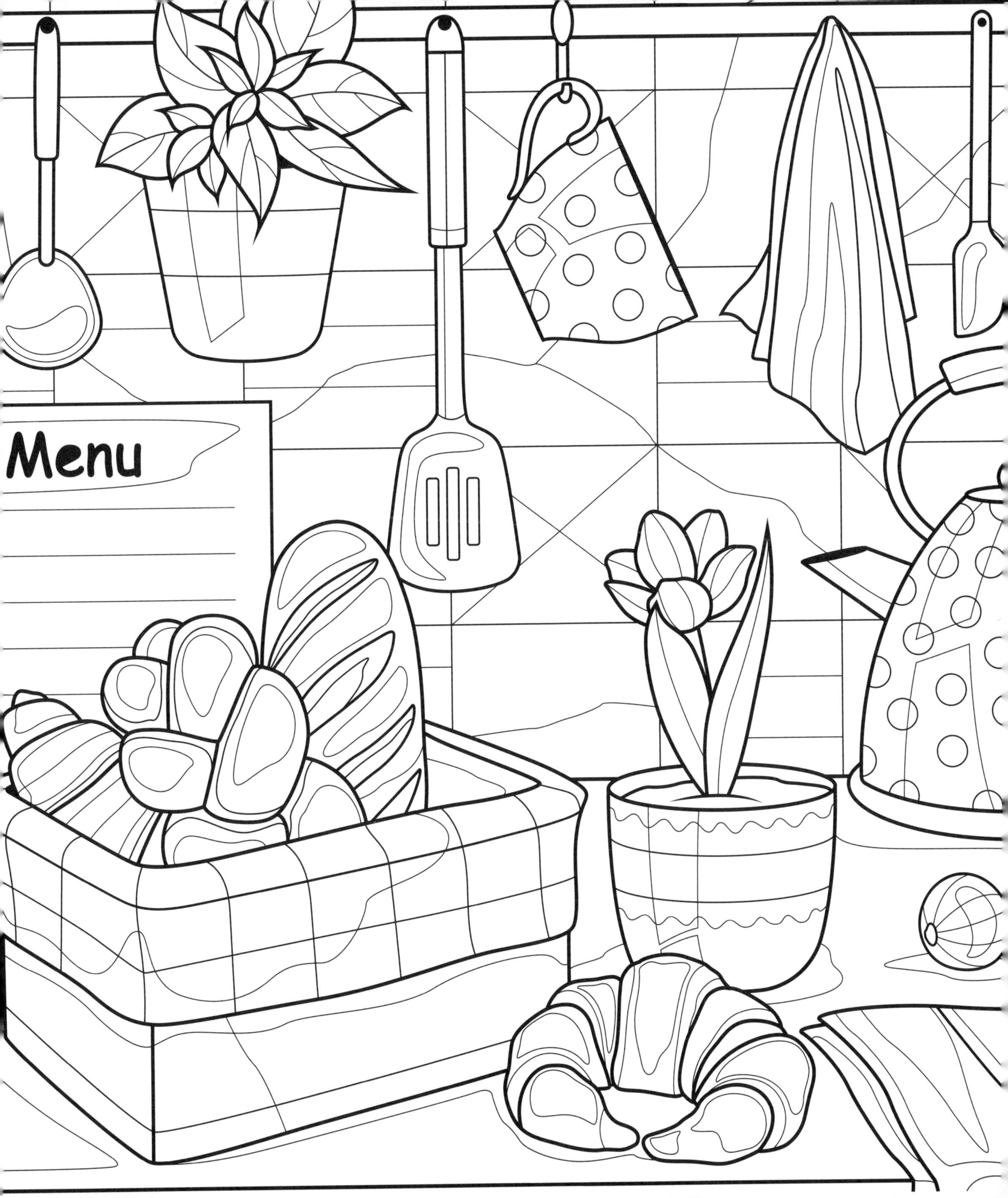
Menu

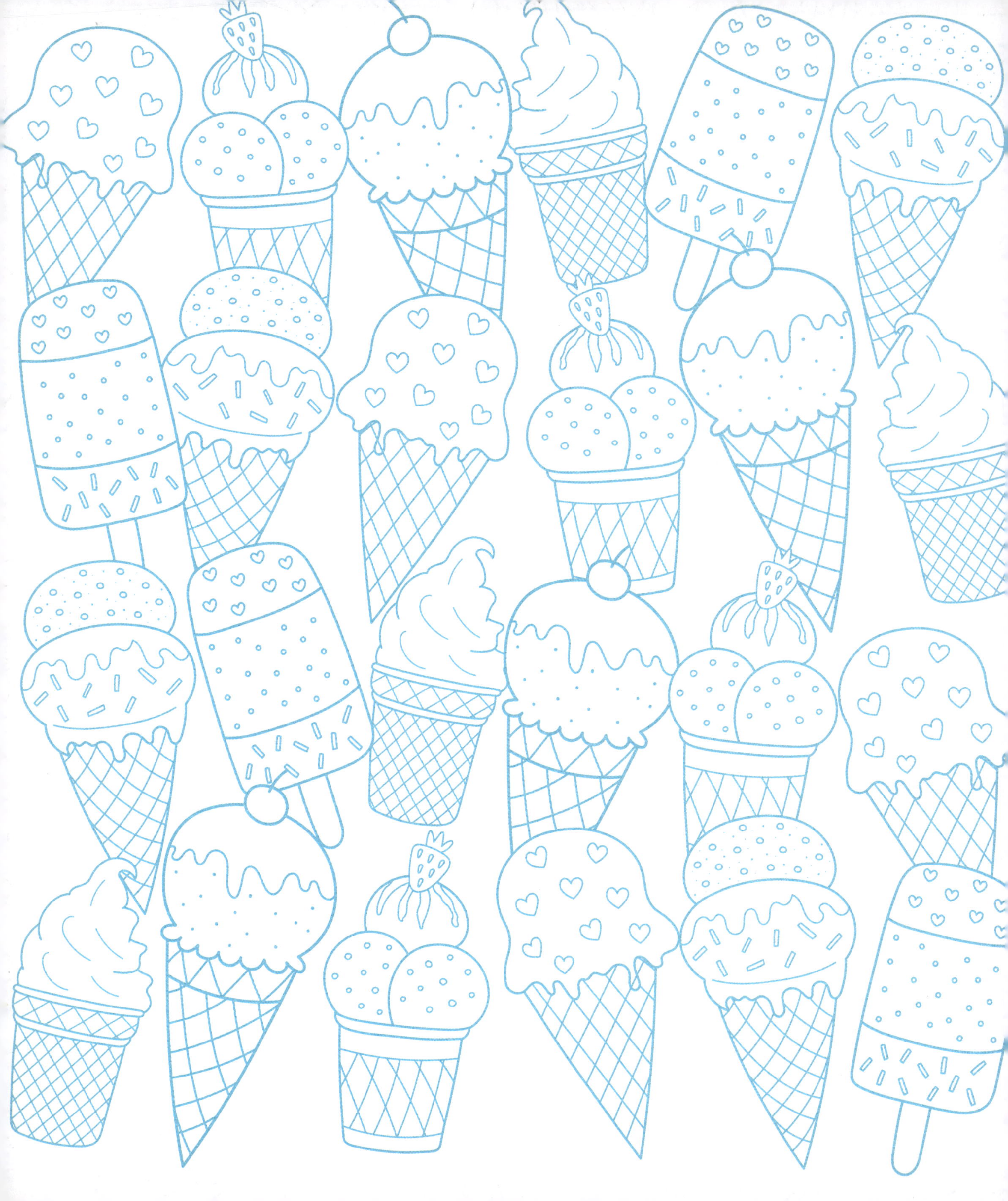

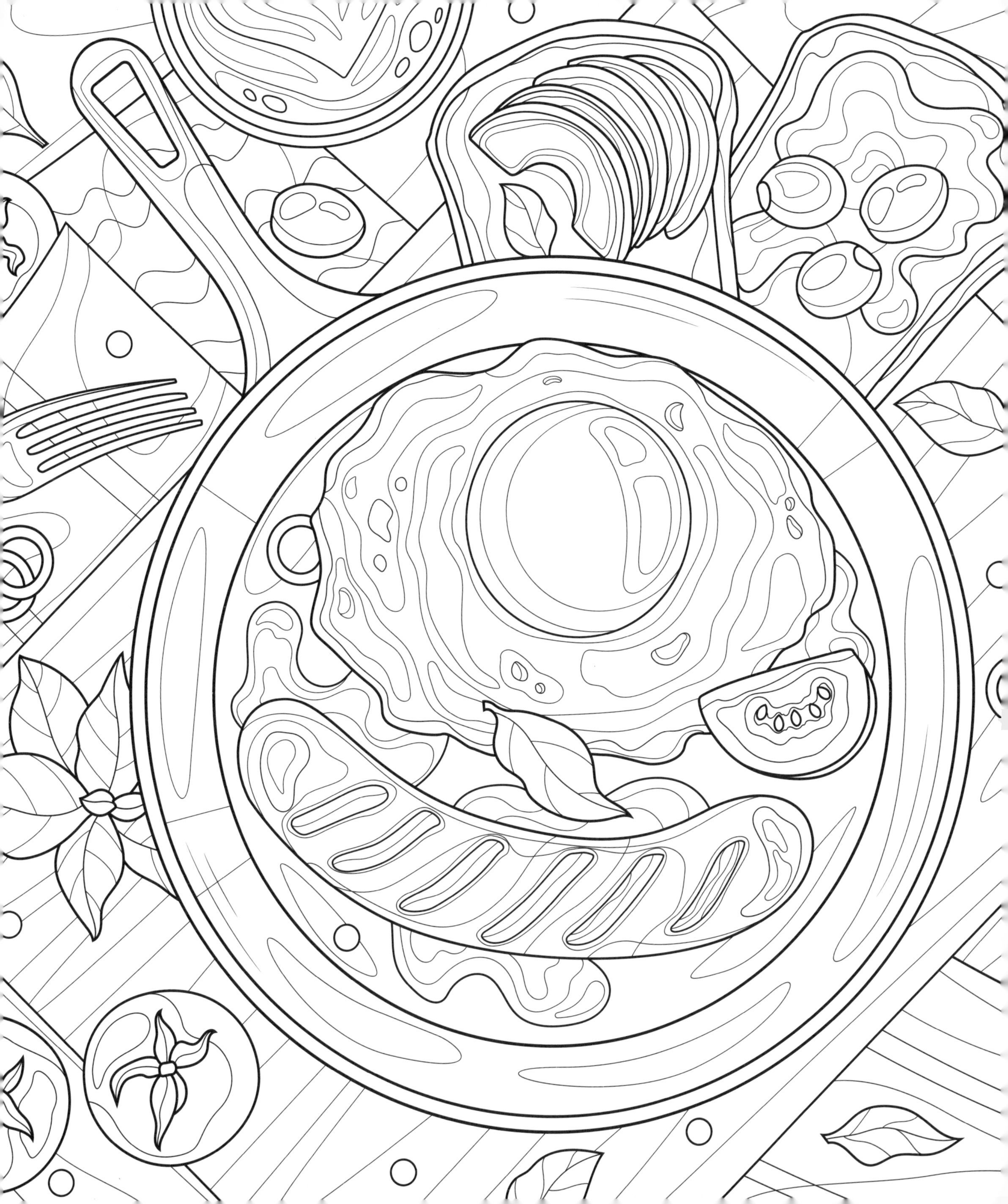

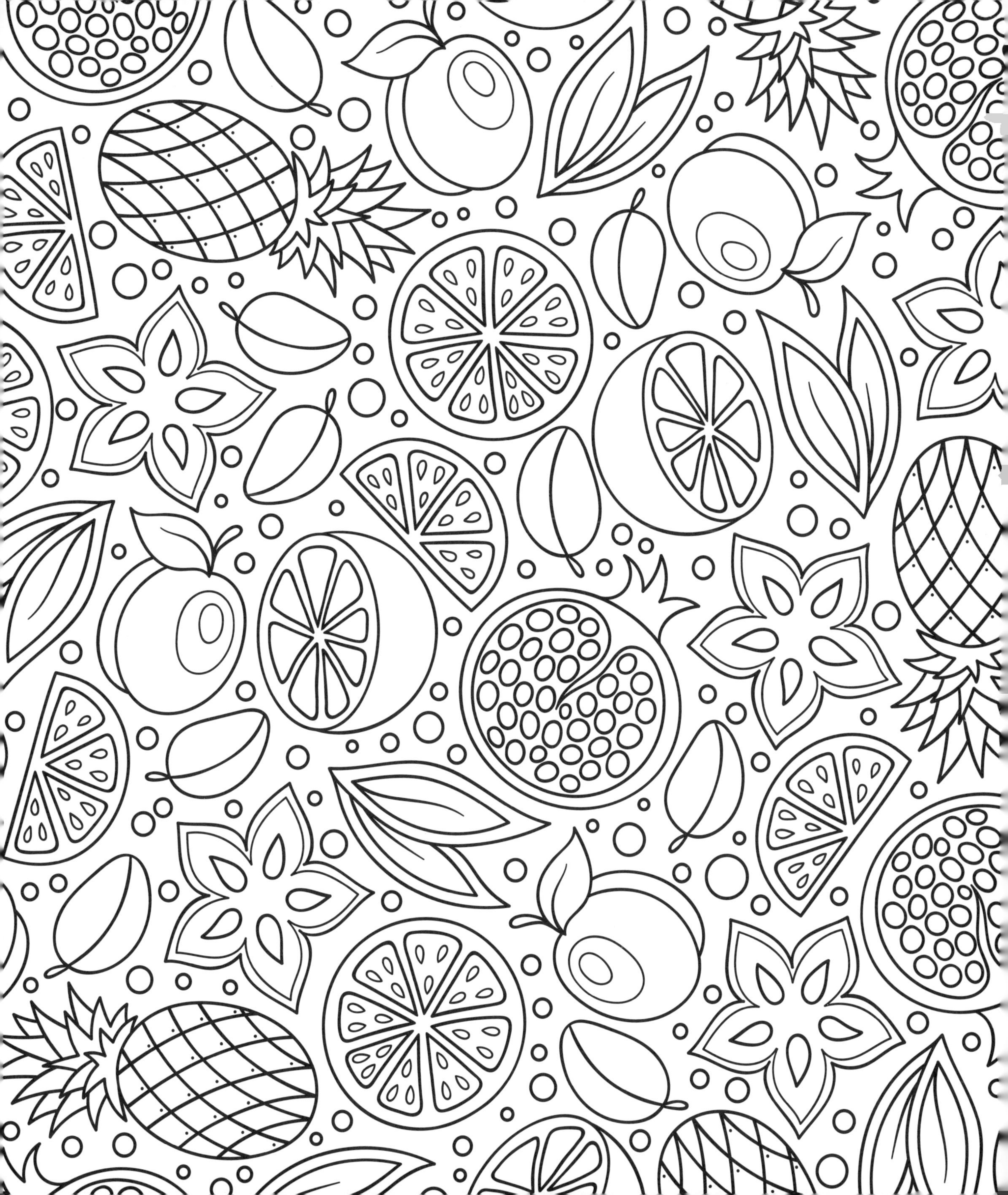

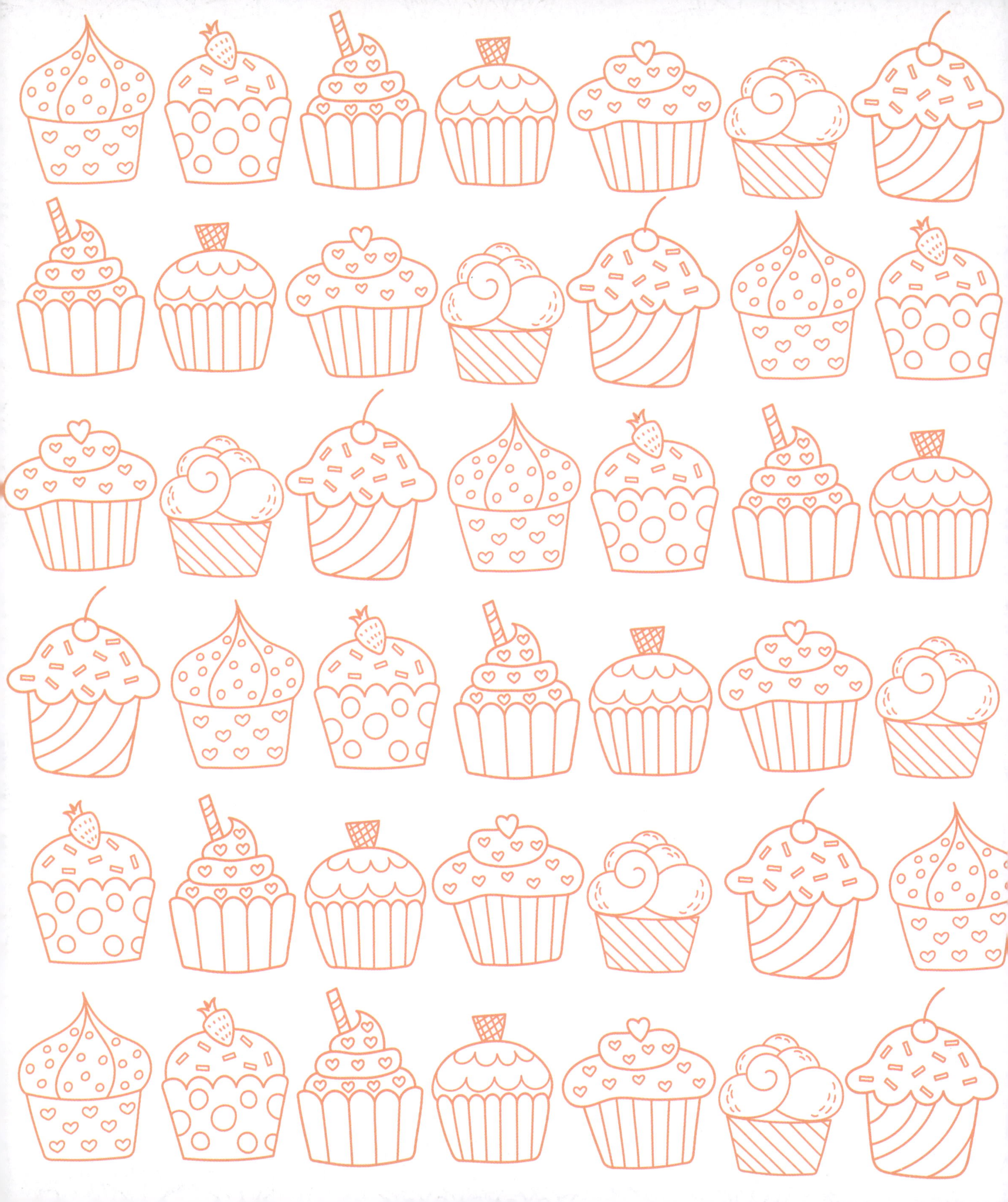

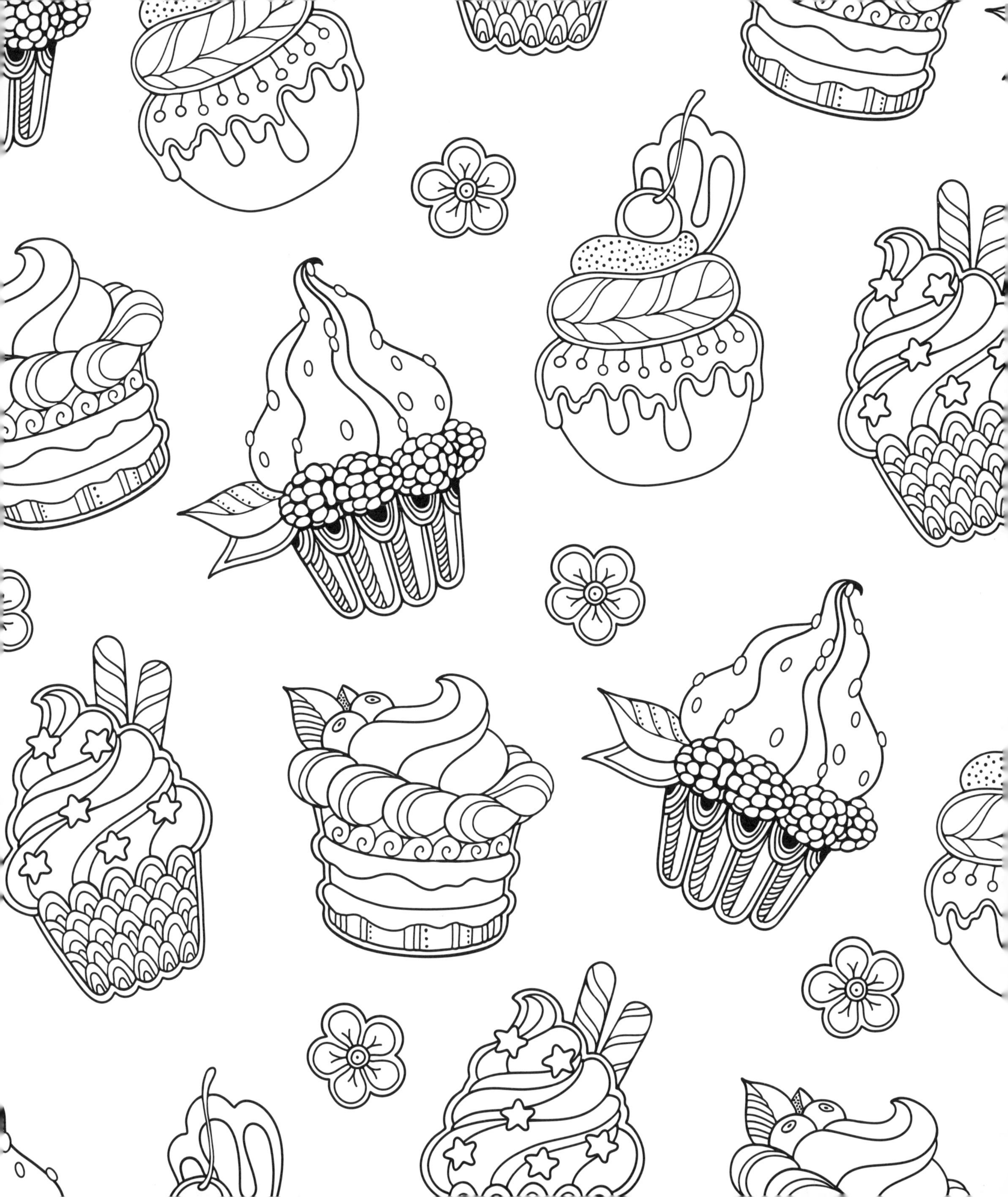

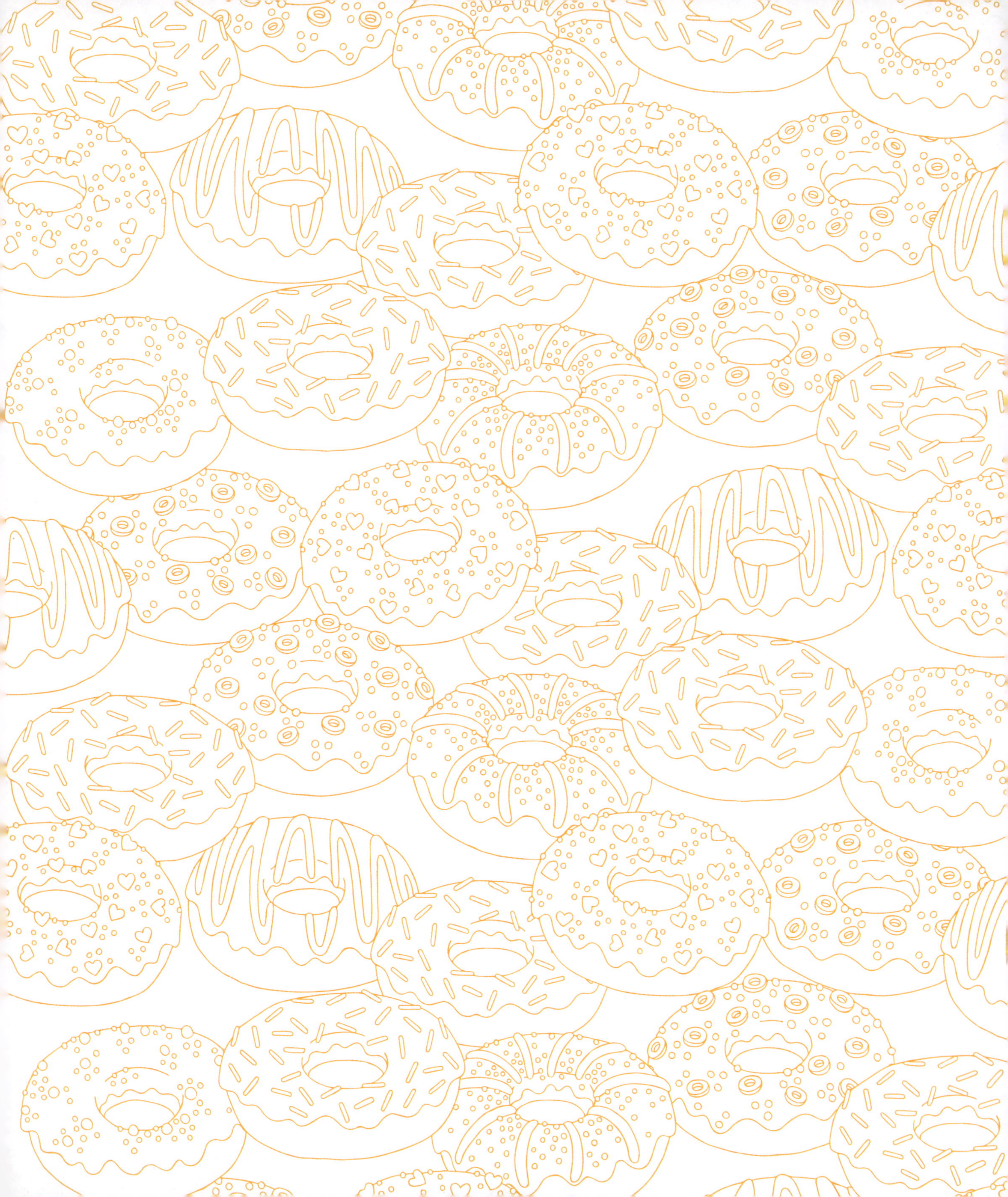

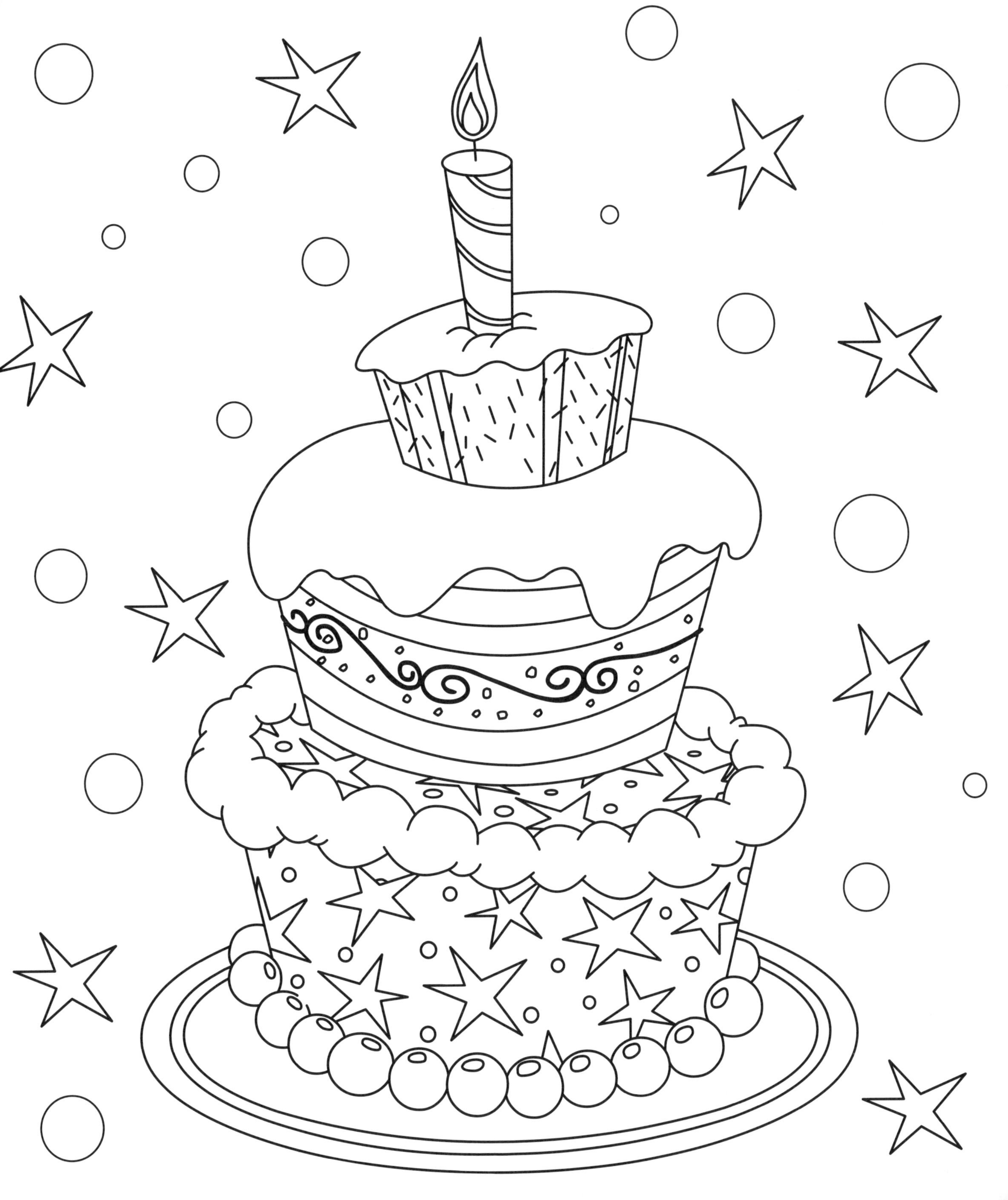

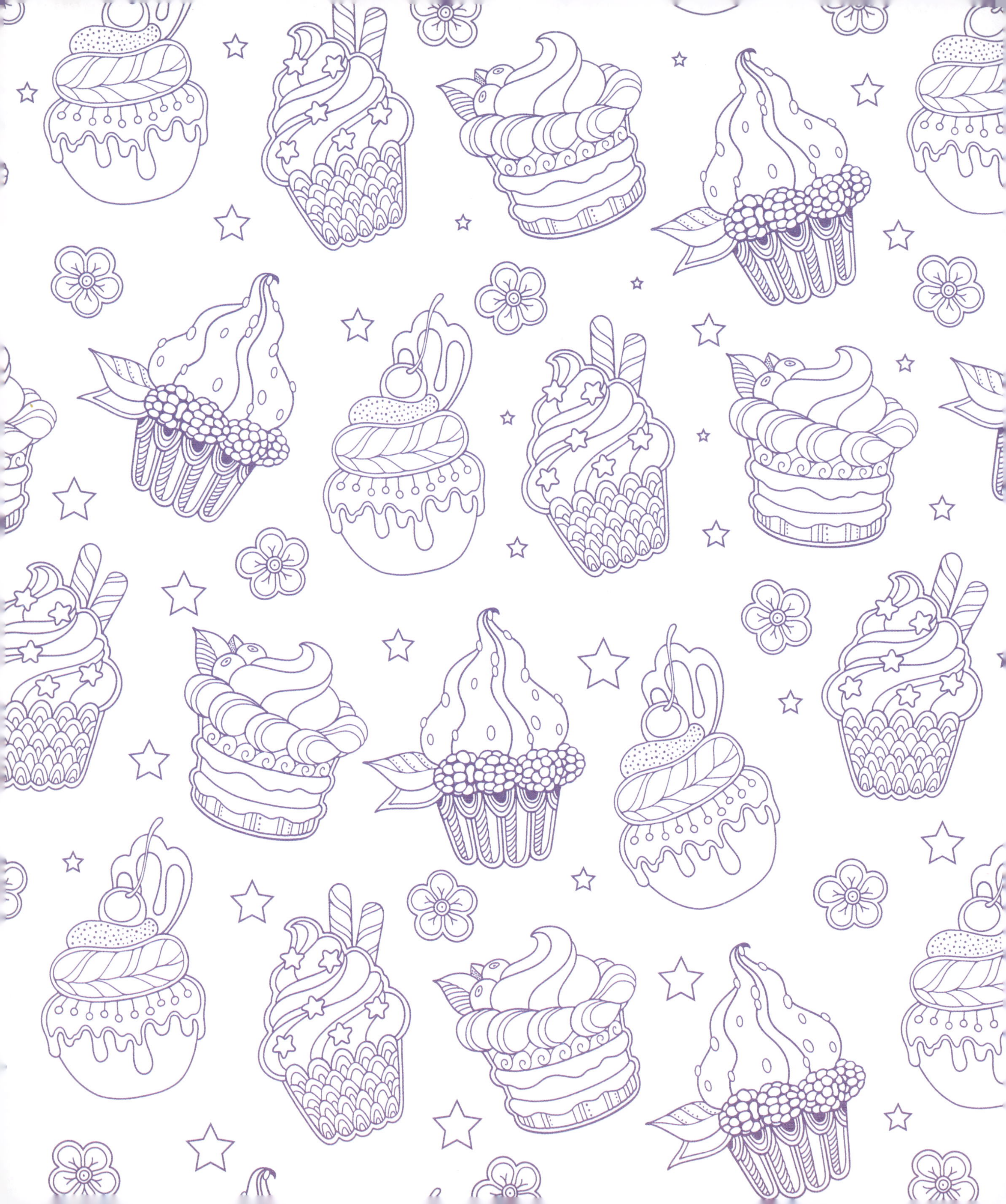

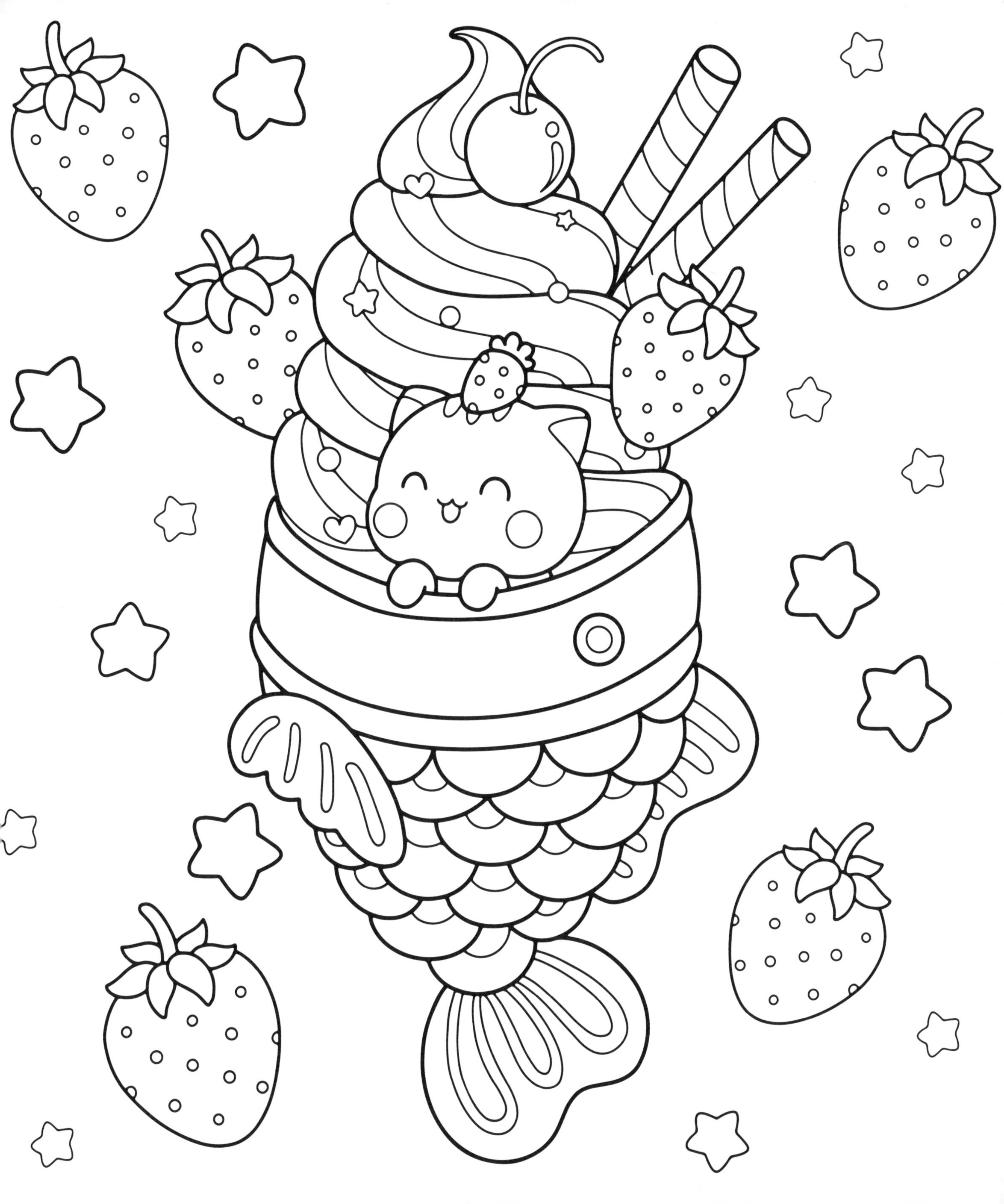

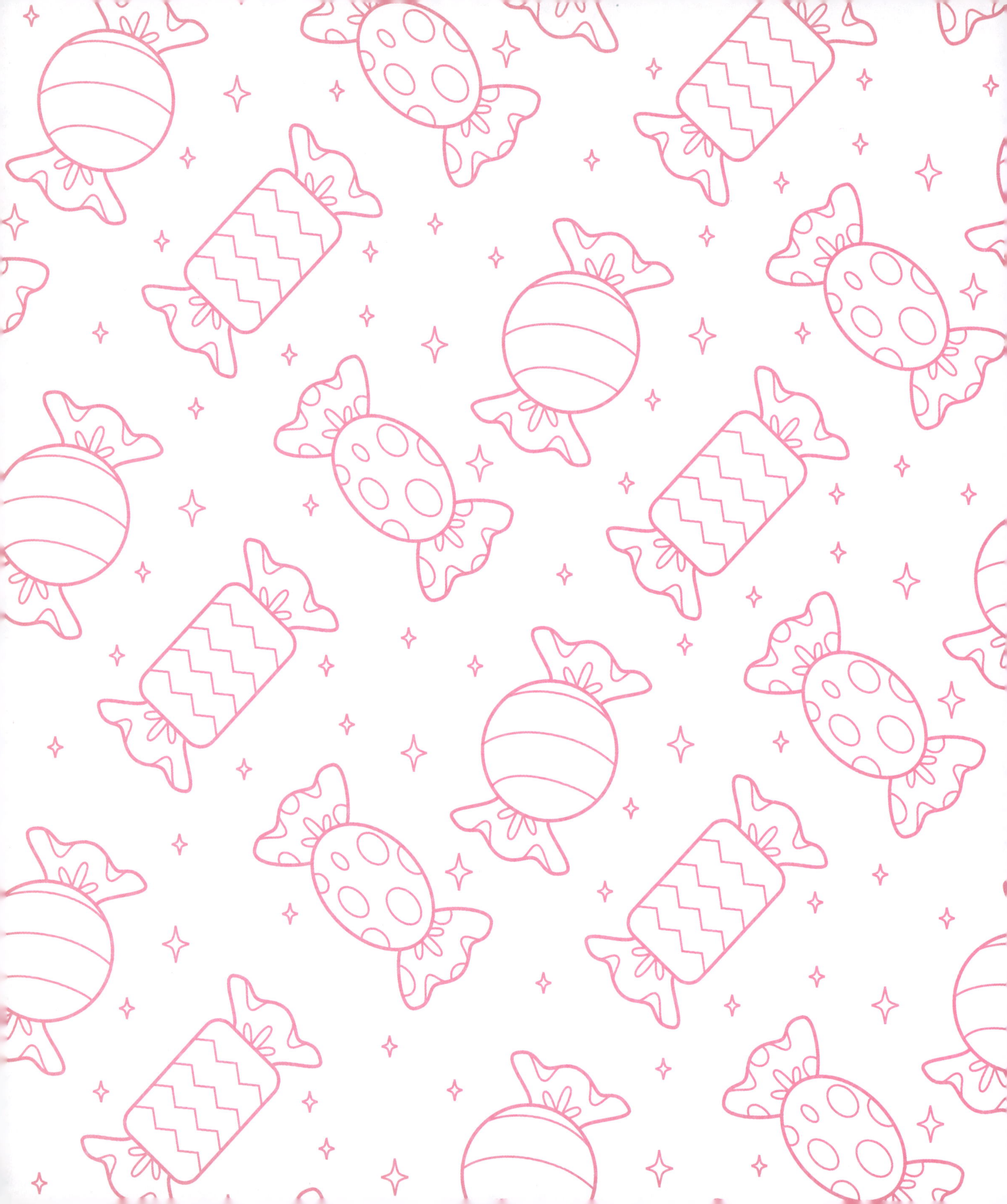

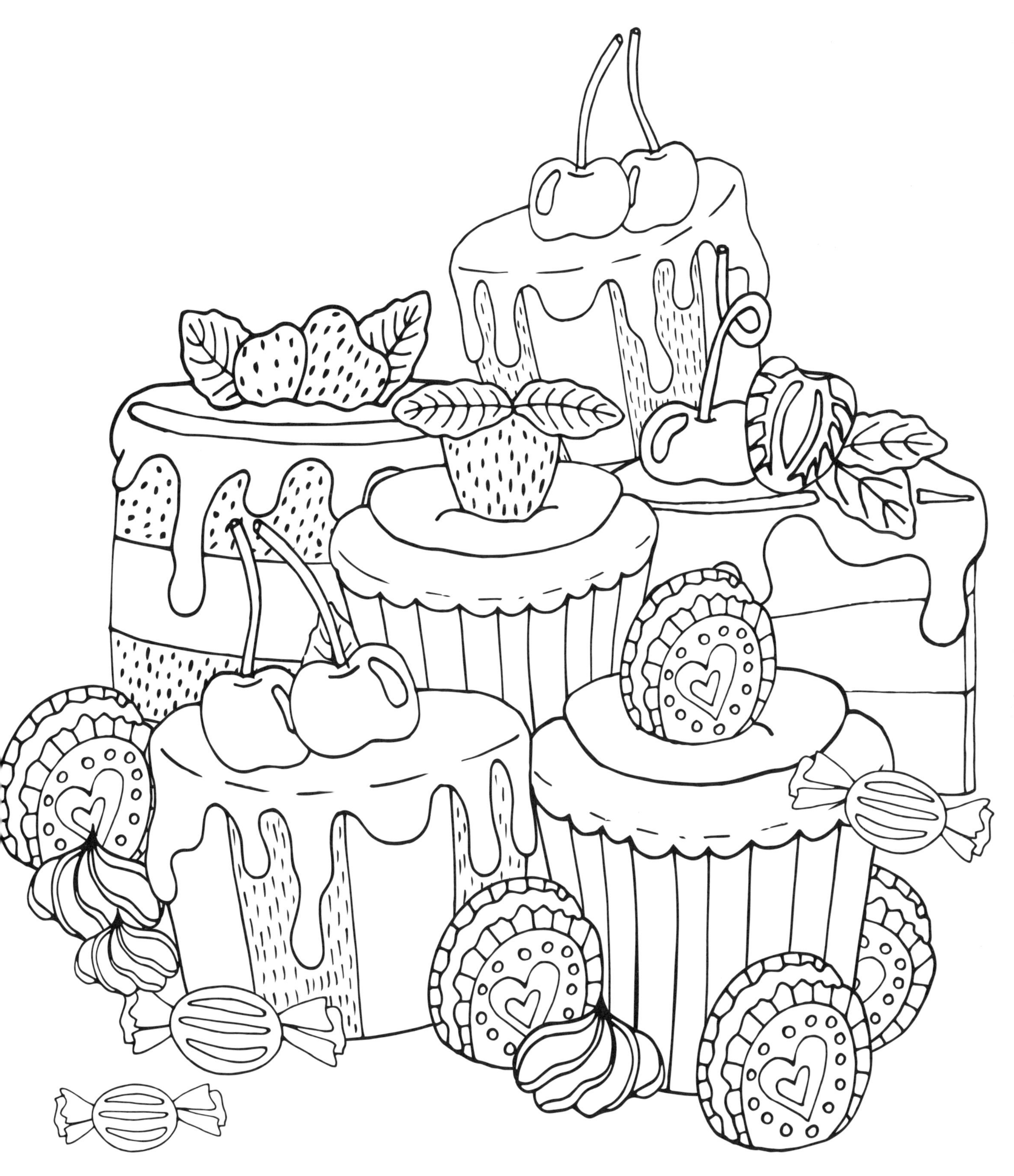

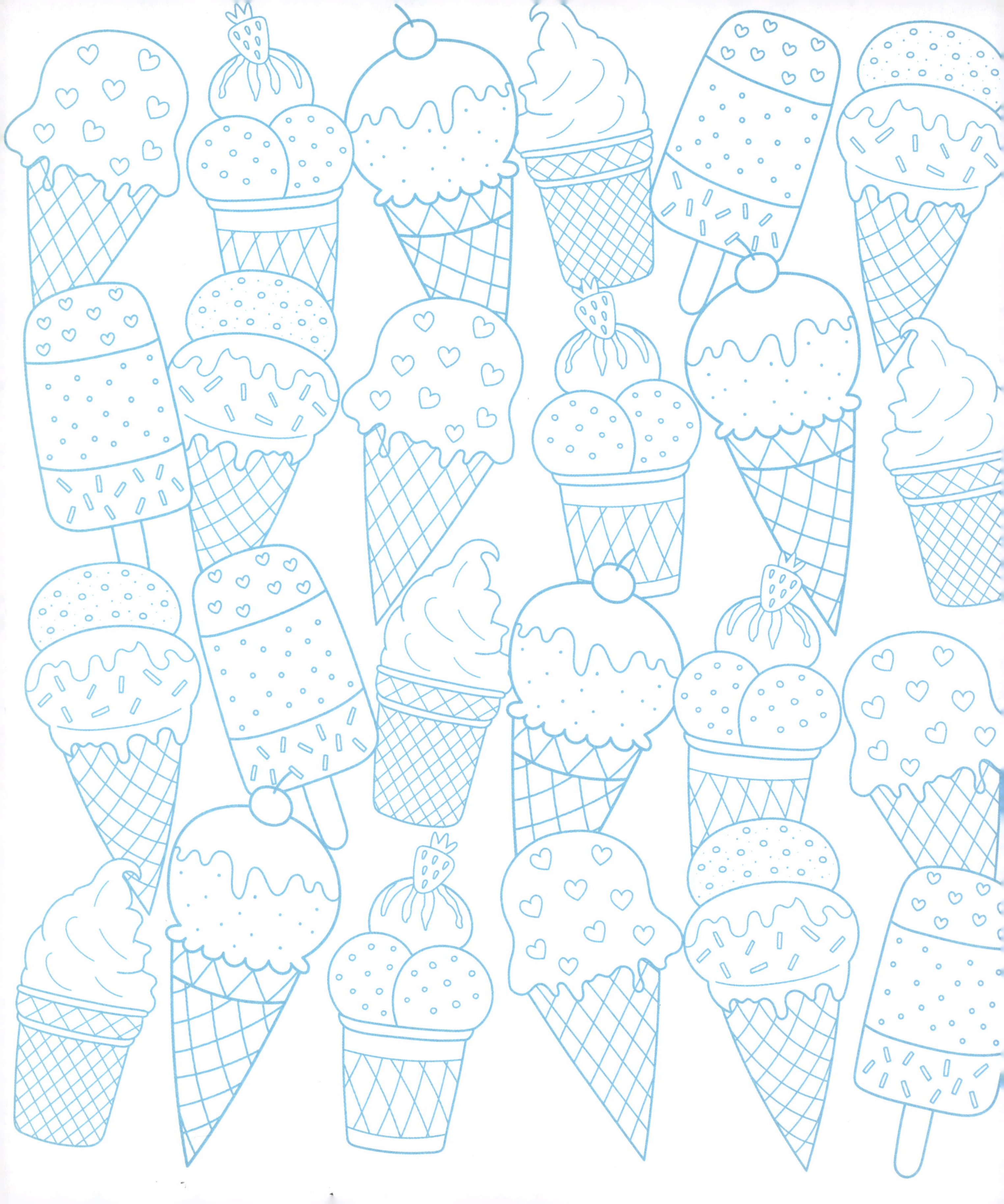

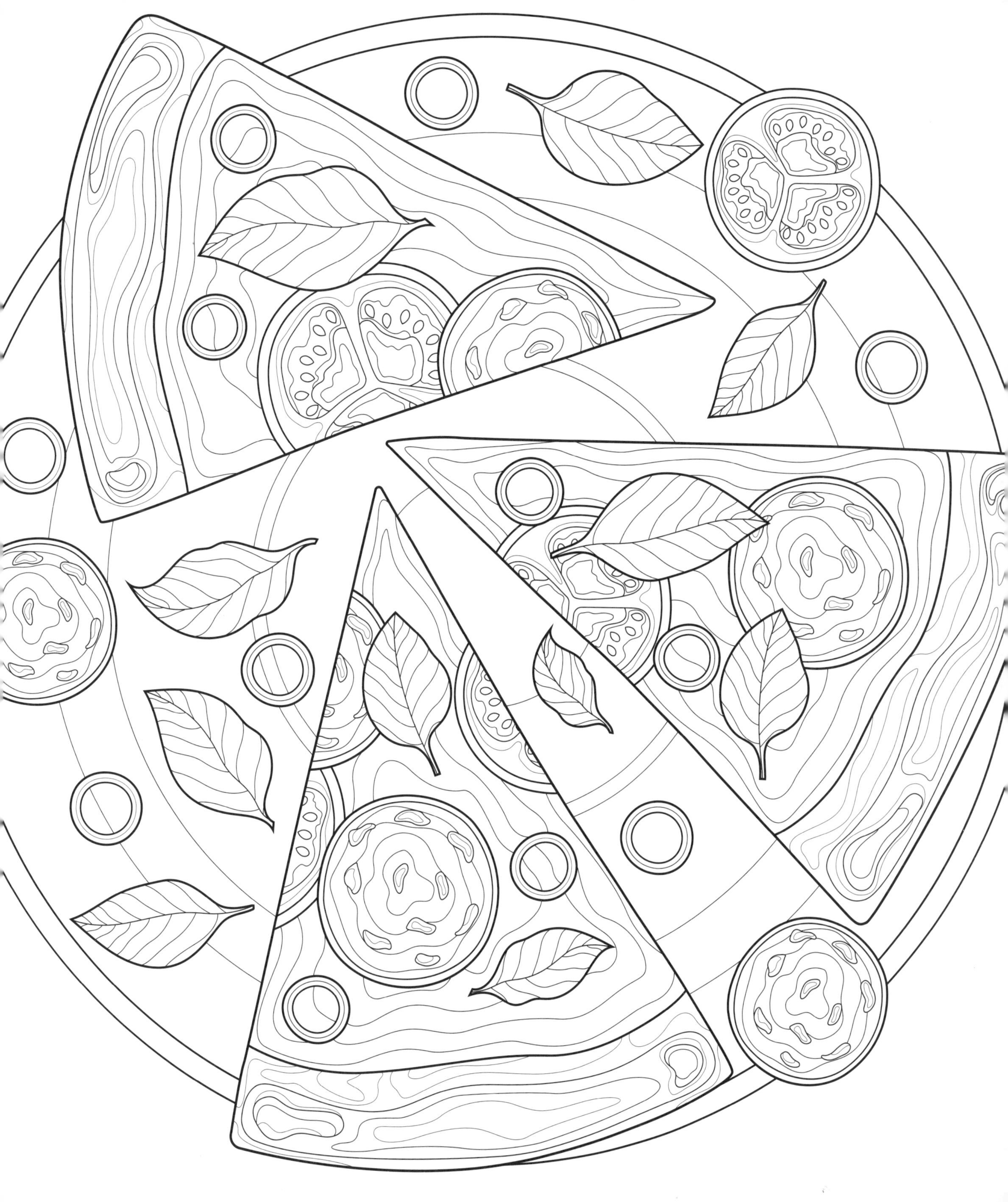

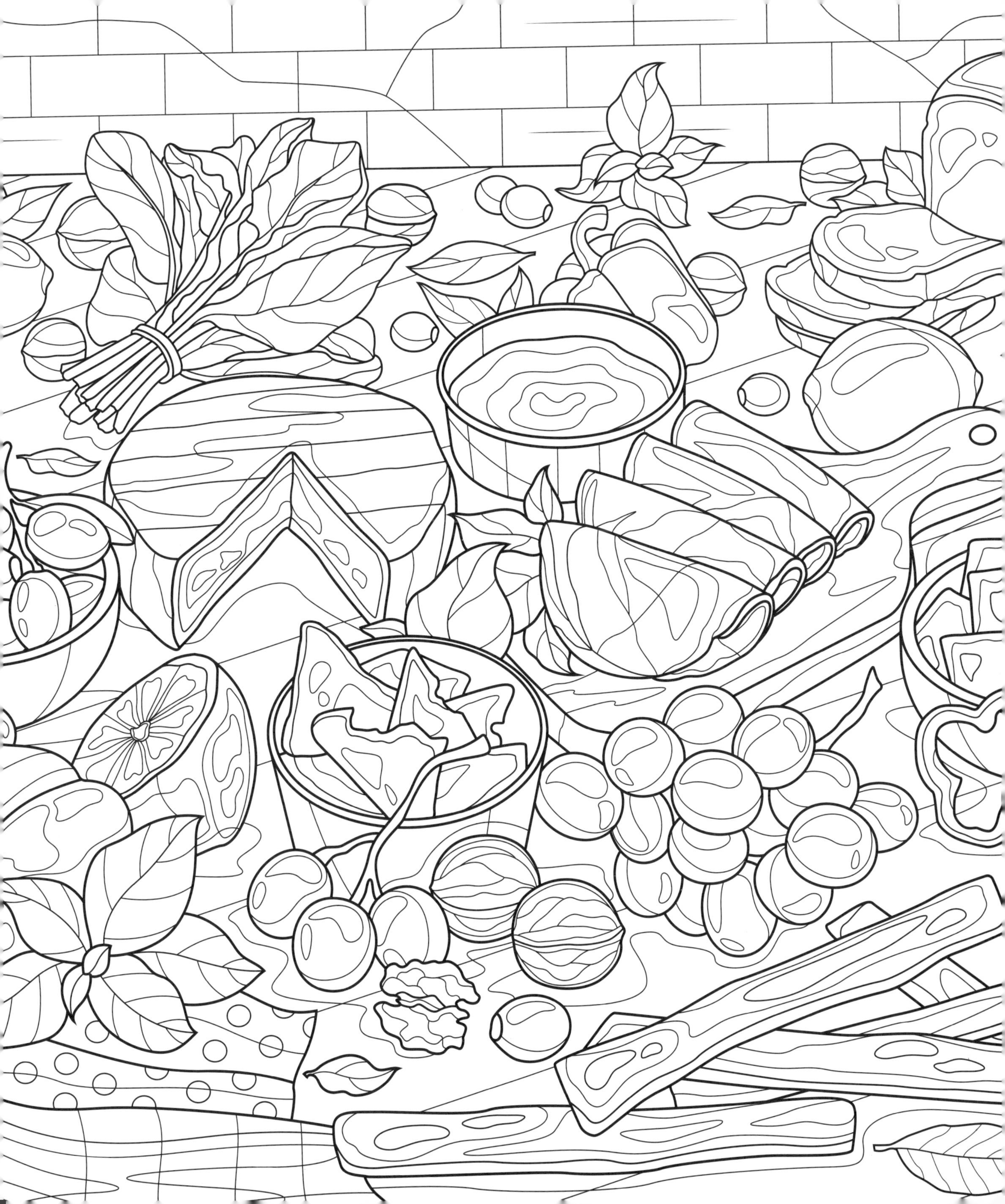

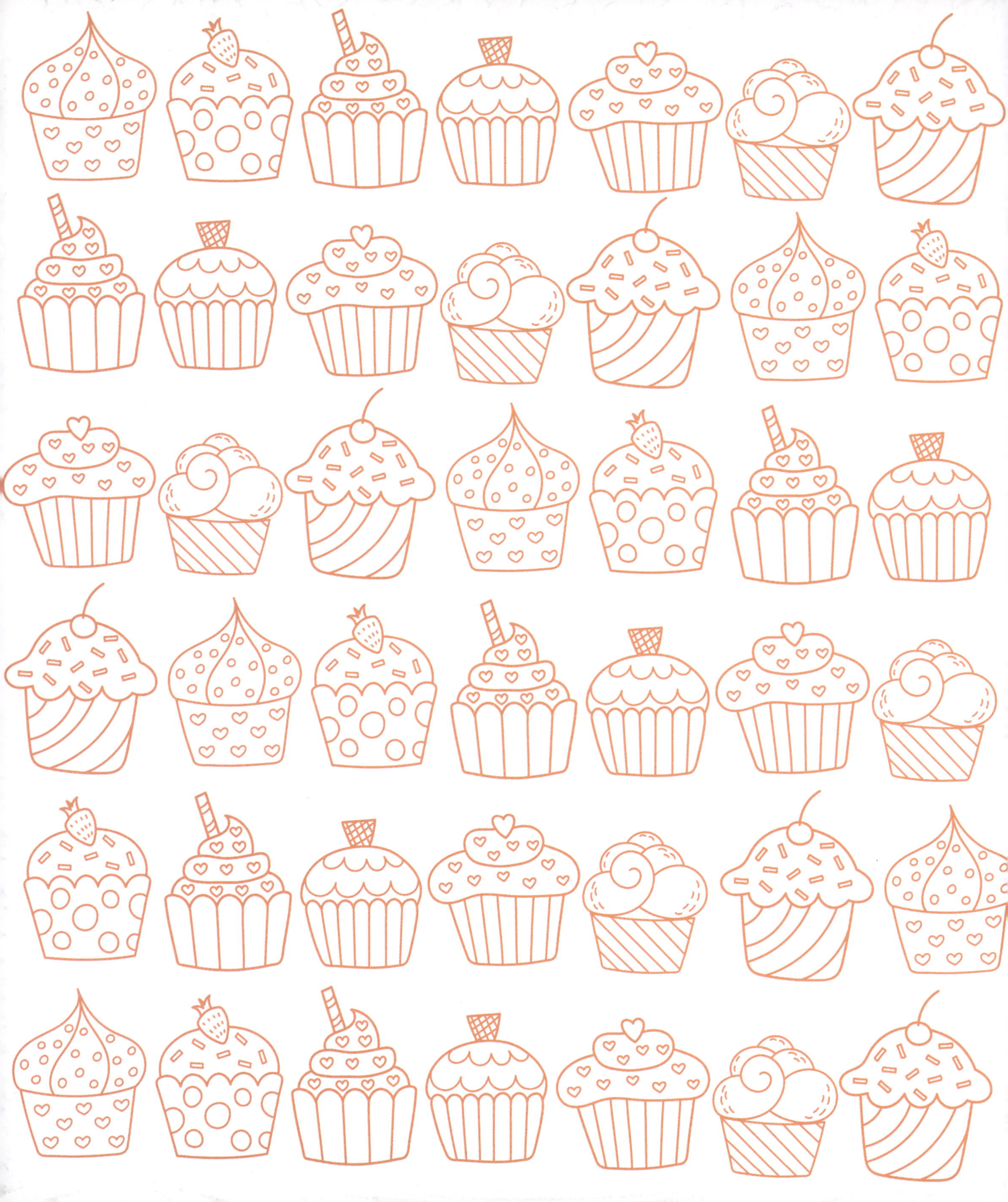

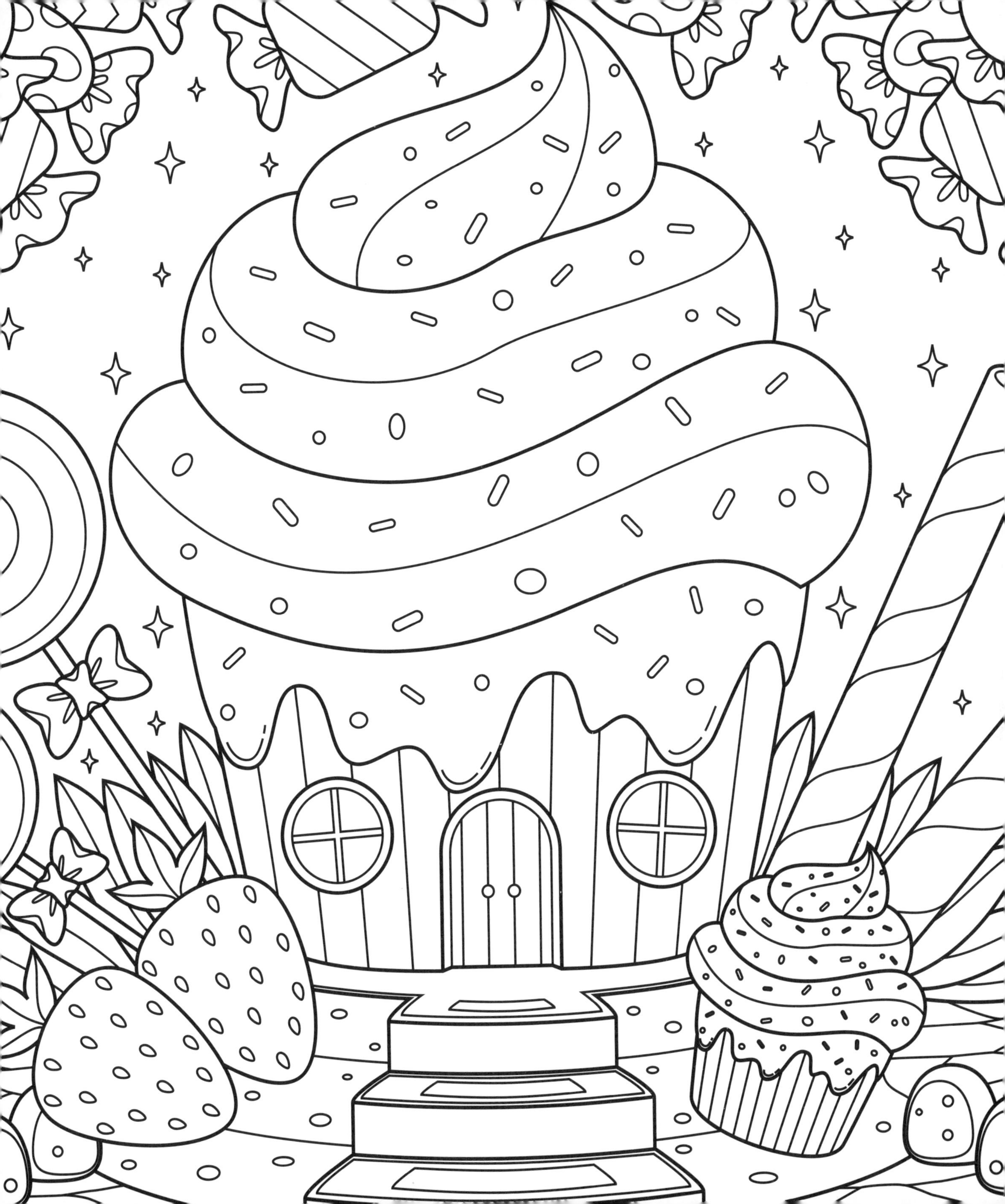

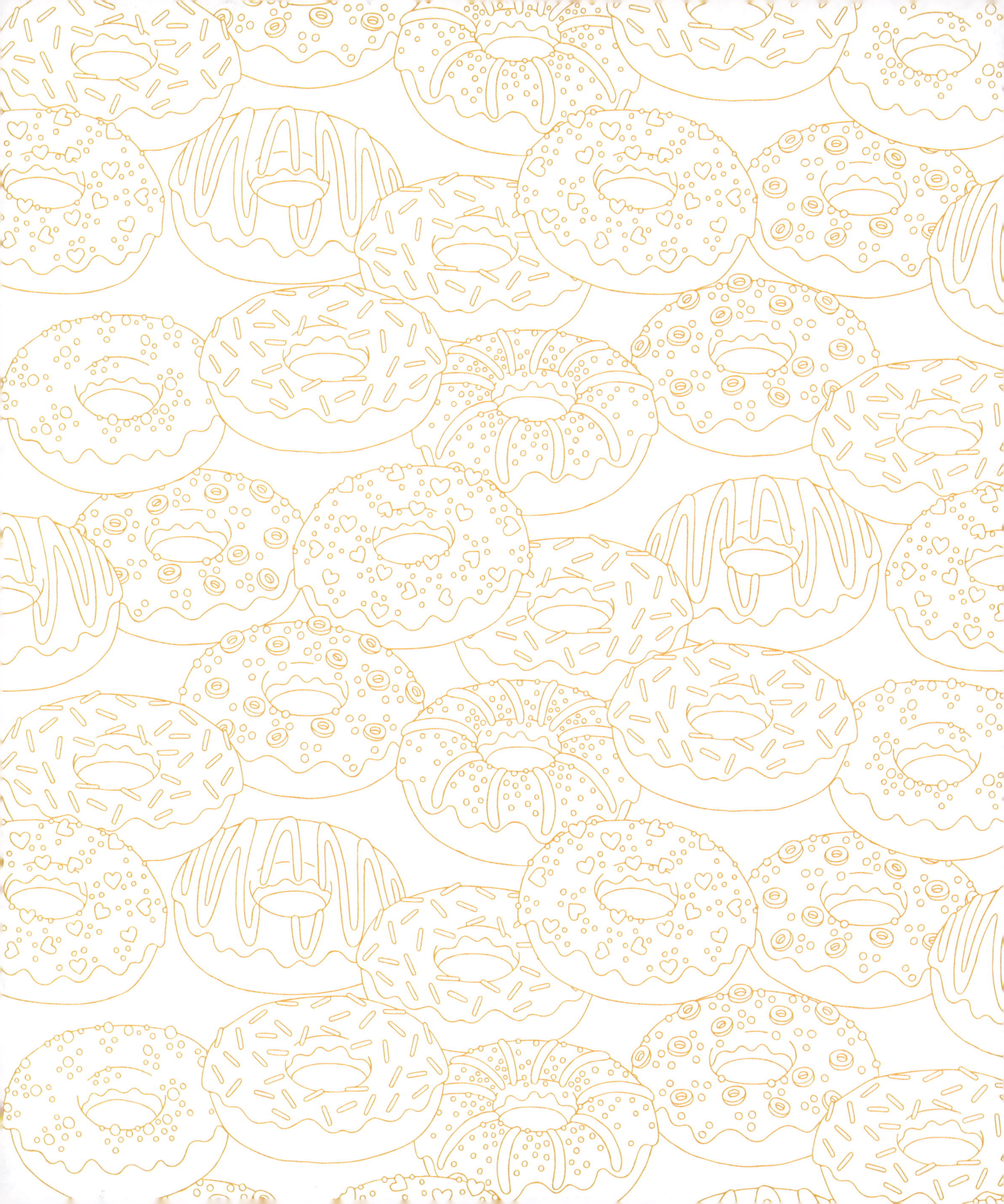

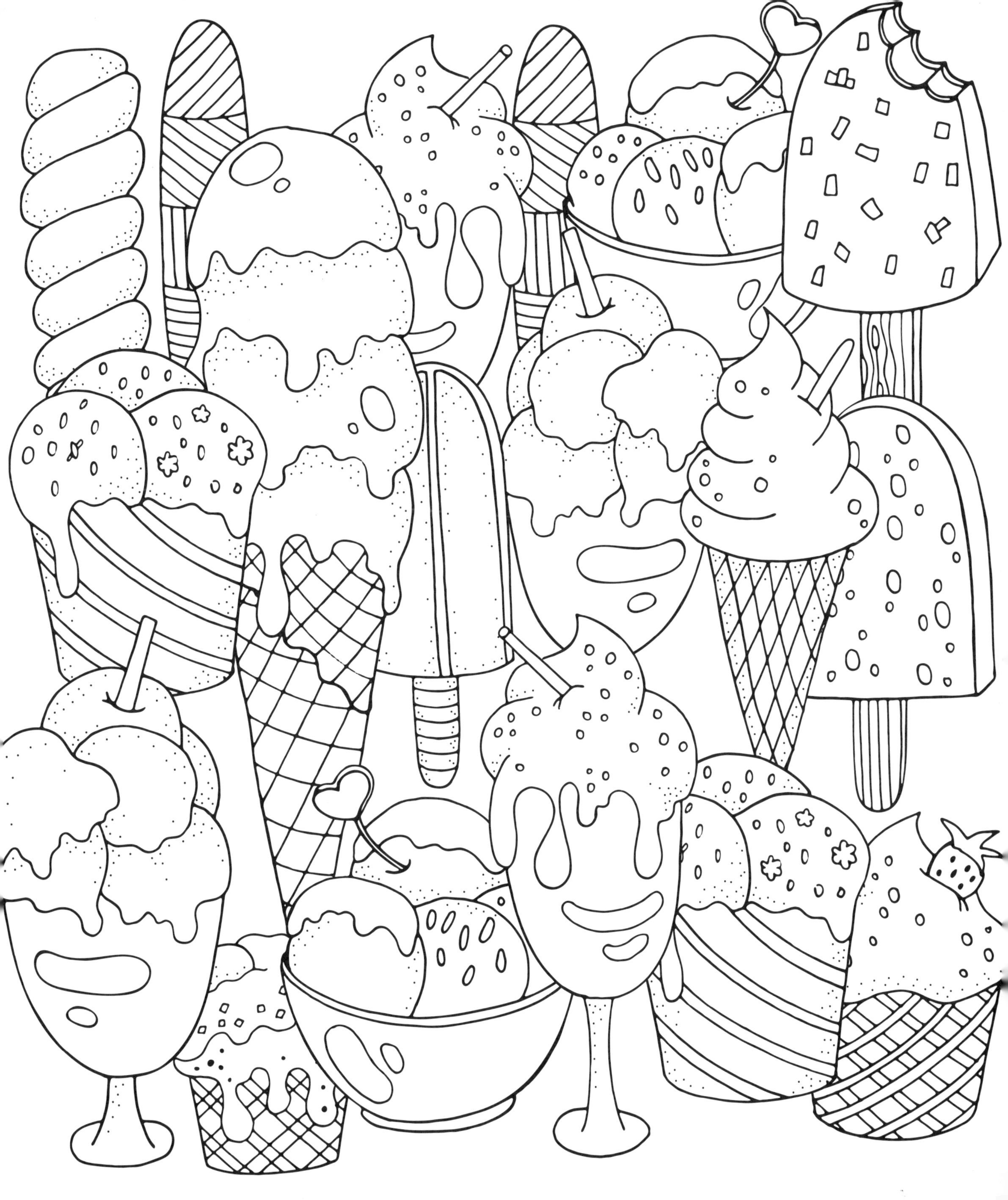

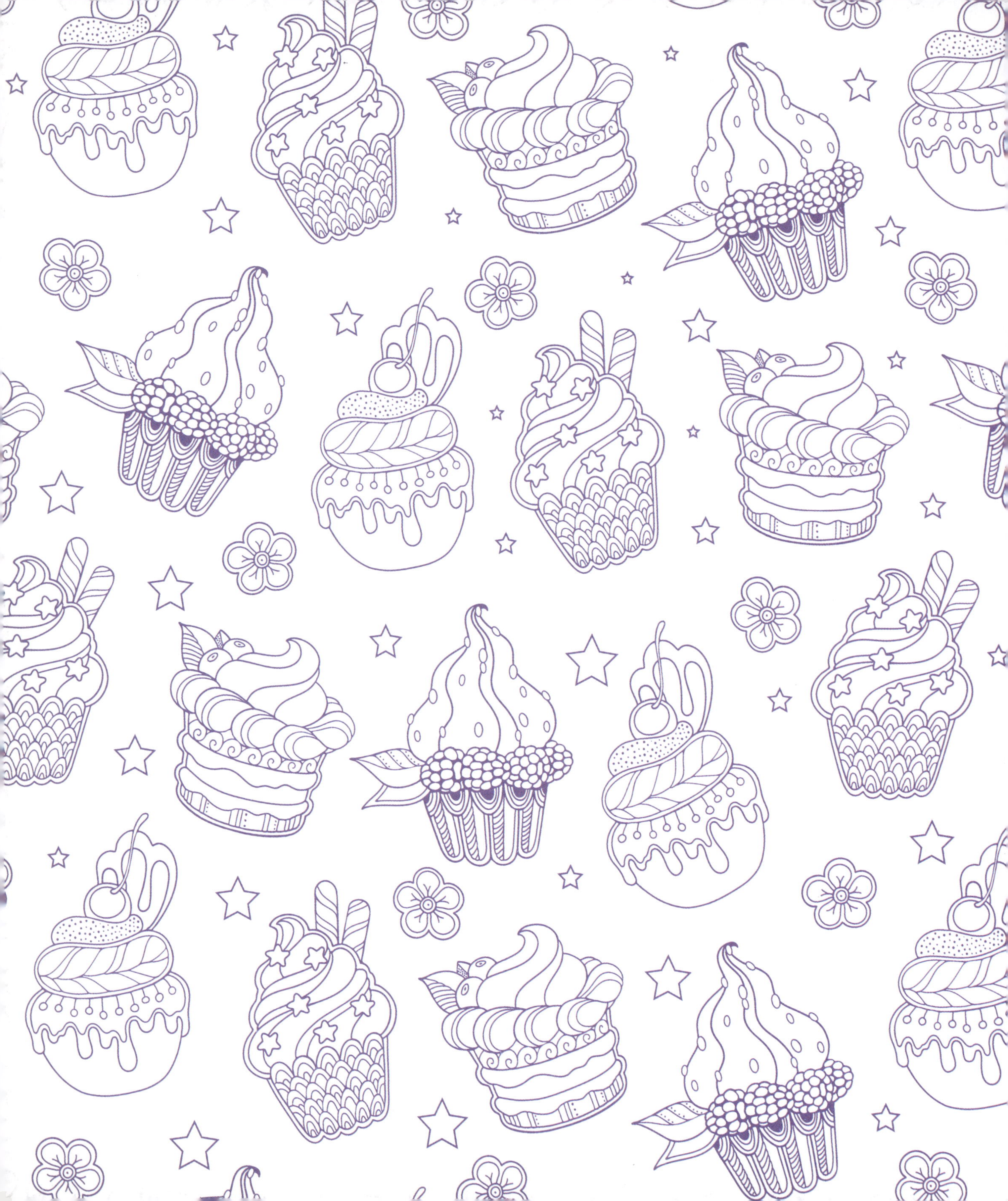

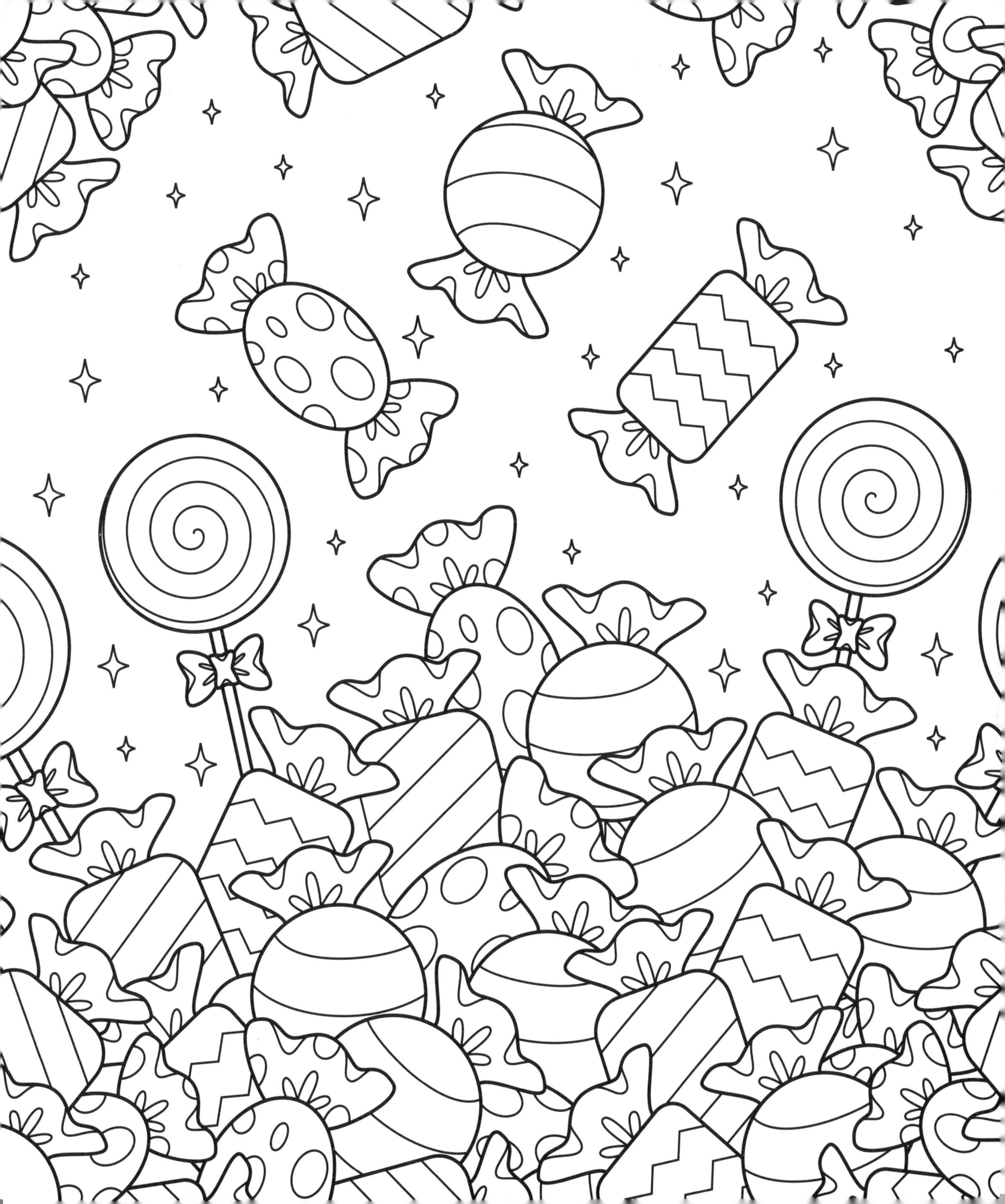

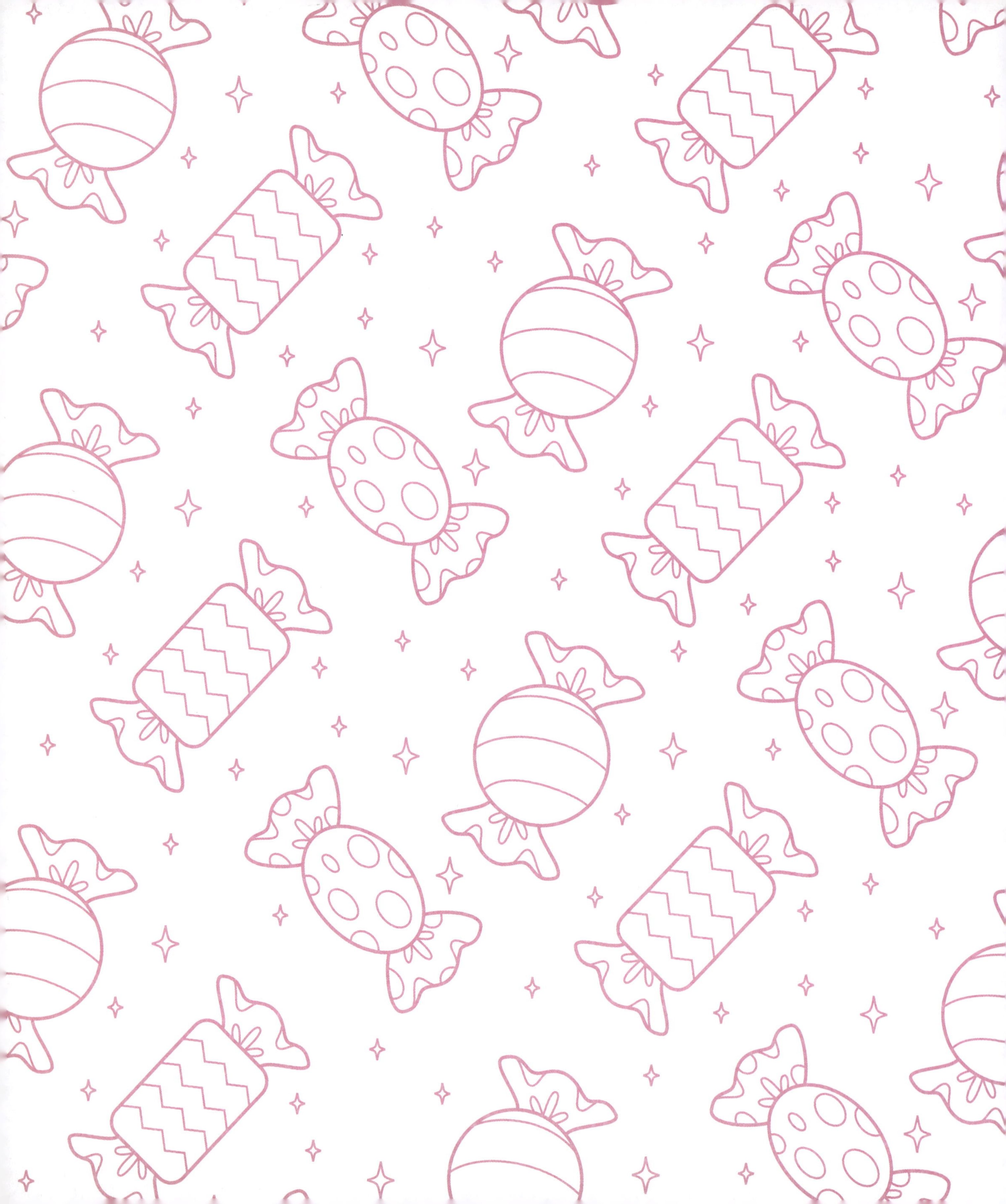

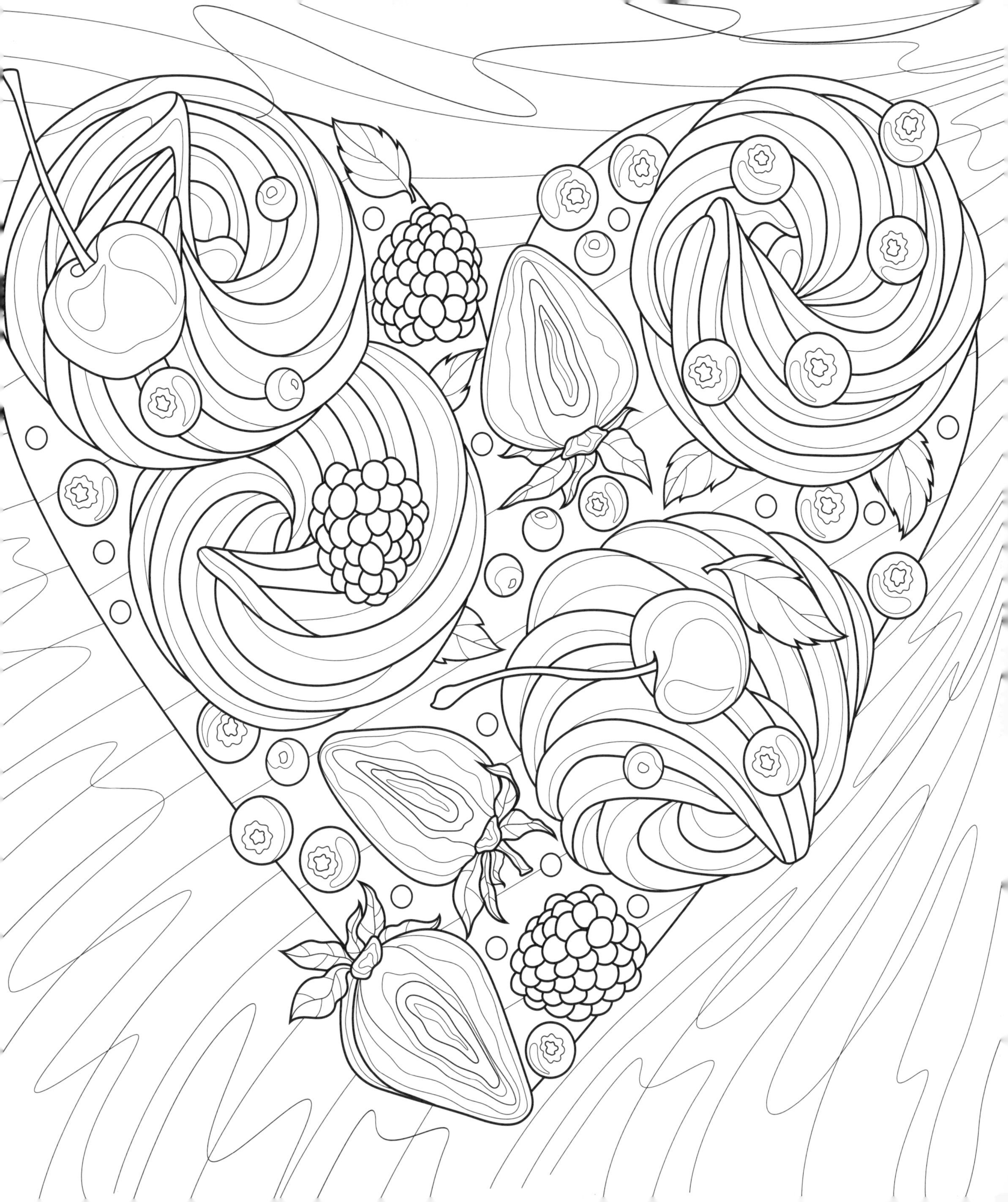

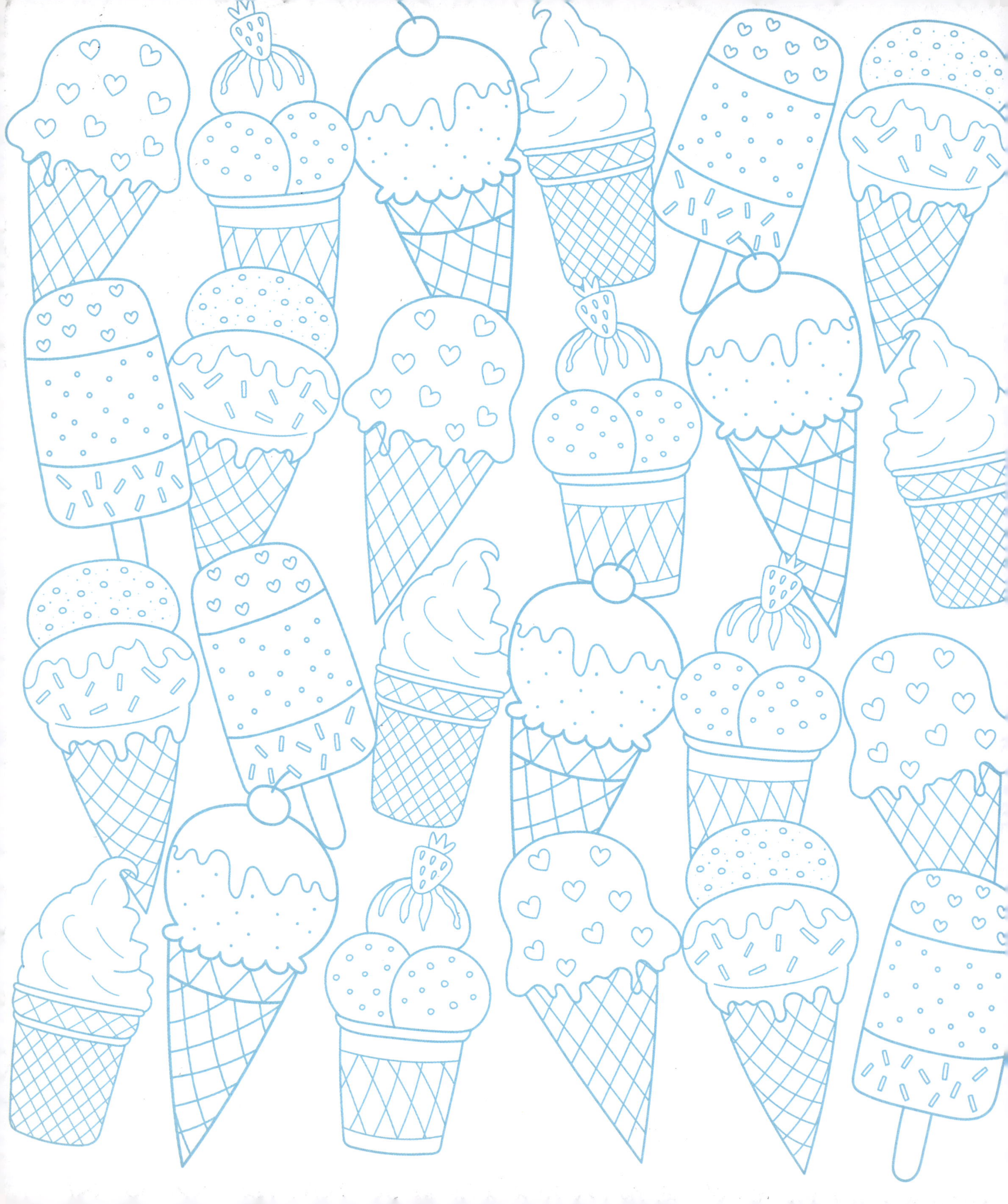

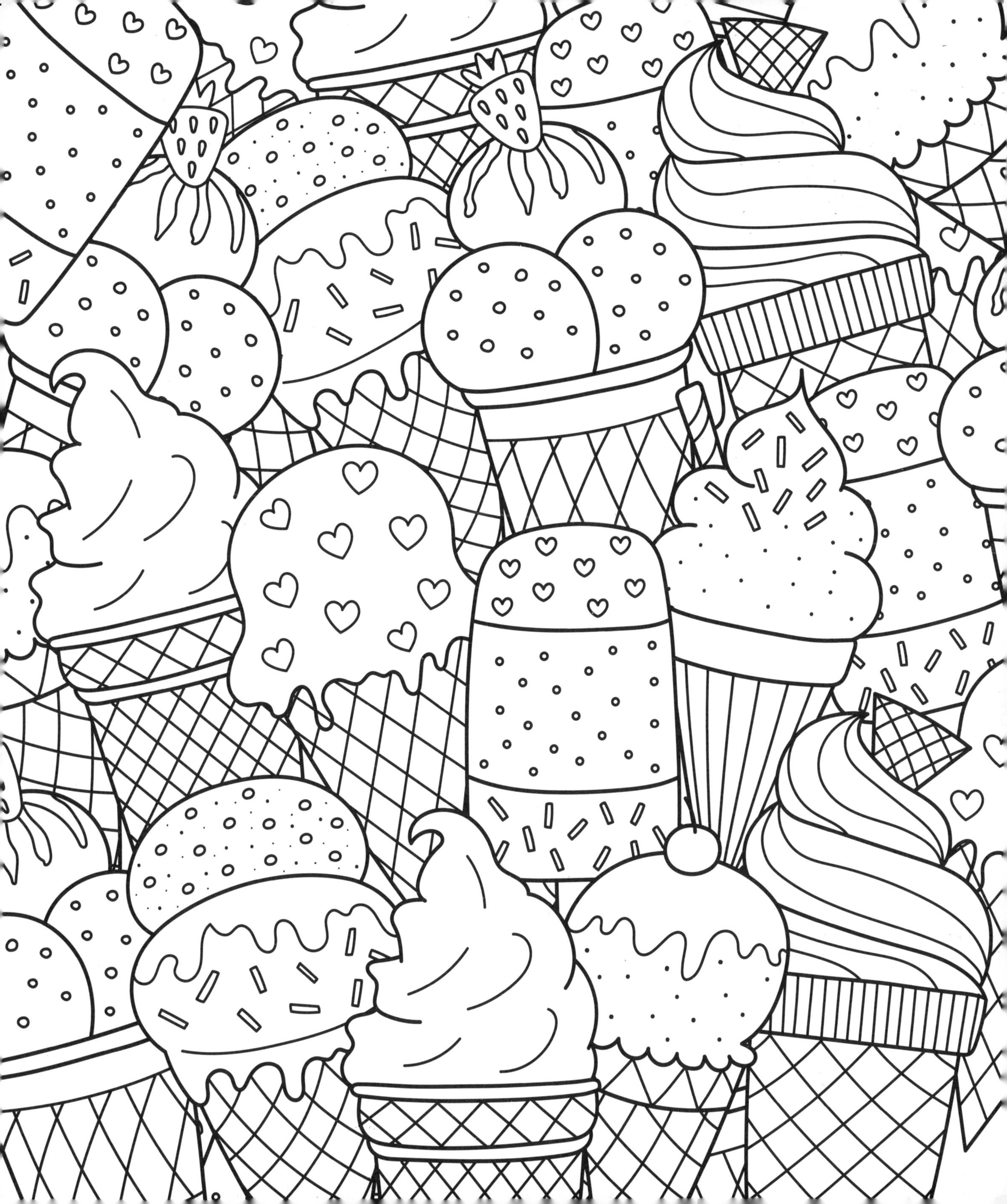